ESSAYS ON BUDDHISM AND PĀLI LITERATURE

ESSAYS ON BUDDHISM AND PĀLI LITERATURE

Prof. ANGRAJ CHAUDHARY,
M.A. (Eng. & Pali), D. Lit.,
Regional Dy. Director of Education,
South Chhotanagpur Division,
Ranchi

EASTERN BOOK LINKERS
DELHI : : (INDIA)

Published by :
EASTERN BOOK LINKERS
5825, New Chandrawal, Jawahar Nagar,
Delhi-110007

First Edition : 1994

Price : Rs. [illegible]

ISBN :-81-85133-68-9

Typesetting by :
Amar Printing Press
8/25, Vijay Nagar, Delhi-9
Phone : 7252362

Printed at : Deluxe Offset Printers, Delhi - 110035

Introduction

The present book is a collection of twentyseven essays written from time to time over a period of more than twentyfive years. Quite a number of them deal with the important aspects of Buddhist philosophy and Buddhist Ethics and some of them treat of the literary and aesthetic aspects of Pali Literature in which the original *Buddhavacana* (the words of the Buddha) is enshrined.

The first essay expounds the four Noble Truths i.e. suffering, the cause of suffering, the assertion that suffering can cease to be and the way leading to the cessation of suffering. In the second essay *Suffering in Buddhist Philosophy*, the nature of suffering has been lucidly explained. It has also been shown here how suffering is an ubiquitous phenomeno an no living being can escape it. Man is destined to suffer in several of his births so long as he does not annihilate his desires *(taṇhā* or *tṛṣṇa)* which are at the root of his suffering. *The Existential Character of Buddha's Philosophy* underlines Buddha's practical and pragmatic attitude to philosophy. He thinks it a waste of time to speculation on metaphysical questions like whether the world is eternal or not and concerns himself with the sixtyfour thousand dollar question of how to put an end to suffering. Buddha did not indulge himself in puzzling out hypothetical answers to hypothetical questions but like a realist he showed that man has infinite capacity to ameliorate his lot. He also shows that man can make or mar himself. How one's *kamma* is responsible for his rebirth is explained with beautiful and homely illustrations in *The Problem of Kamma an Rebirth as Discussed in the Milindapañho.* That Buddhist philosophy is very close to Pragmatic philosophy has been shown in *Buddhism and Pragmatism.* Why matter (*rūpa*) has been defined from the ethical point of view and not from metaphysical point of view has been discussed in *The Concept of Matter in Early Buddhism. Ācārya*

Śāntideva's Humanism brings out the aspects of humanism of early Buddhism and shows how Śāntideva's humanism is equivalent to humanitarianism of Mahāyāna Buddhism. How the principles of Buddhism are relevant in modern times has been set forth in *Buddhism in a Changing World*. Causes of variety in Buddhist thought have been explained in the essay of the same name. That the *Mūlapariyāya Sutta* is a treatise of Epistemology and Ontology has been discussed in *The Mulapariyaya Sutta - a treatise of Buddhist Epistemology and Ontology*. That the elements of Mahāyāna lie embedded in the *Sutta Nipāta* is brought out with ample illustrations in *Elements of Mahāyāna in the Sutta Nipata*. *Ethical Teachings in the Dhammapada* and other three essays following it bring out different aspects of Buddhist ethics and underline their importance in the life of an individual as well as in social and national life. The spiritual progress desends exclusively on following ethical principles enunicated by Buddha has also been shown here. Who is Paccekabuddha and what are the altruistic motives of Bodhisattva have been discuss, in the next two essays. How the *Tipiṭaka* makes a travesty of Nigaṇṭha Nāṭaputta and his view has been amply illustrated in *Jain Culture and Śramaṇa Tradition in the Pali Tipitāaka*. How Nature has been described and what use it has been put to by the *Theras* have been discussed in *Nature in the Theragāthā*. That the similes in the *Sāmaññaphala Sutta* are aesthetically gratifying rich in and suggestive of spiritual wealth is magnificently illustrated in *Similes in the Sāmaññaphala Sutta*. 'The predominant *Rasa* in Buddhist literature is *Śānta*' has been discussed in *Contribution of Buddhism in the Field of Rasa, Buddha's view of Beauty, Buddhist Literature and Śānta Rasa* and *Aesthetics of Buddhist Art*. How harmony in social life can be achieved has been brought out in *Buddha's view of Harmony*. The last essay attempts to prove how *vipassanā* is a distinct contribution of Buddhism to world culture.

Some of these essays were published in different journals and a few oe them were not. Sincere thanks are due to Shri Shyam Lal Malhotra of Eastern Book Linkers for bringing these essays together in a book form.

Angraj Chaudhary

CONTENTS

The Four Noble Truths

More than two thousand and five hundred years ago Buddha was born in Kapilavastu as prince Siddhartha-the son of King Suddhodhan of the Śākya clan. He was born with a golden spoon in his mouth. He had all that are supposed to give pleasure : immense wealth, good health and a beautiful wife. But he was sad amidst plenty.

In course of time he saw a sick man, an old man and a dead man and was very much moved. On enquiry he found out that in this world all without exception suffer from disease, grow old and die. It did not take him long to conclude that his beautiful wife Yasodhara too would grow old and die. The question that arose in his mind was how can *Dukkha* be conquered ? He left home and applied himself assiduously to discover the path which could lead him to conquer *Dukkha* and realize *Nibbāna*.

At Bodh Gaya he attained *Saṃbodhi* (enlightenment) on the full moon day of Āsādha. He realized the profound truths of life. Those truths of life are four in number and are called 'Noble' because they were realized by Buddha-the Noble One.

Lord Buddha was a realist. He never believed in indulging in abstract thinking. He was concerned primarily with the fact of life as he had seen it. And the indisputable fact of life is *Dukkha* from which all beings suffer. So he made it the starting point of his *Dhamma*. Like an experienced doctor he diagnosed the disease of man and also discovered its remedy.

The first Noble Truth enunciates that there is *Dukkha*. Now what exactly is *Dukkha* ? Lord Buddha defines it in the following words :- "Birth is suffering, decay is suffering, illness is suffering, death is suffering. Presence of objects we hate is suffering, separation from objects we love is suffering, not to obtain what we desire is suffering. Briefly, the five fold clinging to existence is suffering."[1]

We can recognise here three kinds of suffering. Birth, old age, illness and death are physical sufferings. Presence of objects we hate, separation from objects we love and not to obtain what we desire characterize the second kind of suffering called mental suffering. The fivefold clinging to existence i.e. *Rupa, Vedana, Saññā, Saṅkhāra* and *Viññāna* which constitute our personality represent the essential form of suffering. Lord Buddha thus puts his finger on the comprehensive form of suffering.

How is it that birth (*Jāti*) has been called *Dukkha* ? Birth in the Buddhist sense is not merely a particular single moment in each life, it is not only the physical process of being born, but it refers to the appearance of the five aggregates of existences again and again.

Jarā (decay) also is called *Dukkha* because with the passage of time the sense - organs decay and become feeble. The bloom of youth gives place to the wrinkles of old age. Similarly *maraṇam* (death) is called *Dukkha*, because it is not only a definite moment of life, but it refers to the decay, dissolution and the continuous change of the physical, mental and psychical elements of existence. In other words, the five groups of *skandhas* (aggregates) continuously undergo a process of decay until they are shattered to pieces.

When we do not get a thing we long for and when we are separated from all the objects we like, this is *Dukkha*.

From all this it is clear that *Dukkha* in the Buddhist sense is not merely hypochondriac discontentment with the world and an emotional weariness of life. It is in fact cosmic suffering as A.B. Govinda has termed it.[2] There is an inexorable cosmic law of *Kamma* which compels us to move in the cycle of birth and death and suffer from *Dukkha*. Buddha did not only propound the first Noble Truth. He also discovered the causes of *Dukkha* which are embodied in the second Noble Truth called *Dukkha Samudaya* i.e. there is cause of *Dukkha*. The first Noble Truth is the diagnosis of disease, the second is the physician's disvovery of its cause. Buddha describes the cause of *Dukkha* in the following words:- *Yā Yā taṇhā ponobhavikā* i.e. craving, that leads to re-birth, accompanied by pleasure and lust finding its delight here and there. The craving is threefold, crsving for pleasure, craving for existence and craving for non-existence or life to end.

Taṇhā or *Tṛṣṇā* is the selfish craving for the things of the world. It is inordinate attachment and passionate clinging to the six kinds of objects of our six sense - organs.

The pertinent question is how does it arise and where does it reside. We are endowed with six sense-organs, of eye, ear, nose, tongue, body and mind and with these sense-organs we enjoy the various objects of the world. We see the beautiful objects of the world with our eyes, hear the melodious sound with our ears, smell good perfumes with nose, taste dainty dishes with tongue and touch soft things with the body. The more we enjoy them, the more we want to have them. Thus our craving increases and multiplies. So craving, infact, resides in these sense-organs and it is also being continually manufactured by them in an endless process not only in one existence but in several existences. In the process of enjoying various objects of the world we become greatly attached to them.

Taṇhā is of three kinds.[3] *Kāma taṇhā* means desire for all sensuous and sexual pleasures. *Bhava taṇhā* means craving for being born again and again in order to enjoy the pleasant sensations arising out of the various objects of the world. *Vibhava taṇhā* is craving for non-esistence. When a man does not want to be born again in this world and suffer all kinds of trouble, he has what is called *vibhava taṇhā*.

In short, it is craving of one kind or another which is responsible for man's suffering in numberless births. It is craving which binds a man to the cycle of birth and death. Lord Buddha has compared *taṇhā* to a seamstress who brings two ends together and joins them i.e. joins the two existences. Craving or *taṇhā* supplies oil. As a result the lamp of life keeps on burning.

It is for this reason that Buddha said *Natthi rāga samoaggi*[4] (There is no fire like lust).

With the help of the law of dependent origination called *Paṭiccasamuppāda* Buddha has explained the cause of craving. If craving, he thought, causes *Dukkha* in life, then *Dukkha* can be eradicated by removing craving. Disease will be cured if the germ is killed. This led him to enunciate the third Noble Truth, i.e. *Dukkha* can cease with the complete cessation of this thirst, a cessation which consists in the absence of every passion-with the abandoning of this thirst, with the doing away with it, with the deliverance from it, with the destruction of desire.

Craving can cease to be when we have no passionate attachment for any object in the world, when we give up our desire for pleasant sensations that we get from the objects we like. When we eradicate our desire completely and when we are fully delivered from it then craving in us will cease to be. How can we give up craving for the pleasant objects of the world? We can do so only when we contemplate the transitoriness of existence, transitoriness of pleasant sensation and transitoriness even of the worldly objects to which we attach ourselves out of ignorance. If we can put an end to craving, grasping will automatically cease to be. Then becoming ceases which is followed by cessation of rebirth and finally by the cessation of old age, sickness, death, pain, lamentation, suffering, sorrow and despair.

Because of Buddha's concern with *Dukkha* Buddhism has been condemned as a doctrine of gloom, despair and pessimism. But Buddhist philosophy is not a philosophy of despair. Buddha has said in unequivocal terms that *Dukkha* can be annihilated.

And how can *Dukkha* be annihilated is the theme of the Fourth Noble Truth. *Dukkha nirodha gāmini paṭipadā ariya saccaṃ* i.e. there is a path leading to the cessation of suffering. "This O, Bhikkhus, is the Noble Truth of the Path which leads to the cessation of suffering, *that* holy eightfold path, that is to say Right belief, Right aspiration, Right speech, Right conduct, Right means of livelihood, Right endeavour, Right mindfulness and Right meditation".

The path prescribed by Buddha is called the Middle path or *Majjhimā paṭipadā* because it steers clear of two extremes - one of indulging in sensuous and sexual pleasures and the other of practising austerities and penances. It contains eight constituents which can be put into the three categoreis of *sīla, samādhi* and *paññā*.

Out of the eight constituents, Right speech, Right action and Right livelihood come under the category of *sīla* i.e. a man can achieve purity of conduct if he exercises restraint over his speech and action. The power of speech which only man is blessed with should never be put to wrong use. Right speech means refraining from falsehood, back biting, harsh speech and idle gossip. Right action consists in refraining from killing, stealing and from sexual misconduct. Right livelihood consists in the judicious earning of one's livelihood. Even though one may be tempted in the struggle for existence to earn one's livelihood by any means, one should not do so. One should not, therefore, trade in arms, trade in animals for slaughter, trade in human beings, trade in intoxicant drinks and poisons.

From the observance of *sīla,* we move on to achieve concentration of mind i.e. *samādhi,* which consists of Right effort Right mindfulness and Right concentration. Right effort consists in destroying the evil that has arisen, preventing the evil from arising, producing good that has not yet arisen and increasing the good that has already arisen. Right mindfulness consists in practising awareness with regard to the true nature of our body, feelings, mind, and mental objects so that we can know their impermanent nature. Right concentration means one-pointedness of mind. Right view (*Sammādiṭṭhi*) and Right thought (*Sammāsaṃkappa*) fall under the category of *pañña.* The first consists in understanding the *anicca, dukkha* and *anatta* aspects of existence and the second in making a firm resolution to get rid of all obstacles that come in our way of realizing the highest good i.e. *Nibbāna.*

In short the eightfold path is the path of progressive self culture. By treading upon this path the creeper of *taṇhā* that has 'cribbed, cabined and confined' us can be cut for good.

Thus we see that the four Noble Truths as propounded by Buddha constitute the quintessence of his teaching and a right understanding of all that is implied by them will guarantee our salvation from the bondage of *Dukkha*.

REFERENCES

1. *Dhammacakkapavattanasutta*, *Vinaya Piṭaka*.
2. A.B. Govind, *The Psychological Attitude of the Early Buddhist Philosophy*.
3. *Dhammacakkapavattanasutta*, *Vinaya Piṭaka*.
4. *Dhammapada*.

Suffering in Buddhist Philosophy

Suffering is one of the four Noble Truths discovered by Lord Buddha and in fact forms the corner-stone of his Philosophy. All that Lord Buddha has said for fortyfive long years after attaining enlightenment centres round this plain fact of life. Suffering is the most universal feature of life and all human beings suffer from it. That it is the most ubiquitous phenomenon is proved by the fact that not only human beings but also animals and birds experience suffering. If we take into account only the physical suffering we are awed by its enormity. But this is not all. There are also mental and cosmic sufferings. These two latter kinds of sufferings are felt more keenly by sensitive persons. The more sensitive a human being is "the mass and the magnitude of the agonies" suffered by mankind become more obvious to him.

Lord Buddha was exceptionally sensitive and compassionate. He started with the plain fact of physical suffering which he saw in a sick man and in an old man and was shocked to see so much pain which is the necessary lot of man. He also came face to face with death when he saw a dead man. In seeing the suffering of others he immediately realised his own lot and the lot of all whom he liked and loved as also of all human beings who are subject to old age, decay and death. It flashed across his mind that suffering is the most universally established principle and human beings are not only subject to physical suffering but also to mental and what A.B. Govind aptly phrases "cosmic suffering".[1] This became apparent to him when he realised that man is born again and again to suffer and he is bound to the cycle of birth and death. This truth was born out of his own immediate, intuitive and insightful perception and does not require anything else to prove it. *Sabbe sankhārā dukkhā ti yadā paññāya passati.* His *sādhanā* and yogic practices enabled him to put his finger on the cause of suffering as also on the way to remove it and thereby eradicate suffering altogether.

The first encounter with physical suffering, as a matter of fact, seems to have inspired him to think deeply over it and achieve deliverance from it by completely annihilating it. He made assiduous efforts, achieved *Nirvāṇa* - a state of desirelessness and showed the path of liberation to the suffering humanity.

The aim of all systems of philosophy particularly of Indian systems of philosophy has been to achieve *mokṣa* i.e. liberation from the bondage od *dukkha*. The professed object of Buddhist philosophy also is to get rid of suffering and attain *Nirvāṇa*.

Suffering is common to both man and animal as has been said earlier. In fact "it is the bridge that unites the human and the animal kingdom. One can, therefore, establish universal brotherhood by recognising oneself in the sufferings of others". It has been said in the *Dhammapada* :

Sabbe tasanti daṇḍassa sabbe bhāyanti maccuno
Attānan upamaṁ katvā na haneyya na ghātaye[2]

"All beings are afraid of pain, all beings are afraid of death. Recognising (lit.comparing) oneself in this, one should neither kill nor cause to kill". Lord Buddha was a practical philosopher and unlike other theoretical philosophers who concerned themselves with metaphysical questions concerned himself completely with knowing the cause of suffering and achieving *Nirvāṇa* by ending it i.e. by extinguishing the flame of desire. It was for this reason that he did not try to answer metaphysical questions. "Suppose a man were wounded by an arrow, will it not be good for him, to consult a physican?", he asked. "Will it be of any advantage to him if he insists on not having the arrow taken out until he has learnt who hit him, what caste he belonged to and whether it was a *cāpa* or a *kodaṇḍa*?" Metaphysical question he does not answer "because it does not promote the higher life in all its purity, because it does not lead to disgust with the world, to annihilation of all lust, to the ceasing of the transitory, to peace, to the higher knowledge, to awakening, to *Nibbāna*" and suffering he expounded because its realization led one to higher knowledge.

To free oneself from the bondage was, according to him, the greatest concern of man and the greatest Philosophy that man will ever need for his solace. We shall not be the poorer for it if we could not answer metaphysical questions but we shall definitely be great losers if we could not understand what suffering precisely is and how to get rid of it.

Buddha defined suffering in the following words " Birth is suffering, old age is suffering, disease is suffering, death is suffering, to be united to the diliked is suffering, to be separated from the liked is suffering, not to get what one desires is suffering... in short, the five groups of grasping are suffering[3]". Here we find that suffering has been most precisely defined by Lord Buddha. It has been viewed as not only physical and mental but also as cosmic. It is true that birth, decay and death are obvious symptoms of physical suffering, but to a sensitive and thinking being they become objects of mental suffering. We at once realise that we will meet the same fate when we grow old and all of us will die. Thus reflecting we bring to us what is called mental suffering. We go one step further and do not take long to realise that birth, decay and death are "the symbols of the essential laws of individual life to which we bind ourselves". This realization that the "suffering of bondage" is really " cosmic suffering" is in fact born of a higher state of consciousness.

Lord Buddha then reflected on the cause of suffering and came to the conclusion that desire (*tṛṣṇā* or *taṇhā*) is at the root of all suffering. And the irony is the more we try to satiate our desires, the more insatiable they become. By virtue of his heavenly insight and on the strength of his peculiarly original experience he discovered the cause of our bondage. It has been nicely put into the formula of dependent origination called *Paṭicca-samuppāda*. This constitutes the second Noble Truth of *dukkha samudaya* i.e. arising of *dukkha*. Had Buddha stopped here, he would have been no better than a pessimist, but he met the challenge put up by suffering. He reflected further and in his meditational practices he realised that whatever arises, ceases i.e. if the cause of *dukkha* is removed, *dukkha* itself ceases to be. This realisation constitutes the third Noble Truth called *dukkha nirodha*. But how to remove the cause of suffering and achieve *Nibbāna* - the *summum bonum* of life according to Buddha by annihilating desires constitutes the fourth Noble Truth (*dukkha nirodha gāmini paṭipadā*). The way of liberation according to Buddha is the eightfold path called *Aṭṭhangiko maggo* in Pali canonical literature and combines in itself *śīla, samādhi* and *paññā*.

Śila is practical ethics, *samādhi* i.e. concentration of mind is practical *yoga* and *paññā* which develops out of the sincere practice of these two helps one realise the true nature of worldly objects. Lord Buddha said that the world is in a constant state of flux and the objects of the world are characterised by *anicca* (impermanence), *dukkha* (pain) and *anatta* (soullessness). A desire for these objects is bound to cause suffering. In order to quench our desire we must have to tread on the eightfold path. Out of its eight constituents Right speech (*sammā vācā*), Right livelihood (*sammā ājiva*) and Right action (*sammā kammant)* together come under *sīla* ; Right concentration (*sammā samādhi*), Right mindfulness (*sammā sati*) and Right effort (*sammā vāyāmo*), come under *samādhi* and Right view (*sammādiṭṭhi*) and Right resolve (*sammā saṃkappo*), constitute *paññā*. All these constituents help strengthen one another and thus a *Bhikkhu* or a *Yogāvacara* goes unhindered on the path of spiritual evolution and ultimately ends his suffering by finally destroying the bondage that binds him to the cycle of birth and death.

Buddha looked upon our bondage as the creation of our own lust and longing for the objects of the world. The fulfilment of our desires is pleasure but if our volitions are impeded, suffering is caused. This has also been observed by Schopenhauer. So the only way to free ourselves from the cycle of birth and death is to root out our desire (*taṇhā).*

Suffering and the cause of suffering form the basic theme of his philosophy, and the way to put an end to suffering and achieve a calm, untroubled and peaceful state of mind and finally liberation from the cycle of birth and death forms the basic theme of his ethics. It is around this fundamental theme of suffering that Buddha's views of ethics and philosophy centre. In the *Aṭṭhangiko maggo* he mapped out a path of liberation for us and asked us to tread on it and work out our salvation. By treading on this path one can purify oneself, extinguish all desires and free oneself from the bondage. This eightfold path is the royal road to *Nibbāna* (*Nirvāṇa*).

Lord Buddha put searching questions concerning the arising of suffering, How does it arise ? Does it come from outside ? Is there any external agency responsible for it and came to the conclusion that it is caused by our own desire. It is "no longer felt as coming from outside, from hostile world but as coming from within. It is no longer something foreign or accidental, but a part of one's own self-created being".[4] This realisation makes us understand that it is in our own hands to overcome this suffering by removing its causes and stopping the inflow of *taṇhā*. Thus Lord Buddha did not take a resigned attitude as the stoics did or did not develop a pessimistic attitude as those pessimists who in their efforts could not reconcile the good and the evil in the world or did not find in suffering something glorious as the Christians did, but showed clearly that we can liberate outselves from the cycle of birth and death. We ourselves create the good and the evil and we do not have to depend upon any god or any other external agency to help remove the causes of our suffering.

Reference

1. See A.B. Govinda's *The Psychological Attitude of the Early Buddhist Philosophy.*
2. *Dhammapada* ; 10, 1.
3. *Dhammacakkapavattanasutta, Vinaya Piṭaka.*
4. See A.B. Govinda's *The Psychological Attitude of the Early Buddhist Philosophy.*

The Message of Lord Buddha

Attā hi attano nātho, ko hi nātho paro siyā /
Attanā hi sudantena nātham labhati ḍullabham // [1]

(The self is the lord of self, who else can be its lord ? If the self is well controlled, there can be no lord greater than it.) This verse from the *Dhammapada* makes it amply clear that man for his salvation does not have to depend upon any god or God with a capital 'G'. He can make or mar his life himself. If he is diligent, he can work out his own salvation. Lord Buddha in one of his last sermons emphasises this aspect of man. *Vayadhammā saṅkhārā. Appamādena sampādetha.* (Decay is inherent in all component things. Work out your salvation with diligence.) What he implies here is that one can put an end to one's suffering by annihilating its cause. Suffering and its cause are all *pratītyasamutpanna* i.e. they arise depending upon other factors. Therefore they can be completely rooted out, as decay is inherent in them.

This is one of the great messages of Lord Buddha. Man has been glorified by him as he sees infinite capacity in him. In another sermon he says *attadīpā viharatha, attasaranā, anaññasaranā, dhammadīpā, dhammasaranā anaññsaranā* which means 'Be ye a refuge to yourselves, betake yourselves to no external refuge. Hold fast to the Truth as a lamp. Hold fast as a refuge to the Truth. Look not for refuge to any one besides yourselves.[2]

Lord Buddha's philosophy was homocentric. *Sabār upor mānus satta, tāhār upor nei* as says Chandidas. He spoke at length about the futility of metaphysical speculations which did not help man in getting rid of suffering which he is subject to and which do not help him in extricating himself from the cycle of birth and death. He said that man can get salvation by treading on the eightfold path. The path as mapped out by him consists of *sīla* (virtue), *samādhi* (concentration of mind) and *paññā* (wisdom). Man himself is the cause of his suffering but in him there is a built- in mechanism which can annihilate his suffering. In order that the built-in mechanism is activated what he has to do is to follow the *aṭṭhangiko maggo* (eightfold path). He should observe *sīla* i.e. ethical precepts in order to attain concentration of mind and then he will be able to attain *paññā* with which he will see into the real nature of things. Knowing the real nature of things he will not be attached to the objects of nature and thus will keep himself from *tṛṣṇā* or *taṇhā* (desire) which is regarded as the root cause of our suffering.

During the time of Lord Buddha society was divided into several castes, high and low, and as a result man belonging to one caste regarded himself superior to another. According to Buddha this was absurd. All men are essentially the same. He said that man is great or small by virtue of his deeds and not by birth.

Na jaccā vasalo hoti, na jaccā hoti Brāhmano /
Kammunā vasalo hoti kammunā hoti Brāhmano //[3]

The theory that man is great by birth was completely demolished by him. In the *Vāseṭṭha sutta* of the *Sutta Nipāta* he has shown it like a scientist that there are classes in birds and beasts but as far as man is concerned, all men are equal. The very idea of class or caste in men is unscientific and illogical. Beasts and birds have characteristics which divide them into different classes, but men do not have any such characteristics. There is not any marked difference in the limbs of men belonging to one country and those belonging to the other.

Na kesehi na sīsena, na kannehi na akkhihi /
Na mukhen na nāsāya, oṭthehi bhamuhi vā //
Na givāya na ansehi, na udarena na piṭṭhiyā /
Na soniyā na urasā, na sambādhe na methune //
Na hatthehi na pādehi, nangulīhi nakhehi vā,
Ṇa janghāhi na uruhi, na vannena sarena vā /
Lingam jātimayam neva yathā aññāsu jatisu.[4]

Men all over the world are the same in respect of hair,

head, ears, eyes, mouth, nose, lips, brows, neck, shoulders, stomach, back, heart, genital organs, hands, feet, fingers, nails, thighs, as also in respect of complexion and voice.

Buddha did not call him a real Brāhmin who was born of Brāhmin parents. But a real Brahmin, according to him, was he who has broken all fetters, who has annihilated all his desires, who has made himself free from greed, ill will and ignorance, who is full of love and compassion and who practises the four *Brhma vihāras* viz. *mettā* (friendship) *karuṇā* (compassion) *muditā* (sympathetic joy) and *upekkhā* (equanimity). If we are friends with all, if we feel compassion for those who are in distress, if we feel sympathetic joy for those who are making progress in life and if we practise equaṇiṃity when troubled and teased by others, the world will be happy and peaceful.

Lord Buddha was very much pained to see what man had made of man in his days but he did not make any distinction between man and man. He showered his compassion and love on all alike. He ordained many low caste people and gave them place in his *saṅgha*. He also did not mind staying in the mango grove of Ambapali who was the courtezan of Vesāli. Thus he gave the glorious message that all men are equal. If we follow this message of Lord Buddha, love one another and do not look down upon others there will be peace in the world, and much of our trouble which is caused when a group of men who rise in revolt against their exploiters, will disappear.

Buddha's ethical precepts, if followed sincerely, can go a long way in establishing peace in our society. He has asked us to practise non-violence and not to injure the feelings of others. We should do unto others as we want others to do unto us. As we love our own selves, so others also love their own selves. Knowing this we should not wound others.

Sabbe tasanti danḍassa, sabbe bhāyanti maccuno /
Attānan upamaṁ katvā, na haneyya, na ghātaye //[5]

(All men tremble at punishment, all men fear death. Likening others to oneself, one should neither slay nor cause to slay).

For various reasons there is so much enmity in the world, between individuals and nations. How can it be appeased ? Not through enmity but through non-enmity.

Na hi verena verāni sammantidha kudācanam /
Averena ca sammanti, esa dhammo sanantano //[6]

(Not at any time are enmities appeased through enmity but they are appeased through non-enmity. This is the eternal law.) One who harbours thoughts like 'he abused me, he struck me, he overcame me, he robbed me', hatred will never cease in his herart but it will cease to be in the case of those persons who never allow such thoughts to strike deep roots in their minds.

Akkocchi maṁ, avadhi maṁ, ajini maṁ, ahāsi me /
Ye taṁ upanayhanti, veraṁ tesaṁ na sammati //[7]

This is practical philosophy of making life happy and peaceful as also an unfailing way to plant peace in the world at large.

It is true that Buddha always talks of human suffering, but he talks about a fact of life. However, his philosophy is not pessimistic. He says suffering can be eradicated by one who follows the eightfold path.

If we practise the ethical precepts prescribed by Lord Buddha we will enjoy heavenly bliss.

REFERENCES

1. *Dhammapada* XII, 4.
2. *Dialogues of the Buddha*, part II, p.108.
3. *Vasalasutta, Sutta Nipāta.*
4. *Vāseṭṭha sutta, Sutta Nipāta.*
5. *Dhammapada* 10, 1.
6. *ibid.*, 1, 5.
7. *ibid.*, 1, 3.

The Existential Character of Buddha's Philosophy

When we make a study of Buddhist philosophy, its similarity with existentialism becomes clear. Not that it is cent per cent existentialism as we know it today, but there are points on which the two hold the same views. Take for instance the modern existentialist's attitude to philosophy. It is not to speculate on metaphysical questions like what is ultimate reality nor is it to discuss whether the world is created by God or not, nor is it to speculate on the existence of God Himself. It is also not to speculate on questions like whether God is eternal or whether the world and the soul live for ever. The existentialists believe that no amount of speculation has led philosophers to any conclusion so far as these questions are concerned. Plato, Aristotle, Locke, Berkeley, Hume, Descartes, Leibnitz, Kant, Hegel and a host of other great philosophers have failed to find out answers to these questions. They speculate but they never arrive at the truth. Their speculations, at best, remain arm-chair speculations which have no bearing on and relevance to the immediate problems of mankind.

Lord Buddha also, like the existentialists, does not believe in speculating on metaphysical problems. To Mālunkyaputta and Poṭṭhapāda Buddha said that questions like "whether the world is eternal or not, whether the world is an ending thing or not, whether the life-principle is the same as the body or different or whether the Tathāgata is or is not or both or neither after dying" are useless because they are "not calculated to profit, they are not concerned with the Norm (*Dhamma*), they do not redound even to the elements of right conduct, nor to detachment, nor to purification from lusts, nor to quietude, nor to tranquillisation of heart, nor to real knowledge, nor to the insight, nor to *Nirvāṇa*". He proves the absurdity of these questions by pointing out that man's real problem is to get rid of suffering which is so ubiquitous that he cannot shut his eyes to it. Buddha makes the absurdity of these questions amply clear by giving the example of a man struck with an arrow who is experiencing great pain. What good it is to him to say that he wont have the arrow pulled out unless he knows who shot it, whether be was a noble Brāhmin or a merchant or a worker or whether he was tall or short or whether he was black or brown or golden skinned or which town or village he came from" and so on. But Buddha says that questions relating to suffering, its, origin, its annihilation and the way leading to it are meaningful because "they are calculated to profit.....and help one achieve *Nirvāṇa*". Buddha had applied himself heart and soul to find out the answers to those questions which concern mankind immediately and cared less for questions which are not relevant to man and his problems. Man finds himself confronted with a large number of serious and immediate problems the slight neglect of which will spell out a disaster never heard of before in the history of human civilization as it is likely to threaten the very existence of mankind.

There was a time when philosophers took it easy, could afford to take hypothetical questions and puzzle out their hypothetical answers. But conditions in modern times have changed a great deal. They compel them not to indulge in such useless activities and apply themselves seriously to find out the answers to those problems facing them instead. What use it is to bother one's head about whether God exists or not or what constitutes ultimate reality ? The real problem before mankind is to live a peaceful and happy life without having the danger of being threatened with total annihilation. Of late, this concern of man has grown increasingly because of the invention of very deadly nuclear weapons with which the two world wars were fought in this century which caused heavy loss of life and wealth. The existentialists profoundly realized that with Industrial Revolution man lost his stature and individuality. Apart from this, there were other factors responsible for the loss of man's individuality and stature. As a reaction to these, existentialism was propounded. Existentialism is a protest against "various forms of dehumanization that it believes result from industrial technology, rationalism, materialism and scientific objectivism."[1] It is also a protest against Hegelian philosophy which creates such a big world of ideas that man is rendered negligible. Thus the loss of subjectivity is caused with the result that human values are in a state of crisis and human freedom is threatened with extinction.

Esistentialism is essentially a man-centered philosophy and individualistic philosophy which emphasizes human existence and its peculiar qualities more than the physical world. The great philosophers of the world devoted much of their time to the unravelling of it. J.P. Sartre who is one of the greatest exponents of existentialism, on the other hand, emphasizes existence much more than essence - an attitude and commitment which is anti-Hegelian. In his lectures on existentialism he defines it as existence preceding essence. What he says in this connection is quoted here *in extenso*.

"Atheistic existentialism, which I represent, is more coherent. It states that if God does not exist, there is at least one being in whom existence precedes essence, a being who exists before he can be defined by any concept, and that this being is man, or, as Heidegger says, human reality. What is meant here by saying that existence precedes essence ? It means that, first of all, man exists, turns up, appears on the scene, and, only afterwards defines himself. If man, as the existentialist conceives him, is indefinable, it is because at first he is nothing. Only afterward will he be something, and he himself will have made what he will be. Thus there is no human nature, since there is no God to conceive it. Not only is man what he conceives himself to be, but he is also only what he wills himself to be after this thrust toward existence"[2]

From this it is clear that the first principle of existentialism is that 'man is nothing else but what he makes of himself'[3] At another place in the same lecture he says that 'man is at the start a plan which is aware of itself rather than a patch of moss, a piece of garbage, or a cauliflower; nothing exists prior to this plan; there is nothing in heaven; man will be what he will have planned to be'.[4]

The last phrase 'planned to be' is very important in so far as it sums up man's entire responsibility of what he makes of himself. He alone is responsible for what he does. Other forces as explained by Karl Marx and other philosophers are not responsible.

As far as this aspect of existentialism is concerned there is a great similarity between existentialism and Buddha's philosophy. Buddha has said again and again that man is wholly responsible for what he does and is also equally responsible for what he becomes. Good and bad actions done by him produce their resultants which create his self.[5] His self, therefore, is created and caused by his own actions. If he chooses to debase and demean himself, he can do so by his unwholesome actions. On the other hand, if he wants to make himself great and exalted the resultants of wholesome actions done by him will pave the way for it.

Like the existentialists, Buddha also says that man is free to make his choice. He is his own master.[6] However, there is a great difference between the import of choice in Buddha's philosophy and existentialism. For the existentislists, choice of an individual has a social implication. "When we say that man chooses his own self, we mean that every one of us does likewise; but we also mean by that that in making this choice he also chooses all men."[7] A man's choice involves the image of man in the larger context i.e. if one chooses to be one thing, he, at the same time, adds to the attributes of man.

Choice, according to Sartre, has twofold meaning. A man is free to choose. In this respect it is close to the import of choice in Buddha's philosophy. The other import, according to Sartre, is that in choosing for himself a man adds to the attributes of man i.e. man is defined by the actions of individuals.

According to Buddha's philosophy man's choice is more individual than social i.e., he is responsible for his own self and not for others. Buddha's concept of choice is spiritual, whereas the existentialists make human beings responsible for all that happens to mankind. If the Head of a state decides to drop a nuclear bomb, it may not be disastrous for him, but it may be very disastrous for a great section of mankind. Therefore, man has to develop his wisdom to make a choice. This import of choice may be seen in Buddha's philosophy indirectly. If we study Buddhism between the lines, it will be clear that if any individual makes a choice of earning his livelihood by honest and right means, its effect will be salutary. Others will imitate him and a sort of peace will be established in the society. According to Sartre man's choice has a direct effect on society. "I am responsible for myself and for everyone else. I am creating a certain image of man of my own choosing. In choosing myself I choose man"[8] Buddha's choice has spiritual bearing more than social.

The other aspect of existentialism is that it is a philosophy which arises out of personal involvement. It is a philosophy from the standpoint of actor or sufferer and not from the view point of spectator. As E.L.Allen says, "Existentialism is an attempt to philosophise from the standpoint of the actor rather than from the standpoint of the spectator." In this respect these philosophers differ from Aristotle and other philosophers who deal with objective things and do not bring in their hopes, aspirations and frustrations in their philosophy. Kierkegaard makes his own individual problems as the starting point of his philosophy. He is not a dry intellectual thinker deriving pleasure from his intellectual activities and imaginative flights but he makes his own anguish and despair the subject matter of his philosophy. Existentialistic philosophy is the philosophy of human anguish and despair and forlornness and indeed, it is a revolt against abstract thinking which lays great emphasis on idea as ultimate reality.

From this point of view Buddha's philosophy is existential in character. Buddha was born a prince with a golden spoon in his mouth, had all kinds of comforts and luxuries to enjoy, but somewhere deep within him discontent was frothing. No amount of worldly pleasure could deter him from raising fundamental questions like why old age ? Why disease ? and ultimately why death ? In short why men suffer at all ? Why does he have to be born again and again and suffer incalculably ?

Buddha raised these questions out of deep discontentment and profound grief. When he saw an old man, a diseased man and a dead man on his rounds to the royal garden, he could not help asking these questions of philosophical importance, "Will my Yasodhara also grow old ? Shall I also grow old and die ?" The questions to which he wanted to find out answers relate to life. They are personal but they have universal application inasmuch as they are questions pertaining to man and his spiritual problems. We never find Plato and Aristotle asking such soul-stirring questions-questions which are born out of anguish and grief. The existential philosophers do ask such questions. Ralph Harper in his book *Existentialism* beautifully and briefly sums up the origin and nature of existentialism. Genuine self-knowledge first came into Western civilization through Judaism, and hosts of religious folk in taking the words of the Psalmist to their hearts have been testifying to a concern for themselves which no Greek philosopher could share. 'Save me, O my God,' 'Hear me when I call, O God.' 'Give ears to my words, O Lord,' 'Have mercy upon me, O Lord.' No Greek philosopher is praying. One cannot imagine Aristotle groaning, 'Out of the depths have I cried unto thee, O Lord'. No, one can point to no crying of the heart in Greek philosophy. The Greek philosophers wished to be saved by reason ; they were not to understand St Paul. In the end we are forced to judge them as failing even to define the nature of man. For, to ignore the person is to ignore the very ground on which humanity lives, moves, and has its being."[9] Thus existentialism is born out of great concern for persons as we find in Christianity, "Come unto me, all ye that labour and are heavy laden and I will give you rest." Existentialism also takes into consideration the seemingly" ineradicable tragedy of human life" which Nietzsche calls 'the eternal wound of existence'.

Existentialism, as a matter of fact, is characterised by a

sense of urgency.What do we mean when we say that one exists? If one begins to ask questions about oneself it means he exists. We find the same urgency in Buddha. "Whether there is the view that the world is eternal, or whether there is the view that the world is not eternal, there is birth, there is ageing, there is dying, there are grief, sorrow, suffering, lamentation and despair the suppression (destruction) of which I lay down here and now."[10]

Like existentialism Buddha's philosophy is not pessimistic. One of the objections raised against existentialism by Christians is that it is a philosophy of despair because it does not believe in God. This attitude of unbelief is despair. But Sartre while refuting it says that the despair of Christains and the despair of existentialists are not the same. Existentialism is a doctrine of actions, it is not a doctrine of quietism. "In this sense existentialism is optimistic, a doctrine of action and it is plain dishonesty for Christains to make no distinction between their own despair and ours and then to call us despairing." And although Buddha talks of suffering, his philosophy is not pessimistic. This becomes very clear from an analysis of the last two Noble truths that he had realized viz., *dukkha nirodha* (suffering can be ended) and *dukkha nirodhagāminī paṭipadā* (the path leading to the eradication of suffering). Besides, Buddha did not believe in non-action or quietism. For long fortyfive years he wandered forth in cities, towns and villages in the length and breadth of the country and preached his *Dhamma* and asked his followers to work for the good of many and for the welfare of many. How can his philosophy be called the philosophy of despair ?

Buddha also propounded his philosophy in sharp reaction to the philosophical views propounded by heretical thinkers like Pūraṇa Kassapa, Makkhali Gosāla, Ajita Kesakambali, Pakudha Kaccāyana, Nigaṇṭha Nāṭaputta and Sañjay Velaṭṭhaputta. Pūraṇa Kassapa did not believe in the existence of merit and demerit; *pāpa* and *puṇya*. Man, according to him, does not reap fruits of his good or bad actions. Makkhali Gosāla was a fatalist. Man, according to him, is helpless. Just as a ball of thread turns round and round till it is completely unwound so a man has to pass through several births before he is liberated. His liberation does not depend upon his efforts for good actions.

A cursory analysis of the views of these philosophers will make it amply clear that there is nothing dignified and exalted about their views. They pictured man as helpless, hopeless and a slave to the circumstances in which he finds himself. If this is the view of man how can we distinguish a good man from a bad one and a wise man from a foolish one ? Buddha rightly calls these views wrong (*micchā diṭṭhi*) and wants us to think, speak and act nobly. He says it again and again that man has infinite capacity to work out his own salvation. He can make himself what he wants to be. Who will say that this is a philosophy of despair ?

From what has been said above, the existential character of Buddha's philosophy becomes clear.

References

1. *Hand book in Social Philosophy,* p.137.
2. Jean-Paul Sartre, *Existentialism,* p.18.
3. *ibid.,* p.18.
4. *ibid.,* p.19.
5. See *Piya Sutta, Saṁyutta Nikāya,* Vol.I p.71. (Nalanda edition)
6. *Attā hi attano nātho.* (The self is the Lord of self). *Dhammapada,* Verse 160.
7. J.P. Sartre, *Existentialism,* p.20.
8. ibid., p.21.
9. Ralph Harper, *Existentialism,* pp.6-7.
10. *The Middle Length Sayings,* Vol.II, p.101.
11. Sartre, *Existentialism,* p.61.

The Problem of Kamma and Rebirth as Discussed in the Milindapañho

Practically all Indian philosophical systems except that of Cārvāka believe in the theory of *kamma* and rebirth. It is taken for granted that good deeds produce good and salutory results and bad deeds produce bad and harmful ones. This is the law of *karma* and this law operates unfailingly and inevitably in the moral world.

Buddhist philosophy also believes in the law of *kamma* but instead of saying that a man must reap what he has sown he says that what a man reaps accords with his deeds. Thus Buddhism is not fatalistic. It allows man freedom to do his work. Buddha was a propounder of humanism and he saw great potentiality in man. He knew it from his own personal experience that man can do a lot, so much so that he can put an end to his suffering and attain *Nibbāna*-the *summum bonum* of life. He refutes the wrong view that "whatsoever weal or woe or neutral feeling is experienced, is all due to some previous action (*pubbekatahetu*)" and says, "So then owing to a previous action man will become murderers, thieves, unchaste, liars, slanderers, abusive, babblers, covetous, malicious and perverse in view. Thus for those who fall back on the former deeds as the essential reason, there is neither desire to do, nor effort to do, nor necessity to do this deed or abstain from that deed."[1] He further says that "If any one says that a man must reap according to his deeds, in that case there is no religious life nor is an opportunity afforded for the entire extinction of sorrow. But if any one says that what a man reaps accords with his deeds, in that case there is a religious life and an opportunity is afforded for the entire extinction of sorrow."[2] The law of *kamma* as envisaged by Lord Buddha is not inexorable in the sense that any *kamma* that a man does must produce its result. If this is accepted then there will remain no possibility of counteracting an *akusala kamma* by a *kusala* one.

According to function there are four types of *kamma* viz. (i) *janaka kamma* (reproductive), (ii) *upatthambhaka kamma* (supportive), (iii) *upapidaka kamma* (counteractive) and (iv) *upaghātaka kamma* (destructive). It is clear from this that a *kamma* can be not only counteracted but it can be destroyed also before it attains the time of operation. When it is accepted that a bad action can be counteracted and destroyed then religious life is possible. Besides, there are some *kammas* which are ineffective i.e. they are *Ahosi kamma*. The *kammas* which produce results are *Diṭṭhadhammavedanīya kamma* (immediately effective), *Upapajjavedanīya kamma* (subsequently effective) and *Aparāpariya vedanīya kamma* (indefinitely effective). From this all this it is patent that the law of *kamma* operates in a very complex manner. The law is not so simple. The *kammas* attain time of operation according to their nature. As far as priority of effect is concerned *Garuka kammas* produce results earlier than *Āsanna, Acinna* and *Kattata kamma*.

If we go a little deeper and try to understand how the law of *kamma* operates, it will become clear that what applies to the vegetable world applies, *mutatis mutandis,* to the moral world. As all seeds sown in the soil do not grow and bear fruits, so some *kammas* also become unproductive and ineffective. But if the seed of a bitter gourd sown in the soil germinates, becomes grown up and produces fruits, it is impossible that it will have fruits like an apple tree. What is clear from all this is that one is not bound to reap all that one has sown and one is also not bound to reap all that one has sown in just proportion. As fried seeds do not germinate so the actions done by an *Arhanta* or a *khīṇāsava* do not bear any fruit. Lord Buddha says that actions done under the influence of desire (*taṇhā*) are capable of producing results.

Lord Buddha made a detailed study of human mind as also of how it works. In the process of explaining the springs of action he happily combined psychology and ethics. Man does various actions in his life under the influence of six *hetus* (roots). *Alobho, adoso* and *amoho* are the roots of good actions and *lobho doso* and *moho* are the roots of bad actions. These roots exist in mind. So mind is the spring of all actions.[3]

The whole canonical literature, I mean, Pali canonical literature is replete with passages where Lord Buddha says that the fruits one reaps accord with his actions.

The *Milindapañho* is an important non-canonical work but the force and clarity with which the theory of *kamma* and rebirth has been expounded here give it the authority and authenticity of canonical literature itself. The explanation given here is ingenious.

In this paper I propose to explain the theory of *kamma* and rebirth as discussed in the *Milindapañho* by Nagasena-one of the fine minds that lived before Buddhaghoṣa. He has very lucidly explained why all men are not equal and alike and who is reborn even though Buddhist philosophy does not believe in a permanent soul.

When king Milinda asks Nagasena to explain the differences that exist among men, Nagasena explains it by giving an ingenious illustration. "Why is it, Nagasena, that all men are not alike, but some are short-lived and some long-lived, some sickly, some healthy, some ugly and some beautiful, some without influence and some of great power, some poor and some wealthy, some low-born and some high-born, some stupid and some wise."[4] In fact, the law of *kamma* is very complex and it is difficult to isolate actions that make one beautiful or ugly. It is staggering to think the permutations and combinations of actions that go to make one rich or poor. Nagasena makes it amply clear by giving one illustration from vegetable kingdom. Just as all vegetables are not alike but some are sour, some pungent, some astringent and some sweet, so are men different. Differences in the case of vegetables are brought about by different seeds. Similarly different actions done by different persons produce different results and make them different. Nagasena quotes what Lord Buddha says in the *Majjhima Nikāya*.

He ascribes differences in men to their different actions. "Beings, O Brahmin, have each their own *karma*, are inheritors of *karma*, belong to the tribe of their *karma*, are relatives by their *karma*, have each their *karma* as their protecting overlord. It is *karma* that divides them up into low and high and the like divisions."[5]

So long as man performs his actions impelled by his desires, his actions will produce results which will follow him like his own shadow. The actions of one who has attained the state of desirelessness, however, are like fried seeds as said above which are incapable of germination.

Milinda then goes on to ask another important question to Nagasena. If the results (*vipākas*) of the actions performed by a man are so powerful as to influence and shape his present life where do they live ? where are they stored ? Nagasena does not talk of Id here as Freud does but he says something like that. Perhaps only unfulfilled desires go to make up Id but results of both *kusala* and *akusala kammas* are called *vipākas* which exist in the form of subtle impressions. To the question where *vipākas* are stored Nagasena replies that they cannot be said to exist at a particular place unless their results become manifest. He makes it very clear with the help of a magnificent illustration. Just as one cannot point out the fruits which a tree has not yet produced so the *vipākas* cannot be pointed out unless they become manifest. The deeds done by one name and form follow it like a shadow.[6]

Nagasena explains the effects of the law of *kamma* in another context. Milinda wants him to explain and resolve the contradiction involved in the two statements made by Buddha. The statements are that "the fire of purgatory is very much more fierce than an ordinary fire. A small stone cast into ordinary fire may smoke for a day without burning and being destroyed but a rock as big as an upper chamber cast into the furnace would be that moment destroyed"[7] and "whatsoever beings are reborn there, though they burn for hundreds of thousands of years in purgatory, yet are they not destroyed."[8] It is in the process of resolving the contradiction that Nagasena explains the powerful effects of *kamma*. He says that "the females of sharks and crocodiles and tortoises and peacocks and pigeons eat hard bits of stone and gravel"[9] and digest them or destroy them but the embryos inside the same animals and birds are not destroyed. Why is it so ? Because the embryo escapes destruction by the influence of *kamma*. With another illustration he makes it more clear. Just as the "females of lions and tigers and panthers and dogs eat hard bits of bones and flesh and digest and destroy them but do not destroy the embryos in their inside similarly the beings who live in purgatory for thousand of years in fierce hell fire are not destroyed."[10] He gives yet another illustration. "Just as tender women - wives of the *yonakas*, the nobles and the Brahmins and the house holders eat hard cakes and digest them but do not destroy and digest the embryos inside them so something is destroyed immediately by the fierce fire of purgatory but others escape destruction by the influence of their *karma*.[11]

In this way Nagasena makes the theory of *kamma* patent not only to Milinda but to all of us. Here a pertinent question arises: to what extent this theory of *kamma* is responsible for fatalism? Shall we say that Buddhism propounds fatalism ? If we just probe a little we will see that if the theory of *kamma* is wrongly interpreted it may give rise to belief in fatalism. The clever leaders and priests of society made it an effective tool to exploit the illiterate masses and said that their misery is due to their bad actions. If they are poor and miserable, they are so because of their past actions. Thus, people started thinking that they are rich or poor by virtue of their own actions and thus they learnt to bear with their destiny. But this interpretation of the theory of *kamma* only tells the half truth as has been said earlier. The law as envisaged in Buddhist philosophy operates in the moral world and does not include only the past lives and the present one but also the life to come. Fatalism leaves no choice open to man. What happens seems to be predetermined, but Buddhism believes in free will. If a man is leading a miserable life now, he is free to choose his life to come and make it better.

If we read between the lines of the passages that occur in the *Milindapañho*, it will be clear that Nagasena clearly talks of a continuous life in the case of those persons whose desires have not been annihilated. So long as their desires are there, their *vipākas* are bound to give birth to another life. Nagasena says that past actions are no doubt responsible for the present life but man is free to make efforts to make his life better. The fresh causes of misery and sorrow can be stopped from rising. To a question put by Milinda as to why Nagasena has taken renunciation he replies that effort in the form of renunciation is now concerned with what still remains to be done. Former effort has accomplished what it had to do. He makes this point clear with beautiful illustrations. Just as a man works to have a well or an artificial lake dug long before he feels thirsty, so a Bhikkhu takes renunciation to stop further sorrow from rising and springing up.[12] One has to arrange for food long before he feels hungry because it will be unwise on his part "to have fields ploughed and seeds planted and crops reaped with the intention of getting some food to eat" in the same way as it will be unwise of a king "to have a moat dug, and a rampart put up, and a watch tower built and a stronghold formed, and stores of food collected"[13] when the battle against him is impending.

From these illustrations it is clear that Buddhists believe in freedom.

Inseparably connected with the theory of *kamma* are two questions. The first is who is born and how rebirth takes place. Let us take the second question first. Buddhist philosophy explains rebirth not in the Pythagorean sense but in a different sense altogether. Pythagoras believed in a soul which transmigrated from one life to another after death. Buddhism does not believe in a permanent soul. The question is how Buddhism explains rebirth. When Nagasena says that there is no being which migrates from one body to another Milinda asks if there is no transmigration how is rebirth possible ? Nagasena makes this difficult point clear by giving a few ingenious illustrations. He says that when a lamp is lighted by another lamp we do not say that the former transmigrates to the latter or when a disciple learns a verse from the teacher we do not say that the verse transmigrates from the teacher to the disciple. Similarly rebirth takes place without transmigration.

The king puts another question : if there is no being then what is reborn will be free from the evil deeds done in the past. Nagasena answers this question by giving the simile of a thief who steals mango from a mango tree and when he is charged with theft and informed that he would be punished for it, he makes a plea that the mango he stole is not the same mango as was planted in the soil. But he deserves punishment all the same because the mango that he stole is the result of the mango set in the ground. We can never imagine this mango without the first one being planted in the ground. And so just as the thief deserves punishment so one name and form performs deeds either *kusala* or *akusala* and another name and form is reborn by the influence of that *kamma* and suffers. If the being is not reborn he will be free from evil deeds but if he is reborn he will not be set free from his evil deeds because they are the results of his past actions.

Nagasena explains the question 'who is reborn' with magnificent and ingenious illustrations. He says that what is reborn is name and form and this name and form is the result of the previous *kammas*. He again takes the help of the simile of a thief stealing mangoes from a tree and says whatever the thief might say he cannot be absolved from the guilt because the mangoes that he stole have resulted from the last mango set in the ground. If a man after warming himself leaves fire burning although inadvertently and if from this fire a whole village is set on fire he is bound to pay for the loss the people have suffered. No amount of his plea that the fire he warmed himself with was not the same fire which burnt the village could make him free from the guilt. He is definitely guilty of the subsequent flagration that resulted from the previous fire. He gives another illustration to make it clear. Suppose a man takes the hand of a girl in marriage by paying price and goes away and comes back when she has grown up. Now at that time another man marries her and refuses to give her back to the man who on return claims her as his wife. Will the second man be justified in saying that the girl grown up to full age whom he has taken her as his wife is not the same young girl whom he had married. This convinced king Milinda and he saw how rebirth takes place. Nagasena makes this point clear by giving yet another illustration. He says that a man who buys a pot of milk and refuses to pay the price to the milkman because the milk that he bought from him turned into curd will not be justified because it is from the milk he bought that the curd came into being.

There is another very important and relevant question connected with the theory of *kamma* and rebirth." Does he, who is born, remain the same or become another ?" Nagasena replies that he is neither the same nor another. Just as the grown up man is not the same as the child from whom he had developed and derived, he is not different either. Similarly one who is born is neither the same nor different. The different states and phases from childhood to manhood are included is one by means of the same body. Just as a man who commits a crime is the same who gets the punishment so what is born is not completely different from one who grows up. A child is born, he grows up, he goes to school, he learns from a teacher and when he grows to manhood he may look different but, as a matter of fact, all these states are included in one growing process. Just as in a burning lamp continuity is maintained through change, so continuity in name and form is maintained through changes. To make it more clear just as continuity is maintained through changes when milk turns into curd and curd into butter and butter into *ghee* ,similarly the continuity of a person or a thing is maintained. One phase or state comes into being and another passes away and the rebirth is as it were simultaneous.

It is really an intellectual treat to go through these illustrations which make the most complex problems connected with the theory of *kamma* and rebirth very patent to us. All these illustrations are dynamic connected as they are either with chemical process or biological one and throw a flood of light on this complex problem. Just as 'the bird in a cage' simile beautifully illustrates the permanent soul leaving this body and entering another after death so these similes and illustrations very clearly and convincingly make it patent to us how rebirth takes place and he, who is born, is not something permanent. Rebirth, as a matter of fact, is a dynamic and a living process.

References

1. A.N. i, 173; *Gradual Sayings*, i, 157.
2. A.N. i, 249
3. *"Cetanāham, Bhikkhave, kammam vadāmi." Manopubbam gamā dhammā mano seṭṭhā manomayā*....D.P1.1.
4. *The Questions of King Milinda*, p.100,
5. *"Kammassakā, mānavā, sattā kammadāyādā kammayoni, kamma bandhu, kamma paṭisaranā, Kamma satte vibhajati, yadidaṃ hīnappaṇitatāyā ti. Majjhima NIkāya* p.280 (Nalanda edition).
6. *The Questions of King MIlinda*, pp. 112-113.
7. *ibid.*, p.103.
8. *ibid.*, p.104.
9. *ibid.*, p.104, *ibid.*, p. 105.
10. *ibid.*, p.105.
11. *ibid.*, 105.
12. *ibid.*, p.101.
13. *ibid.*, p.102.
14. *ibid.*, p.111.
15. *ibid.*, p.111.
16. *ibid.*, p.112.
17. *ibid.*, p.63.

Buddhism and Pragmatism

Is Buddhist philosophy pragmatic ? This is a very intriguing question for scholars of Buddhist philosophy. Those who study modern philosophy like pragmatism feel compelled to interpret it in terms of pragmatic philosophy inasmuch as they see the seeds of pragmatism in it.

What is pragmatic philosophy ? Robert N. Beck in his book entitled *Handbook in Social Philosophy* defines it in the following words:-

"As a philosophic revolt, then, pragmatism is a movement that rejects philosophies which speculate on abstractions or empty first principles. It looks to concrete cases, to particular consequences, and to ideas and meanings that will 'make a difference'. It is also against monistic and absolutistic positions : there are no 'wholesale views' of reality (Dewey) or single solutions for the problems of men. Pragmatists also reject purely logical procedures such as coherence as a method of thought for either facts or values. Thought is experimental, and its full meaning includes active manipulation and control beyond logical inference."[1]

It is clear from this definition of pragmatism that the soundness or otherwise of a philosophical theory can be judged on the basis of its consequences in our life. If a theory has got a practical utility in solving our problems it is meaningful for us. But if it merely speculates on abstractions which have no practical bearing on our life then it is no longer a philosophy worth the name. William James explains it in the following words:- "A pragmatist turns his back resolutely and once for all upon a lot of inveterate habits dear to professional professors.

He turns away from abstraction and insufficiency, from verbal solutions, from bad *a priori* reasons, from fixed principles, closed systems, and pretended absolutes and origins. He turns towards concreteness and adequacy, towards facts, towards action and toward power."[2] At one place he explains it as an anti-intellectualist tendency because it lays emphasis on practical consequences rather than on abstract thinking. Pragmatism according to him is "the attitude of looking away from first things, principles, 'categories', supposed necessities ; and of looking towards last things, fruits, consequences, facts."[3]

All this explains pragmatism as a philosophy which is a revolt against Hegelian abstract thinking which led people no where in the sense that it did not prepare them to grapple with their immediate problems and solve them. It, at best, remained an arm-chair speculation.

If we look at Buddhist philosophy in the light of the characteristics of pragmatic philosophy, it will be immediately clear to us that Buddhism as a philosophy is largely pragmatic inasmuch as it lays emphasis not on abstract thinking but on solving the practical problems facing human beings.

Buddha's attitude to philosophy becomes thoroughly clear from what he says to Poṭṭhapāda who put ten questions regarding the soul and the world to him to answer. Buddha did not answer those questions. He said that questions like "Is the world eternal ? Is the world not eternal ? Is the world finite ? Is the world not finite ? Does Tathāgata live after death or does He not live ?" have no bearing on human life and its problems. So why waste one's time and energy to try to find out their answes? He thought it better to leave them unanswered. But he very gladly expounded the four Noble truths which he had realised in his life and explained their significance at length. Buddha did not care to answer the question put by Poṭṭhapāda because "this question is not calculated to profit, it is not concerned with the Norm (*Dhamma*), it does not redound even to the elements of right conduct nor to detachment, nor to purification from lusts, nor to quietude, nor to tranquillisation of heart, nor to real knowledge, nor to the insight (of the higher stages of the path), nor to *Nirvāṇa*."[4] But he expounds what suffering is as also its origin, its cessation and the way leading to its cessation because "that question...is calculated to profit, is concerned with the Norm, redounds to the beginnings of right conduct, to detachment, to purification from lusts, to quietude...to *Nirvāṇa*"[5] His pragmatic attitude is also clear from what he says to Malukyaputta about the man struck with an arrow.[6]

The best thing for a philosopher, according to him, is to try to know the cause of suffering and the way to put an end to it. The four Noble truths about which he spoke at great length explain in great depth the cause of our suffering and the way to get rid of it. His philosophy, therefore, is practical in the sense that it shows mankind the path that leads to annihilation of suffering as also to attaining light and liberation. Had it been speculative, it would have tried to answer questions like "Is the world eternal or not eternal" and so forth. Instead he expounded the four Noble truths. The first Noble truth makes a statement of fact. Suffering is ubiquitous and has universal appeal. The second Noble truth puts finger on its cause. The third is an assertion born out of his personal realisation that suffering can be eradicated and the fourth maps out the eightfold path which leads one to liberation.

If we look at the Noble eightfold path we shall find that it consists of *śila* (virtue or ethical conduct), *samādhi* (concentration of mind) and *prajñā* (wisdom or insight into the real nature of things). All three individually and together are of great value in our life. That is why it is said again and again that Buddha has preached *Dhamma* which is 'lovely in its origin (*ādi kalyāṇaṃ*), lovely in its progress (*majjhe kalyānaṃ*) and lovely in its consummation (*pariyosāna kalyānanṃ*). The observance of virtue enables one to exercise control over his physical, mental and vocal actions. It also enables one to keep the doors of sense-organs well-guarded and helps one to drive away greed and develop contentment. Practising meditation helps one to control the unsteady mind and achieve concentration which, in turn, can lead one to gain insight into the true nature of things. Besides, observance of virtue plays a great role in improving the society of mankind. It has both individual and social bearings. A man who observes virtue and whose conduct is ethical becomes a useful citizen of society.

In short, Buddhist philosophy is practical. It lays emphasis on the concrete rather than on the abstract. It is a philosophy which has good results both in this life and in the life to come. Therefore, it is practical and not speculative.

But there is a great difference between Buddhism and pragmatism as we know it today. The difference is due to the background of the birth of pragmatic philosophy which is not the same as that of Buddhist philosophy. Buddhist philosophy concentrates much on spiritual problems confronting man. But pragmatism concerns itself with man's social, economic, political and above all existential problems. Man suffers largely because of economic, social and political injustice. Besides, his scientific achievement has put into his hands very powerful and sophisticated weapons which threaten his very existence. The economic imbalance that grew up in the wake of Industrial Revolution caused economic injustice. The two world wars with all their horrors compelled man and legitimately so to bother his head about what is going to happen in the present life and not to think of life to come. It is in this background that pragmatic philosophy grew and developed. Thus, it kept in view the consequences, the results and never bothered itself about abstract speculations.

It is for this reason that pragmatism is essentially connected with education. Dewey who is a pragmatist gives the basic meaning of pragmatism in the following words :- "The theory that the processes and the materials of knowledge are determined by practical or purposive considerations-that there is no such thing as knowledge determined by exclusively theoretical, speculative, or abstract intellectual considerations."[7] The soundness or otherwise of an educational system is determined by its results. If it helps mankind in solving the problems of life, it is good, if it does not, it is not. Similarly whether a philosophy is good or not is determined by what it does to mankind.

Judged from this point of view, Buddhism, as I said earlier, is pragmatic. But it is pragmatic in a different sense. It is a pragmatic philosophy in so far as it takes into consideration the spiritual problem of mankind-the problem of *karma* and rebirth-the problem of being born again and again under the influence of one's desires and suffer incalculably. Pragmatism as we know it today does not take into consideration man's spiritual problem. Instead, it takes into consideration problems arising out of his social, economic and political situations. In other words, it does not think of the other world but thinks only of this world. The pragmatism that we find in Buddhism is spiritual. It is not speculative and escapistic but it is realistic and teaches mankind to face the problems of life squarely and find a way out of them.

Buddhism, at least early Buddhism, never allows itself to think of and speculate on the first principles. Instead, it always concentrates on the consequences. If treading on the eightfold path does not give one the desired results why tread on it at all? But each constituent of the eightfold path when observed and practised produces good results and has ennobling effect on the individual who treads it. Therefore, we can say without any doubt that Buddhist philosophy is pragmatic.

References

1. Robert N.Beck, *Handbook in Social Philosophy,* Macmillan Publishing Co., New York, 1979, p.123.
2 William James, *Pragmatism,* Longmans Green and Co., London, 1949, p.51.
3. *ibid.*, pp. 54-55.
4. T.W.Rhys Davids, *Dialogues of the Buddha* Vol.I Oxford Umiversity Press, 1899. pp.254-55.
5. *ibid.*, p.255.
6. *Cūlamāluṅkya sutta, Majjhima Nikāya* Vol.2 pp. 107-113 (Nalanda edition).
7. Robert N. Beck, *Handbook in Social Philosophy,* p. 121.

The Concept of Matter in Early Buddhism

In early Buddhism, analysis of matter has been made with an express ethical purpose in view. Buddhist Ethics lays emphasis on getting rid of *taṇhā* which is at the root of our repeated existence and sufferings of all kinds, physical, mental and cosmic. *Taṇhā* is caused by our desire for the various objects of the world. We are attached to the various forms of *rūpa* (matter) and our passionate attachment to them gives rise to *taṇhā*. The irony is that no amount of the enjoyment of the worldly objects can quench our thirst for them. The more we have of them, the more we still desire of them. *Taṇhā*, as a matter of fact, is an ever-going dynamo; the more it is constantly fed on by *taṇhā, the more it produces ever increasing taṇhā.*

Lord Buddha, unlike other theoretical philosophers, was a practical philosopher and the *Dharma* preached by him contains practical doctrine. His greatest purpose was to get rid of suffering which we are heir to. Suffering, as we have seen, is caused by our attachment to *rūpa* i.e. by our *chandarāga* for it. But we are hardly aware that the *rūpa* we attach ourselves to, is in a constant state of flux. Though it looks permanent and unchanging, it is merely appearance. The reality is far otherwise. Therefore attachment to *rūpa* would inevitably lead to unrest and sorrow. In the *Saṁyutta Nikāya* Buddha advises us to give up all kinds of desire and passion in respect of *rūpa*.

Yo, Bhikkhave, rupasmiṁ chandarāgo taṁ pajahatha.[1]

Rūpa (matter) is not a *saṁyojana* (fetter) in itself, but it is *Saṁyojanīya* i.e, it creates fetters. So long as we have avid greed and passion in our mind for the various objects of the world, we will always be bound by fetters created by them. Therefore, if we want to put an end to suffering, we must destroy the various warps and woofs of our passion for the objects of the world. *Rūpa* is productive of fetters that bind the living being to worldly existence. *Rūpaṁ saṁyojanīyo dhammo.*[2]

It is chiefly and perhaps solely in this context that the Buddhists have made an analysis of matter. Because *rūpa* is *saṁyojanīya,* so its true nature must be comprehended. Our ignorance of its true nature will make us crave for it, remain attached to it and as a consequence, our spiritual progress will be impeded.

There are a number of passages in the Pali canon which describe this aspect of *rūpa*. It is a source of dangers that arise from attachment to it. How do we get attached to it ? Because we are ignorant of its real nature. *Ajānaṁ apassaṁ sārajjati.*[3] In the *Saṁyutta Nikāya* Lord Buddha says : *Rūpaṁ, Bhikkhave, anabhijānam, aparijānam abhabbo dukkhakkhayāya.*[4]

Rūpa (matter) is not permanent. Its origination and dissolution are manifested. In the *Saṁyutta Nikāya*[5] its true nature is described. It is *Paṭiccasamuppanna, saṁkhāta, aññathābhāvi, khayadhammā, vayadhammā* and also it is *nirodha dhammā.*

In the profoundly religious context, it has been described as *māra, roga, gaṇda, salla, ogha* and *āditta. Suññam, tuccha, ritta* and *asāra* form another set of characteristics describing *rūpa*. It has been compared to *Pheṇapiṇḍa* (bubble) to bring out its impermanent nature.

Analysis of matter by the early Buddhists has been done in the above mentioned way so that no one may feel like being attached to *rūpa* which is short-lived like froth.

The early Buddhists do not so much describe the metaphysical concept of *rūpa* as they describe its that aspect which causes our worldly existence. Human personality is made up of *nāma* (consciousness) and *rūpa* (matter). The early Buddhists have described both of them from a pragmatic point of view which is to end our suffering.

The Buddhists like the Vedantins do not regard this external world as non-existent. Nor like the other idealists, do they show that the world is mind-made or a projection of subjective thought as held by Berkeley. Throughout the Pali texts it is maintained that matter or *rūpa* does exist independent of one's mind.

This is the position taken by the early Buddhists. They start from the obvious. According to them when an individual comes into being in this world, he comes in contact with this external world which acts on him and to which he reacts. Thus, attachment to those objects of the world which are pleasing to him and repugnance for the objects which do not do so arise in him. As a consequence, he is inextricably bound by his passions and desires.

The immediate problem before the early Buddhists was how to annihilate passions and desire. It was, therefore, very necessary for them to understand the real nature of *rūpa* which acts on human beings and causes interminable grief.

According to Buddhist philosophy, human personality is composed of five *khandhas* in their dynamic relationship with one another. They are *rūpa, vedanā, saññā, saṁkhāra,* and *viññāṇa.* The last four are mind and the first one is matter. How the two entirely opposite elements are related has been graphically described by Buddhaghoa. He gives the illustration of a lame man going on the path on the shoulders of a blind man. None of them can do without the help of other. Both depend on each other.

Such a human personality naturally reacts to the external world with the six sense-organs he is endowed with. The dynamic contact between the sense-organs and their objects gives rise to myriads of complex sensations which cause fetters that bind an individual to the wheel of existence unmistakably characterised by suffering.

The *summum bonum,* according to Buddhist Philosophy, is *Nibbāna* which means the extinction of all passions and desires. It has been time and again pointed out that whatever is in a state of constant flux can hardly afford any lasting happiness. *Rūpa* is transmutable and has been defined in the following words :

Ruppatīti kho, Bhikkhave, tasmā rūpaṁ ti vuccati.
kena ruppati ? sīten pi ruppati, uṇhen pi ruppati,
jigacchāya pi ruppati, daṃsa makasa vātātapa sirinsapa
samphassena pi ruppati.

T.W. Rhys Davids explains the most important word *ruppati* in this passage as "to be vexed, oppressed, hurt, molested". According to the *Vibhanga Aṭṭhakathā*, it is *kuppati, pīliyati* and *bhijjati*. Although *ruppati* refers to a psychological disturbance, it also refers to the physical change that an object undergoes. The whole purpose is to show the changeable and transmutable nature of *rūpa*. There is nothing like the metaphysical entity called matter. But any given material is analysable into *rūpadhammas*, which have been regarded as the ultimate reducible factors that make up the physical world. A *rūpa dhamma* does not have any independent existence. It always exists inseparably with a set of other *dhammas*. It is for this reason that the *mahābhūtas* (primary) are called *sahajāta*.

According to Buddhist Philosophy, there are twentyeight types of *rūpas*, four of them are primary and the rest twentyfour are secondary.

Paṭhavī, āpo, tejo and *vāyo* are primary elements and they are called *mahābhūtas*. *Paṭhavī dhātu* is characterised by *kakkhalatā* and *kharigatā*. One may say that *kakkhalatā* is itself *paṭhavi*. So is the case with *āpo dhātu* which is defined as *rūpassa bandhanattā* i.e. viscidity and cohesion that bind the matter together. There are two other characteristics of water, *paggharaṇa* i.e. flowing and *nissandabhāva* i.e. state of streaming.

In the *Nikāyas*, the *mahābhūtas* are defined in simple and general terms and they are illustrated with reference to the constituents of body. Hair of the head and body, nails, teeth, flesh and skin etc. are examples of *paṭhavī dhātu*, because they are hard and rigid. Blood, bile, cough and phlegm are examples of *āpodhātu*. Heat in the body is an example of *tejo dhātu* and inhalings and exhalings and other kinds of winds are examples of *vāyo dhātu* which is airy.

Such definitions of the *mahābhūtas* may be called popular. It is only in the *Abhidhamma* that abstract and detailed definitions of these *mahābhūtas* are given. According to the *Nikāyas* what is *kakkhala* is *paṭhavī*, whereas according to the *Ābhidhammika* definition *kakkhalatā* itself is *paṭhavī*. Not only *kakkhalatā* but *kharatva* and *gurutva* also are said to be *paṭhavī*. It is also defined as that which spreads up, *pattharatīti paṭhavī*. Buddhaghoa says that *paṭhavī dhātu* acts as a foundation in so far as the other three elements are established on it.

Āpo dhātu is *rūpassa bandhanattā* i.e. it is that which binds the *rūpa kalāpas* together. It is represented by the fact of *sineha* or viscidity. How are the particles of iron or for that matter the particles of stone closely bound together ? It is the function of *āpo dhātu* to bind all the particles together. Two other characteristics of *āpo dhātu* are flowing and streaming. These account for the fact that *vāyo dhātu* and *tejo dhātu* also have *āpo dhātu* in them, because they spread and flow. According to the Vaiśeṣika philosophy, *āpo* has two characteristics i.e. liquidity and viscidity, *āpo dravah snigdhah* but unlike the Vaiśeṣikas, the Buddhists do not recognize the dichotomy between substance and quality.

Tejo dhātu means the phenomenon of heat or *uṇhattā*. The Buddhists, unlike the upholders of Vaiśeṣika philosophy, believe that *uṣṇa* and *sīta* really come under *tejo dhātu*. It is true that cold or *sīta* is known by the sense of touch, it is really *tejo dhātu* because cold is really relative absence of heat. This is indeed an ingenious explanation given by the Theravādins.

The *Dhammasangani* defines *vāyo dhātu* in terms of *thambhitattā (inflation) and chambhitattā (mobility). As distinct from the rest three of mahābhūtas*, it represents the dynamic aspect.

Thus seen, the *mahābhūtas* are not qualities and attributes of the *bhūta rūpa* i.e. they are qualities not inhering in any substance. In other words, the qualities themselves constitute the *mahābhūtas*.

One of the fundamental features of the *mahābhūtas* is that none of them can exist in isolation. In fact no *mahābhūta* (primary element) can exist independently of the other three *mahābhūtas*. They are, therefore, called *sahajāta* and *sahabhū*. On further analysis it becomes clear that the *upapatti* (origination), *ṭhiti* (existence) and *bhanga* (dissolution) of one always synchronize with those of the others. The *mahābhūtas* cannot be separated from one another. In short, they rise together, exist together and are destroyed together. They are, therefore, called *abbinibhoga rūpa*. It means that every instance of matter contains all the four primary elements. Thus all material aggregates are tetra-*bhautic*. Although the Vedānta philosophy believes in mono-*bhautic* substance, it holds that in each *mahābhūta* there are five *sūkṣama* (subtle) *bhūtas* present.

As against the *Sāṁkhya* system of philosophy where *mahābhūtas* are not ultimate constituents of matter (they are believed to evolve immediately from the *tanmātrās* and ultimately from the *prakṛti* which is the uncaused first cause of the world of non-self), the early Buddhists assign them a comparatively primary position.

Vedānta philosophy, as we have seen, holds that *mahābhūtas* are gross which come into being from the *sūkṣama bhūtas*. According to Jaina philosophy, not the four elements but the *paramāṇus* are the constituents of *pudgala*. So according to them *paramāṇu* is given a comparatively primary position. The Nyāya-Vaiśeṣika system of philosophy has postulated four kinds of atoms corresponding to earth, water, air and fire.

Besides the above explained four primary elements (*mahābhūtas*), there are twentyfour secondary *rūpas*. They are called *uppādā rūpas* in so far as they depend on the *mahābhūtas*. Five sense-organs, four objects of the senses, two faculties of sex, one faculty of life, *āhāra, hadaya vatthu* (the physical basis of mental activity), the two modes of self expression (*kāyaviññati* and *vacīviññati*), three characteristics like *lahutā, mudutā* and *kammaññatā*, four phases of matter like *upacaya, santati, jaratā* and *aniccatā* and the element of space are the twenty four *uppādā rūpas*.

The first five sense-organs viz; *cakkhu, sata, ghāna, jivha* and *kāya* are respectively the organs of sight, hearing, smell, taste and touch. In the *Abhidhamma* they have been described as *pasāda* which means clearness and brightness. These sense-organs are not only receptive, but they also gratify our sensual pleasures. They react as well as gratify. They are very subtle and delicate and they can be known by no other sense-organ than by mind which is the subtlest of all. They are composed of subtler matter and their corresponding objects are made of gross ones.

According to the early Buddhists, the relationship between the sense-organs and their corresponding objects is that between the subtle and the gross. The Sāṁkhya philosophy holds more or less the same view. According to it, the development of matter takes place along two different lines. Where there is predominance of *sattva* that evolves into sense-organs and where there is predominance of *tamas* or dead matter that becomes sense objects. But there is a basic difference. As Prof. Stcherbatsky has pointed out, the two groups of matter are not conceived as modification of an eternal substance by the Buddhists.

It has been held by most of the systems of Indian thought that the sense-organs are something which are very fine and very subtle. The Jains speak of two kinds of *indriyas* viz., *dravya indriyas* (the physical sense-organs) and *bhāvendriyas* their - psychical correlates. The Mimāṁsakas mention that "the sense-organs consist in the faculty of potency abiding in their sockets." According to the Vedānta system of philosophy, different sense-organs consist of *sāttvic* parts of light, ether, earth, water and air.

From all this, it is clear that sense-organs as they are subtle, transparent and translucent, develop sensitivity to external world of objects as a looking glass has to all objects.

The sense objects have been enumerated as four viz., *rūpa* (the visible), *sadda* (sound), *gandha* (smell) and *rasa* (taste). Although there is another sense object called the *phoṭabba* (the tangible), it has not been enumerated here because it consists of three of the four primary elements, water being excluded. The *rūpāyatana* (the sphere of the visible) includes colour like blue, yellow, red, etc. and figures which are circular, oval, square, hexagonal etc. The *saddāyatana* (the sphere of the audible) includes different kinds of sounds of drum, of tabors, of conch shells etc. The *gandhāyatana* (the sphere of the odorous) includes all kinds of odour *ṣugandha* and *durgandha* and the *rasāyatana* (the sphere of the savoury) includes tastes like bitter, pungent, saline and acrid etc.

It is interesting to note here that the early Buddhists have discussed the problem as to how the sound travels. Does it require a medium to travel ? The answer is in the affirmative.

The two faculties of sex which are responsible for distinguishing the male from the female also come under *uppāda rūpa* (secondary matter). According to the *Dhammasangani,* the *purisindriya* (faculty of masculinity) is responsible for the physical appearance, marks, traits and deportment that are peculiar to a male. Similarly the *itthindriya* (faculty of femininity) gives rise to the marks and traits of a female.

Jīvitindriya (the faculty of life) is also a kind of *uppāda rūpa.* Its function is to stabilize and sustain the *kammasamuṭṭhāna rūpa* i.e. matter that rises as a result of *kamma.* There is *Jīvitindriya* in a piece of paper so long as it is not friable. The moment it becomes so, it has lost the faculty of life. *Kabaliṅkāra āhāra* is also a form of secondary *rūpa.* Although it literally means gross food taken in morsels, its *Ābhidhammika* meaning is that aspect of matter which is nutritive i.e. which helps one in growth.

Hadaya vatthu, not recognized as a form of *rūpa* even in the *Dhammasangani* but mentioned in the *Paṭṭhāna,* is a post canonical development. It is called the heart basis which is the physical basis of *mano dhātu* (mind) and *mano viññāna dhātu* (mind consciousness).

The two modes of self expression (*viññati rūpa*) *kāyaviññati* (bodily expression) and *vacīviññati* (vocal expression) are also *uppāda rūpas.* Because they make the thoughts known or they help in communicating thoughts, they are called *viññati.* *Kāyaviññati* is not identical with bodily expression but it refers to the bodily tension that rises in response to a thought, moral (*kusala*), immoral (*akusala*) or indeterminate (*avyākata*). In the

Dhammasangani, it has been defined as the state of bodily tension or excitement (*kāyassa thambhanā, santhanbhanā samthambhitattam*). *Vacīviññati* menas expression or communication through voice of speech or articulate sound. It rises like *kāyaviññati* in response to a *kusala, akusala* or *avyākata* thought.

The three characteristics of matter viz., *lahutā* (lightness), *mudutā* (softness) and *kammaññatā (pliability) are qualities of matter in general. This triad of lahutā, mudutā* and *kammaññatā* represents the healthy and effcient position of a being.

There are also phases of matter which are four in number viz., *rūpassa upacaya* (growth of matter), *rūpassa santati* (continuity of matter), *rūpassa jaratā* (decay of matter) and *rūpassa aniccatā* (impermanence of matter). Obviously these four phases indicate growth of matter, its continuity, its decaying state and its complete annihilation.

These phases of matter clearly point out that there is no justification for our being attached to any object for true happiness. They rise only in order to be annihilated. When they are in a constant state of flux, how can they give true happiness?

The last item of *uppāda rūpa* is *ākāsa* (element of space). It is *ākāsa dhātu* which gives room to all material things for movement. It is regarded as a bounded space.

Thus, it is clear that the early Buddhists have defined matter more from the ethical point of view than from the metaphysical point of view. In spite of this bias, however, the metaphysical point of view is also not blurred and indistinct.

References

1. *Saṁyutta Nikāya*, Vol.2 pp. 375.
2. *ibid.*, Vol.2, pp. 262.
3. *ibid.*, Vol.3, pp. 389.
4. *ibid.*, Vol.2, pp. 262.
5. *ibid.*, Vol.2, pp. 261.

Ācārya Śantideva's Humanism

Humanism[1] of early Buddhism is apparent from what Buddha said about man as also from what he wanted to do for mankind after he became enlightened. He says that man is his own master. He is his own lord.[2] Whatever a man is, he is so by virtue of his own deeds, good or bad or both. As a matter of fact, the self of a man is made of the *vipākas* of his actions. These he takes with him wherever he goes. In other words, the actions performed by him follow him like a shadow.[3]

In practically all his important *suttas* this is the burden of his teaching. Man is what he does or he becomes what he thinks to be. Therefore, man is responsible for his pollution or purification. He is the cause of his suffering as he is the cause of his happiness. Lord Buddha never brings in 'God' or any god or any other force to account for the misery and happiness of mankind. Man creates his own chains to bind himself to the wheel of birth and death and he himself can cut them and free himself. He does not have to depend upon any power outside himself for his liberation. Lord Buddha says it again and again that man can put an and to his sufferings by his own efforts. The efforts that he makes in treading on the eightfold path enable him to achieve *Nibbāna* (*Nirvāṇa*). Nobody else can tread on the path for him and end his suffering. Lord Buddha says clearly that even the Tathāgatas are there to show the path of salvation. They will not tread on the path for others.[4] Salvation depends upon his own efforts and will not be the result of blessings or boons granted by gods and Tathāgatas. Every man will have to work out his own salvation. It is, therefore, necessary that each one of us should become his own refuge. Lord Buddha wants every body to be his own refuge and his own lamp to guide himself.[5]

Another aspect of the humanism of early Buddhism is closely allied to what has been said above. Man cannot blame others for his miserable state and for what he does. He is cent per cent responsible for all that he does. He will also have to reap the consequences of his actions. But at the same time it should be borne in mind that man is not helpless. He is not like a straw tossed on the angry waves of a stormy sea. On the other hand, he has immense potentiality to do good and at the same time, he is equally capable of doing too many evils. It depends upon his wisdom and energy to do good and shun evil. In short, Lord Buddha has spoken gloriously of man and his potentiality. He agrees with Protagoras[6] and other Greek philosophers who regard man as the measure of all in the universe and anticipates the view held by thinkers and poets like Chandidas who raises man to a lofty position.[7]

Yet another aspect of The humanisn of early Buddhism is its altruism. A man should not think only of his own self but he should rise above narrow selfishness and think of doing good to others. Inspired by this noble and sublime feeling Lord Buddha exhorted his Bhikkhus to go from one place to another in all directions and work for the welfare and happiness of all.[8]

The four *Brahmavihāras* (love, compassion, sympathy and equanimity) are the cardinal sublime attitudes a man must develop in order to love all creatures, to sympathise with all suffering creatures, have compassion on them, to be happy at their achievements and successes and lastly to develop equanimity towards all, even towards his enemies. Thus, early Buddhism exhorts man to ennoble himself so that he can practise altruism in the world.

Śantideva's humanism takes up this aspect of early Buddhism and lays great emphasis on it. From this point of view his humanism is not very different from the humanism of early Buddhism but it is definitely a long way from that from the view points of other aspects of early Buddhism. Lord Buddha did not consider himself a superman, let alone God. He did not want others to depend upon God for blessings or upon him for help for his own liberation. But Śantideva has deified Lord Buddha. Lord Buddha has now become the embodiment of all that is good and great. He is, therefore, fit for being worshipped and revered. Man must worship him in order to achieve spiritual heights. By worshipping Buddhas and Bodhisattvas he will achieve power and strength to help all suffering creatures get rid of suffering. In other words, a man may have altruistic motive to serve others but he will derive strength by making offerings to the Buddhas and Bodhisattvas. In the second chapter of *Bodhicaryāvatāra* Śantideva is seen offering all flowers and fruits, gems and waters, all trees laden with fruits, all kinds of incenses and perfumes and all lotuses to Buddhas and is seen praying to them to accept them and grant him blessings.[9] It is clear from this that Buddhism at the time of Śantideva has come a long way from early Buddhism. As early Buddhism did not believe in the existence of God, it gave a supreme place to man whose dignity was upheld, but with the deification of the Buddhas and Bodhisattvas man came to have a subservient place, although his welfare has become the primary concern of the Buddhas and Bodhisattvas.

Śantideva's *Bodhicaryāvatāra* is the best example of Mahāyāna Buddhism that flowered by the time of Śantideva. The welfare of all suffering creatures is still uppermost in the mind of a Bodhisattva but the method to ameliorate their condition is different. He does not now intend to become the Buddha soon and exhort man to work out his own salvation but he now postpones his entering into *Nirvāṇa* and takes immense trouble for the sake of others. The ideal of a Bodhisatta in early Buddhism was to get rid of all desires and achieve a state of desirelessness called *Nibbāna.* This ideal, practically speaking, is narrow inasmuch as Bodhisatta here is primarily concerned with his own salvation but the Bodhisattva ideal as conceived by Mahāyāna is to postpone his entering into *Nirvāṇa* till all creatures are free from misery, disease and sin; till all creatures achieve *Nirvāṇa.* The Mahāyāna ideal finds best expression when Bodhisattva says that his pious desire is to see that no creature remains miserable and diseased, none remains a sinner, none is despised and none develops a wicked mind.[10] This is the exalted ideal of a Bodhisattva which has replaced the narrow and selfish ideal of a Bodhisatta of early Buddhism. In early Buddhism the anxiety of a Bodhisatta, if I may use this word, was to attain Buddhahood, but in Mahāyāna Buddhism this anxiety is not for his own self but it is now for all suffering creatures. Here a Bodhisattva is not keen and eager to work out his own salvation. His motive has become altruistic. His glorious aim is to free all creatures from suffering. For this he tries to develop his immense concern and love for all creatures without any distinction between good and bad or wicked and saintly. He does not have the patience now to teach man that he can attain *Nirvāṇa* by his own efforts. Instead, he becomes very impatient out of compassion to do all that he can to ameliorate his sufferings. He forgets in his anxiety that he has made men subservient to Buddhas and Bodhisattvas but this also shows his great devotion to them. Lord Buddha himself never did anything in his life to make people feel that they can liberate themselves by his blessings. But Śantideva who greatly and avowedly cherishes the Mahāyāna ideal always gives us the impression that it is Buddhas and Bodhisattvas who can pull us out of the great depth of darkness we are in and lead us to light.

A Bodhisattva practises six *pāramitas*[11] to be strong and meritorious enough to help creatures get rid of sufferings. He knows full well that many in this world cannot achieve merits which will end their suffering. So he thinks of transferring his own merits to them so that they can by virtue of the merits earned by him and transferred to them can end their miseries, live in peace and plenty and attain liberation.[12] He takes a vow to become a doctor to the diseased, medicine to the disease and to see to it that no disease ever visits any man.[13]

This idea of transfer of merit is quite strange to early Buddhism. There the accepted theory is that what a man reaps accords with what he sows. But in Mahāyāna it is not so. By the grace of Buddhas and Bodhisattvas it is possible that a sinner can absolve himself of all sins and reap something quite different from what he has sown. It is true that early Buddhism saw man as his own master but the humanism of Mahāyāna Buddhism has more compassion and generosity in that the Bodhisattvas here are eager to help all and sundry irrespective of their levels of spiritual development. He earns merit by performing *kuṣala kammas* so that he can be able to transfer it to the needy. A Bodhisattva here takes a vow not to be angry even with those who do him a lot of harm.[14] He practises what is called *kṣānti pāramitā* (forbearance). He wishes well even to those who are his sworn enemies and despise him. Ill-will he regards as the greatest stumbling block in his spiritual path. Therefore, he wants to get rid of it by all means. He never allows it to take hold of him even for a fraction of a second. He believes in forbearance and forgives even those who do him harm. Ill - will is a sort of sin according to him and forgiveness is a sort of penance. Therefore, he practises *kṣānti pāramitā*.[15] He knows that with the thorn of ill-will rankling in one's mind one can never get peace and happiness nor can he have sound sleep nor patience to do anything.[16]

A Bodhisatta in early Buddhism is zealous to annihilate his suffering but a Bodhisattva according to the Mahāyāna ideals sees great merit in suffering inasmuch as it does not allow one to become proud and egoistic. It is through suffering that one comes to realize the importance of compassion. He develops this sublime feeling, fears sin and becomes devoted to the Buddha and Bodhisattva.[17]

This element of devotion is also a very pronounced element in Mahāyāna Buddhism. Perhaps the teachings of early Buddhism were meant for a few people who were spiritually developed and who had uncommon amount of reason to take to the eightfold path and zeal enough to work out their salvation. The kind of humansim that we see in Mahāyāna Buddhism becomes the sheet anchor of all men endowed or unendowed with reason and spiritual zeal. Thus, this humanism has extended its scope and covers all men high or low, highly rational or less rational. *Bhakti*, by and large, is a sure means of liberation and it is easy for all to practise. Śantideva's humanism which is nothing but Mahāyāna Buddhism is more broad-based than that of early Buddhism inasmuch as it holds out a ray of hope to all people and not only to the selected few.

While practising forbearance a Bodhisattva argues rightly that if he cannot be angry at the humours[18] of his body which cause his physical ailments why should he be angry with those people who are angry with him because their anger is also caused by humours.[19] They lose their temper because of some pressure. There are causes for their doing so. Just as one does not like suffering, yet one suffers, so one does not like to be angry, yet he becomes angry because anger like suffering is subject to the law of dependent origination. He reasons out that both the weapon with which his enemy inflicts pain on his body and his body are causes of his suffering, so why should one be angry and with whom.[20] So, knowing the causes of his enemy's anger a Bodhisattva never becomes angry with him. This attitude of a Bodhisattva is greatly humanitarian inasmuch as all persons including his enemies come within the ambit of his compassion.

The humanitarian ideals of a Bodhisattva are clearly seen expressed in some of the *kārikās* (verses) of the third chapter of the *Bodhicaryāvatāra*.[21] His pious wish is that all those who abuse him and laugh at him should attain enlightenment. He expresses this exalted wish when he says that he wants to help those who are helpless and he wants to act as a raft or a boat or a bridge for willing people to cross the stream. He is even willing to be the servant of one who requires his service. His wish finds most exalted expression when he says that just as the earth and the sky provide all things needed for the use of infinitely great number of creatures so he also wants to do the same for all creatures till they do not attain liberation.[22]

Ācārya Śantideva was a saint of the first order. Therefore, he very subtly rouses in man the feeling of non-attachment to things of the world which are normally supposed to be delightful. In a style which resembles that of Bhartṛhari of the *Vairāgyaśataka* he makes it amply clear that we should not cling to the body which is ultimately devoured by worms, dogs and jackals and what remains is a skeleton which is useless. Several *kārikās* of the eighth chapter (*Dhyāna pāramitā*) bring the impermanence and transitoriness of human body home to us.[23]

Thus the humanism that we find in Ācārya Śantideva has a great concern for ameliorating the miserable conditions of man and for his liberation from the bondage of suffering, although he may not in his eyes be the measure of all things in the universe as said by Protagoras and other Greek philosophers and tenaciously held by early Buddhism to underline his dignified position. He does not regard man as his own master but what the great Bodhisattvas can do is all directed towards ameliorating his sufferings. In short, man and to ameliorate his miserable condition plus his liberation from the bondage of suffering are still the greatest concerns of a Bodhisattva. Thus the humanism of Mahāyāna Buddhism as we find it elaborated and spelt out by Ācārya Śantideva has more of humanitarian qualities like warmth and love, compassion and sympathy; has more of the desire on the part of a Bodhisattva to suffer for others and has infinite amount of keenness and eagerness to earn merit so as to be able to transfer it to those who badly need it for their salvation. Humanism of easrly Buddhism seems to be supplanted by Humanitarianism of Mahāyāna Buddhism.

References

1. It is a view in which interest in human welfare is central. It also includes August Comte's "worship of Humanity". It also refers to Religious Humanism which does not consider belief in a deity vital to religion. It is based on respect for the dignity of man, concern for his welfare and all round development.
2. *Attā hi attano nātho ko hi nātho paro siyā /*
   Attanā hi suantena nātham labhati dullabhaam //
   Dhammapada, 12.4.
3. *Ubho punnam ca pāpam ca, yam macco kurute idha /*
   Tam hi tassa sakam hoti tam vā ādāya gacchati /
   Tam vassa anugam hoti chāyā va anapāyini //

   S.N. Kosala saṁyutta.

4. *Tumhehi kiccamātappam, akkhātāro tathāgatā /*
Paṭipannā pamokkhanti jhāyino mārabandhanā // D.P., 20.4.
5. *Attadipā viharatha attasaranā anaññasaranā.* D.N.I. *Mahāparinibbāna Sutta.*
6. Man is the measure of all things-Protagoras.
7. *Sabār upara mānusa satta tahār upara nei.* Candidasa.
8. *Caratha,. Bhikkhave, cārikam bahujana hitāya bahujana sukhāya.*
9. *Yavaṇti puṡpāṇi phalāni caiva bhaisajyajatani ca yani santi /*
Ratnani yavanti ca santi loke jaiani ca svacchamanoraman i/3
Devadilokesu ca gandhakupah kalpadruma ratnamayasca vrksah /
Saransi cambhoruhabhusananai hansasvaratyantamanoharani //
10. *Mā kaścid duhkhitah sattva mā pāpī mā ca rogitah /*
Mā hīnah paribhūto va mā bhut kaścicca durmanah //
Bodhicaryāvatāra 10.41.
11. *Dāna, Sīla, Nekkhamma, Pañña, Viriya, Kṣānti.*
12. *Evam sarvamidam kṛtvā yanmayāsaditam śubham /*
Tena syam sarvasattvānām sarvaduhkhaprasantikṛt // op. cit. 3.6.
13. *Glānanāmasmi bhaiṣajyam bhavetam vaidya eva ca /*
Tadupasthayakaścaiva yāvad rogapunarbhavah // ibid., 3.7.
14. *Abhyakhyasyanṭi mam ye ca ye cānye 'pyakarinah /*
Ut prasakasthanye' pi sarva syurbodhibhaginah // ibid., 3.16.
15. *Na ca dveṣasamam pāpam na ca kṣāntisamam tapah /*
Tasmātkṣāntim prayatnena bhavayadvividhairnaye // ibid., 6.2.
16. *ibid.*, 6.3.
17. *ibid.*, 6.21.
18. Blood phlegm choler, melancholy were regarded as humours.
19. *ibid.*, 6.22.
20. *ibid.*, 6.43.
21. See Third Chapter of the *Bodhicaryāvatāra.*
22. *ibid.*, 3.20.
23. See the verses of Chapter eight.

Buddhism in a Changing World

Buddhism was preached more than two thousand and five hundred years ego, but it has not lost its relevance at all. Rather it seems to have become more significant and relevant than ever in the present circumstances that obtain in the world. With armament rące, proliferation of deadly nuclear weapons, ever spiralling stockpiling of them, the world is on the brink of an unprecedented catastrophe. One act of folly and all that mankind has achieved in the name of civilization and culture is destined to be destroyed and all that are nice and valuable for mankind will be lost for ever.

The question is how to live in this world and how to act so that the valuable gems of human thought can be preserved and the world can be saved from going to war and losing all the 'sweetness and light' that man has achieved in his arduous journey from a dark age up till now. Man's aspiration has been succintly expressed in these words of the *Kaṭhopniṣad* -

Lead me from untruth to truth
Lead me from darkness to light
Lead me from death to deathlessness !

But what will happen to his aspiration if he gives a free play to his emotions like hatred and jealousy, anger and other negative feelings. Man should cultivate love and think that because all persons like to be loved, so one must give love to others. As is said in the *Dhammapada*, "All beings are afraid of pain, all beings are afraid of death. Recognizing oneself in others one should neither kill nor cause to kill."[1] If a man does this, then a peaceful atmosphere in the world can be created and people may devote themselves to thoughts which might lead them to further heights of glories.

All religions of the world set themselves the task of making human life nobler, more charitable, more generous and more loving. Their main task is to point out those good seeds in man which when watered and nurtured carefully will sprout forth and produce cool shade for mankind to rest. In case it is otherwise, people will burn in hatred. Man, as we know, has good as well as bad motives for his action According to Buddhist psychology greed, hatred and ignorance are at the root of all immoral actions and their opposites are at the root of moral actions. Whereas these need to be developed, the former *akusala hetus* must be exterminated.

Looked at from this point of view, Buddhism seems to have contributed a lot to help us achieve this end. Buddha was a philosopher of a different kind. Unlike other philosophers he did not like making speculations about the eternality or non-eternality of the world and about its finiteness and infiniteness, because he was fully convinced that no amount of speculation will help one arrive at the true answer. There are ten such questions which he called indeterminate and declined to answer. He declined to answer because such question is "not calculated to profit, it is not concerned with the Norm (*Dhamma*), it does not redound even to the elements of right conduct, nor to detachment, nor to purification from lusts, nor to quietude, nor to tranquillisation of heart, nor to real knowledge, nor to the insight of the higher stages of the path, nor to *Nirvāṇa*"[2] Buddha was primarily concerned with getting rid of suffering which is the inevitable lot of all beings. He realized that the genuine problem of life is suffering (*dukkha*) which is ubiquitous. As has been explained by A.B. Govind, there are three clearly recognisable kinds of suffering viz. physical, mental, and the essential form of suffering which is rightly termed as cosmic. Whereas the cosmic suffering is the concern of one who is on his way to enlightenment and the mental suffering is the concern of the average human being, suffering as physical pain and bodily want is the concern of all forms of primitive consciousness. Buddha has very deeply analysed all the levels of suffering and although he was primarily concerned with the suffering implicit in the cosmic law which chains us to our deeds, good as well as bad, and drives us incessantly round in the restless circle from form to form,[3] he did not ignore the other two but has always spoken about them. In fact, he was led to the essential form of suffering from the other two. In this connection he made two important observations. First, suffering does not come from outside but it comes from within. It is we who cause our suffering, and second all kinds of suffering proceed from our lust or *taṇhā*. He propounded the theory of *pratītyasamutpāda* which explains the cause-effect relationship between lust and suffering.

The path that Buddha prescribed to put an end to suffering is not only concerned with the annihilation of cosmic suffering but it equally applies to annihilating physical and mental sufferings. The *aṭṭhaṅgiko maggo* by which his path is styled consists of right view, right resolve, right speech, right action, right livelihood, right effort, right mindfulness and right concentration and these eight constituents can be classed into *sīla*, *samādhi* and *paññā* which are the three important milestones in the Buddhist path of *sādhanā*. If one treads on this path, one is likely to get rid of suffering but even if one does not end his suffering in this life, one is sure to minimise it to a great extent.

Buddha's religion is the religion of mental culture. If one observes *sīla* and practises meditation *(samādhi)* one will attain *paññā*, i.e. insight into the real nature of the things of the world and attain *Nirvāṇa*.

Most of the ills of the world today have stemmed from giving free play to our enotions of hatred and jealousy and anger, as I have said earlier. We have also become more egoistic. The result is we do not put a premium on the views of others. We look down on them. A chain reaction of hatred sets in and we become more and more involved. If we do not learn to control our emotions, we are likely to be doomed. Buddha taught us how to control our emotions of anger and hatred and jealousy and devlop love and friendliness. If we develop right view we shall be able to understsand what is good for us and what is not and then we shall have right resolve to act accordingly. We must put in right effort to act properly.

Buddha has explained in great detail the importance of *sīla* for our spiritual life but observance of *sīla* is equally good for our leading a peaceful life in this world. He laid great emphasis on right livelihood, right speech and right action. What does right livelihood mean? Right livelihood means purity of livelihood. It means abstaining from all such trades and occupations which cause injury to other beings, deal in flesh, in intoxicating drinks, in arms and in poison. I think that most of our ills proceed from our not having right means of livelihood. Trading in arms is now done on a very large scale. The developed nations sell their deadly weapons to the underdeveloped nations and set them one against the other. They think that weapons alone will drive out their fear. But they do not seem to know the basic thing that enmity can never end enmity.[4] Apart from these means of earnings their livelihood, people indulge in other means such as deceit, treachery, sooth-saying, trickery and usury.[5] Buddha has spoken at length about them in the *Brahma jāla sutta* and has said that these means of livelihood must be avoided. If livelihood is earned by right means, we can live in peace. Greed will be driven out if one sticks to the right means of livelihood and the world will become a veritable paradise.

Right speech is the real ornament of a man. No ornament can beautify him as much as right speech which consists in abstaining from telling lies, from making slanderous speech, from speaking harsh language and from vain talks. Right speech also means speaking the truth, to be devoted to truth, to be reliable and worthy of confidence. For his own advantage, or for the advantage of others he never tells a lie. If a man never causes dissension amongst people but unites those that are divided and strengthens the unity between them he makes good use of his speech. He should never speak harsh language, but should speak "such words as are gentle, soothing to the ear, loving, going to the heart, courteous and dear and agreeable to many". Language distinguishes man from animal and if we can make good use of it we can be friends with all. We shall not make a man angry if we do not speak a harsh language. We shall not incur the displeasure of others and create enemies if we do not back bite.

We must avoid making vain talks. If a man speaks at the right moment with moderate arguments and full of sense he is likely to create good atmosphere. Buddha knew the ill consequences that follow from not making right speech. Therefore, he asked to exercise control over one's tongue. Right action is also very important, so far as it prevents us from indulging in violence, stealing and sexual misconduct. Non-violence is the need of the hour. The world today badly needs to observe the principle of non-violence. Then only the world can be saved from disaster.

Science has progressed a great deal and has put many kinds of deadly weapons at our disposal. But we have not made proportionate progress in our moral life. In the words of Einstein a man today can be compared with a giant whose one arm has grown much bigger than the other. It is high time we exercised control over our emotions of anger and hatred and we had learnt the method to do so, otherwise the whole humanity is likely to be doomed. What is most important today more than ever is to develop wisdom, otherwise we cannot survive.

One may say that Buddha's religion is meant for an individual. But a nation consists of individuals and if what Buddha has preached is practised by a large number of people or even by a small number of people who are at the helm of affairs, the nations of the world can go a long way towards achieving peace. Today much of our suffering is our own creation because we are ignorant, egoistic and greedy. A nation is said to be greedy if it has its eyes on another nation. A nation is jealous if it does not rejoice at the progress of another nation. All these can be minimised, if not altogether annihilated, if the mental culture is developed by the individuals of a nation. We have seen what happens when an atom bomb is dropped. There are many powerful bombs in the arsenals of the developed nations and if we and particularly those who have them do not exercise control over their jealousy, anger and egoism, much of value and a great part of humanity will be wiped out. Therefore, the time has come when the tenets of Buddhism must be followed in right earnest. The practice of four *Brahmavihāras* viz.

maitrī, *karuṇā*, *muditā*, and *upekṣā* as taught by Buddha are very relevant today. We must have the feeling of friendliness for those who are happy, have compassion for those who are miserable and wretched; we should feel pleasure for those who are virtuous and we should develop equanimity for those who are sinners and who perform immoral actions.

Apart from the importance of Buddhism in those respects there is one more respect in which Buddhism has become relevant. The *vipassanā* method of meditation is becoming increasingly popular today and people belonging to all religions enjoy practising *vipassanā* and get rid of mental tension and other severe diseases like migraine and other nervous diseases. Buddhism, therefore, has a far greater role to play in saving human beings individually and collectively.

References

1. *Dhammapada, vagga* X, 1.
2. *Dialogues of the Buddha,* Vol.1, p.255.
3. *The Psychological Attitude of the Early Buddhist Philosophy,* p.69.
4. *Nahi verena verāni, sammantīdha kudācanaṁ-Dhammapada.* 1,5
5. *Dialogues of the Buddha,* vol.1 pp. 15-26.

Causes of Variety in Buddhist Thought

There are only a few religions in the world which have not undergone any change in course of time. The philosophy which is associated with a religion also undergoes change over the years. Such is practically the case with all religions where there is freedom of thought. Buddhist thought-the basis of Buddhist religion is no exception to this law of change. If we look at the different Buddhist sects that came into being in course of only a few centuries, it will be amply clear that Buddhist thought in some respects, at least, underwent a sea change. This is greatly illustrated even from the literature of different sects, which is scantly available. The *Kathāvatthu* which was compiled in the Third Buddhist Council at Pāṭaliputra records as many as two hundred and twenty seven philosophical views held by the Buddhists of different sects which have been examined from the *Theravādins'* point of view. The different views illustrated in the *Kathāvatthu* have not been expressly set down to particular sects. Buddhaghoṣa, the great commentator, however, in his commentary has identified them as the views held by different sects.[1]

On an examination of these philosophical views, it is clear that the differences that are seen among them are not fundamental in the sense that they do not differ from one another in respect of the cardinal teachings of Lord Buddha. They do not dispute about the four Noble Truths, the *Paticca samuppāda*, the three characteristics of *Dhamma* viz. *amicca*, *dukkha* and *anatta*, eightfold path comprising *śila*, *samādhi* and *paññā* and the thirtyseven *bodhi-pakkhiya dhammas*[2]. It is only in some cases that differences in metaphysical speculations are seen. For example, both the Vajjiputrakas and the Sammitiyas believed in the existence of *Pudgala*[3]. Otherwise they show their differences only in minor details. Whereas the Rājagirikas and the Siddhārthikas did not believe in the existence of *caitasika,*[4] they, at the same time, believed that to make a gift is a *caitasika*[5]. The Pūrvasailiyas believed four Noble Truths to be an *asaṁkṛta dharma* (*cattāri saccāni asankhatā iti,* p.106), the Andhakas believed *nirodhasamāpatti* to be *asaṁskṛta* (p.107). They also believed that *Nirvāṇa* can be attained without removing and eradicating all the fetters (*sañyojanas*)[6]. The Mahāsāṅghikas, on the other hand, held that attainment of *arhathood* is possible without destroying all the fetters (*atthi kiñci saṁyojana appahāya arahattappattī ti*).

There are some other respects in which the sects differed. The Vaitulyakas held that Lord Buddha was born in Tāvatiṁsa and he always lives there. He never comes to this world inhabited by human beings. He sends his created image to this world to preach. Ananda once heard his teachings and gave them to the world. (*Tusitapure ṭhito Bhagavā dhammadesanatthāya abhinimmita pesesi, tena ceva tassa ca desanaṃ sampaṭicchitvā āyasmatā Ānandena dhammo desito, na Buddhena Bhagavatā ti*)[7].

There were other very minor details in which the sects differed and wasted their time in proving their points. Some of the Uttarāpathakas and the Andhakas believed that the urine and excreta of Lord Buddha had a divine fragrance (*Bhagavato uccārapassāvo aññe gandhajāte ativiya adhigaṇhāti, natthitato ca sugandhataram gandhajātam,* p.189). The Andhakas believed that there were fauna and flora in the Devaloka and there was no gatekeeper at the gate of the hell. (*Atthi devesu tiracchangatā*[8]. *Natthi nirayapālā nāma sattā*[9]).

Although Buddha propounded his philosophy and explained the path for attaining *nirvāṇa,* he never asked anybody to follow blindly what he said. He expressly asked that whatever he preached should be followed only after carefully examining it. This freedom granted by Buddha gave a scope to his followers to examine and weigh the pros and cons of a philosophical view and accept or reject it according to their conviction. In the centuries that followed the *Mahāparinirvāṇa* of Lord Buddha, naturally his teachings were given several interpretations by different philosophers and hence divergent views came into being.

We know that in the first Buddhist Council the *Sutta* and the *Vinaya* were respectively recited by Ānanda and Upāli and they were, indeed, brilliant disciples of Lord Buddha, but is it possible to conclude that they recited all that Lord Buddha had preached for fortyfive long years after attaining *bodhi* at Bodha Gayā[10] ? It is on record that Lord Buddha went to many villages, cities and *janapadas* and came in contact with many persons to whom he preached and who listened respectfully to his teachings, sometimes even abstruse ones and, therefore, it is likely that many of his teachings were not collected in the first Buddhist council. There must have been some *suttas* or some rules of *Vinaya* which were in a fluid stage and could not be incorporated in the First Council. This assumption is proved by what Porāṇa said after the first synod was held. Porāṇa did not wholeheartedly accept the proceedings of the council and expressed his inability to accept the same as the words of the Buddha. In the *Cullavagga* Porāṇa has been recorded as saying that he would not accept what has been recited as the words of the Buddha, but he would believe only that which he had heard from Buddha with his own ears. He also insisted on the incorporation of eight rules relating to food into the *Vinaya* rules.

This proves beyond any doubt that the seeds of dissension had already been sown in the *Sangha* immediately after the *Mahāparinirvāṇa* of Lord Buddha and they sprouted forth in full vigour two hundred years after and the Buddhist *Sangha* painfully experienced the first split.

The split in the *Saṅgha* which took place in the Second Council was due to the fact that some Vajjian monks of Vesali regarded certain acts as lawful, although really speaking they were un-Vinayic acts. What actually were minor matters gave rise to events of great consequence.

Buddha did not put a premium on these matters of physical discipline. He laid emphasis on *paññā* and *citta* rather than on *sila*. In the *Brahmajāla Sutta* he has expressly said that *sila* is *appamattakaṃ and oramattakaṃ*, i.e. trifling and he has said again and again that the *Dhamma* he has realised is profound, deep and subtle and is not exhausted by *sila*. How could, therefore, Buddha who put less premium on *sila*, regard any act of physical discipline as very important? He was, as a matter of fact, concerned more with internal discipline rather than with external one. In his scheme of mental and spiritual culture, controlling of *citta* plays a greater role than external acts of discipline.

Even during the life time of Buddha there were some monks who insisted on practising rigorous physical disciplines and asked Buddha to prescribe them.

Devadatta insisted on Buddha's making compulsory for all monks to follow five kinds of austere discipline such as : (i) 'the monk should live in forest, (ii) should subsist solely on doles collected from door to door, (iii) dress themselves in rags picked up from dust heap, (iv) dwell always under a tree and never under a roof and (v) never eat fish and flesh'. But Buddha did not abide by the suggestions of Devadatta and left to the monks the option of observing them or not. After his demise some monks made these rules of discipline a great issue, which went so for as to cause split in the *Sangha*.

There were other causes also which were responsible for the split in the *Saṅgha*. While giving his preachings to the monks and laymen, Buddha always kept in view the mental capacity of the chief persons to whom he preached. He had a thorough understanding of human psychology and gave his preachings accordingly. To some who would not understand his doctrine of no-soul, he would talk about *pudgala* as if it were permanent and carried the *khandhas* with it[12]. But those who took it literally argued later that Buddha talked of a permanent *pudgala*. It became a dogma with the Sammittiyas and Vajjiputiyas, although Buddha simply wanted to make them understand the complicated theory of *kamma* and rebirth with the help of his doctrine of *pudgala*. To others who were mentally more advanced, he would explain it in a different way. In other words, his teachings have two kinds of meanings viz. *nītārtha* (direct meaning) and *neyārtha* (indirect meaning). But because the liberty to examine his teachings was given to all, they interpreted his teachings differently and hence the coming into being of different Buddhist sects.

In the centuries that followed the *Mahāparinirvāṇa* of Lord Buddha, Buddhism had to keep pace with new thoughts and ideas that rose in the land and the Buddhist philosophers had to exercise their minds to interpret Buddhist philosophy in a way so that it would not appear to be an anachronism, but would very much serve the intellectual and spiritual needs of the people. As N. Dutta has rightly pointed out that although interpretations were undesirable from the orthodox point of view, "they were indicative of the deep interest taken by the disciples in ascertaining the real teachings of Buddha as also of the attempts to interpret the old teachings in a new way, and to adapt them to the changed circumstances brought about by the advancement of knowledge for over a century."[13]

Buddhism had to keep pace with new thoughts and ideas. There came a time when the need of the hour was to conceive of a Buddha who would be so full of compassion for suffering humanity that he would take a vow not to enter into *Nirvāṇa* unless and until all beings are rid of their suffering. The Hindu concept of God was that He was all ommipotent and omniscient and He would protect him who would go to His refuge [14]. The common people naturally felt drawn towards such a God. Buddha also was conceived in such a way as to possess divine qualities. Thus Buddha was gradually shorn of human characteristics and superhuman qualities were bestowed on him. He was deified. He was made the embodiment of infinite compassion. In the *Jātaka* and *Avadāna* literature that developed, attempts were made to show Bodhisattva making great sacrifice in order to perfect ten *pāramitās*. Thus the stories in the *Jātaka* and *Avadāna* served more than one purpose. In the first place, they served to glorify Bodhisattva who now appeared as a being endowed with superhuman qualities. In the second place, the stories also went a long way in proving the theory of *kamma* and rebirth and finally they inspired in the minds of the people faith in Buddhism. Buddhism is a religion which glorifies man. Man can make or mar his own fortune. He can work out his salvation without depending upon any god[15]. Even Buddha declared it many a time that he only shows the path. Man will have to tread on this path himself in order to attain *Nirvāṇa*. With the development of Mahāyāna, man became more glorified inasmuch as it was said that the seed of *bodhi* is in every one of us. This gave rise to the concept of Bodhisattva which, in turn, led to the evolution of the concept of *pāramitās*, which a Bodhisattva must perform in order to attain perfection. *Pāramitā* means perfection in any of the ten virtues such as *dāna*, *śīla*, *kṣānti*, *vīrya* and *prajñā* etc. In the process of deifying Buddha the Mahāsanghikas introduced and formulated them.

The evolution of Hīnayāna into Mahāyāna marks a further stage of development in Buddhist thought. The Mahāyānists claimed superiority over the Hīnayānists by saying that whereas the latter are satisfied with the removal of only *kleśāvaraṇa* (veil of impurity) they go so far as to remove *jñeyāvaraṇa* (veil covering the *parmārtha* truth) and realise both *pudgalaśūnyatā* and *dharmaśūnyatā*. The *Prajñāpāramitā* literature that developed, made an attempt to explain clearly the voidness of *dharmas*, but always with a warning that this *dharmaśūnyatā* also should not be taken as a dogma. The real purpose was to enable one to get rid of one's ego which is the greatest obstacle in the path of one's spiritual development. Unless one rises above one's ego, one cannot make spiritual progress.

The growth of Mahāyāna ultimately led to the development of the concept of three *kāyas-Rūpa-kāya*, *Nirmāṇa Kāya* and *Dharmakāya*. Buddhism as a religion never remained static but it adapted itself to the needs of the people and hence Buddhist thought also underwent great changes. When it came in contact with other thoughts, it enriched itself in the process of adapting itself to them.

Even this cursory view, therefore, makes it amply clear that there were many causes for the variety in Buddhist thought. The causes ranged from very frivolous ones to serious philosophical ones. Attempts to deify Lord Buddha gave rise to new metaphysics, and its contact with other religions of the country and abroad revitalized it all the more.

But as I said in the beginning, in spite of the variety, there is unity in Buddhist thought which is borne out by the fact that the cardinal teachings of Buddha remained almost the same.

References

1. Vajjiputraka, Sammitiya, Sarvāstivādi, Mahāsanghika Kāsyapika, Andhaka, Pūrva Śailiya, Aparaśailiya, Gokulika, Bhadrayānika, Mahīsāsaka, Uttarāpathaka, Rājagiriya, Siddhārthika, Hetuvādi, Vaitulayaka, Mahāsūnyavādi.
2. (i) Four *Satipatthānas,* (ii) Four *Sammappadhānas,* (iii) Four *iddhipādas* (iv) Five *indriyas,* (v) Five *balas* (vi) Seven *bojjhangas,* (vii) Eightfold path.
3. *Puggalo upalabbhati saccikaṭṭha paramatthenāti,* K.V.A., p.11.
4. *Cetasikena pi nabhavitabbaṁ,* Ibid, p.110.
5. *Cetassko va dhammo dānāni,* Ibid, p.111.
6. *Yasmā Arahā Sabbaññaviṣaye appahīnasaṁyojano va. Pariñibbbāyati, tasmā atthi kiñci sanjoyanaṁ appahāya parinibbānaṁ.*
7. *Pañcappakaraṇa Aṭṭhakathā* (2nd part), Nalanda Edition, p.188.
8. *ibid.,* p.203.
9. *ibid.,* p.202.
10. *Etadaggaṁ, Bhikkhave, mama Sāvakānaṁ Bhikkhunaṁ bahussutānaṁ yadidaṁ Ānandam, gatimantanāṁ, satimanṭānaṁ, dhitimantānaṁ, yadidam Ānandaṁ,* A.N.I.,25.
11. The eight rules (as translated by Suzuki from Chinese) are : (i) cooking food indoors, (ii) cooking indoors, (iii) cooking of one's own accord, (iv) taking food of one's own accord, (v) receiving food when rising early in the morning, (vi) carrying food home in compliance with the wish of the giver, (vii) having miscellaneous fruits and (vii) taking things grown in a pond.
12. *Bhārahārasutta* should be consulted for an explanation of it.
13. N. Dutta, *Buddhist Sects in India,* p.219.
14. See the *Gita.*
15. Like Lord Shri Krishna, Lord Buddha never says, *sarvadharmān parityajya māmekaṃ śaraṇaṃ braja.*

The Mūlapariyāyasutta - a Treatise of Buddhist Epistemology and Ontology

The *Mūlapariyāyasutta* occupies a unique position in the *Nikāyas* in so far as it is a sermon delivered by the Buddha with regard to the fundamentals of all *dhammas* (*sabbadhammamūla*). As a matter of fact, it contains the quintessence of his metaphysical speculations and ethical teachings inasmuch as he explains the nature of reality, mentions the necessary conditions of attaining true knowledge of reality and says who can get true knowledge. In short, the relationship between the knowable and the knower and the nature of the knowable have been given here in detail.

It is because of all these points discussed here that the learned Bhikkhuus could not make out its meaning. They found its subtle and profound metaphysical implication beyond their comprehension and so they did not express their appreciation at the end of the *sutta* as is usually done at the end of other *suttas*.[1]

Lord Buddha has spoken of two kinds of reality, conventional and ultimate which were later termed as *saṁvuti sacca* (*saṁvṛti satya*) and *paramattha sacca* (*paramārtha satya*). What appears to be real is not really real. Appearance is conventional reality. Ultimate reality can be known only by tearing the veil of appearance and penetrating deep into the nature of things. Buddha says that the ultimate reality can be known only by the Arhats and the Tathāgatas, because they are completely free from desires and passions. Deep attachment to and great passion for the worldly objects which appear real do not let a man have a true insight into the real nature of *dhammas* and hence he is unable to get the true knowledge and become a wise man.

He speaks of three broad types of persons viz., *puthujjana* (untrained and unskilled in the real *dhamma* propounded by an ārya), *sekkha* (who receives training in the *dhamma*) and Arhat or Buddha or Tathāgata (who has annihilated all his desires, got rid of all polluting factors, broken all fetters[2] that bind all beings to the cycles of birth and death and has freed himself from all *āsavas*)[3]. These three types of persons are apparently at different stages of spiritual evolution and hence view reality differently. All terms such as earth (*paṭhavī*), water (*āpo*), fire (*tejo*), air (*vāyo*), man, god, Prajāpati, Brahmā...one, many and *Nibbāna* are only conventional symbols. They are not real. The common man (*puthujjana*) of the world and the Arhat both use them in their day to day life and in this respect there is no difference between them. But yet there is a great difference between their attitudes towards the objects. The *puthujjana* regards them as real but the Arhat who has penetrated into their true nature with his *tīraṇapaññā*, understands their nature and does not take them to be real; they are only conventional reality.

It is by making such a distinction between a *puthujjana* and an Arhat that Lord Buddha sheds considerable light on the necessary conditions of getting real knowledge. Real knowledge which is nothing but wisdom depends on one's being able to drive out all one's desires (*taṇhā*) which make him strongly grasp the objects of the world. And for annihilating desires one has to follow the eightfold path (*Aṭṭhangiko maggo*) as mapped out by the Buddha. The eightfold path consists of *śīla*, *samādhi* and *paññā*. If one observes *sīla* and practises meditation one can develop one's *paññā (insight)* and penetrate into the real nature of things. All the objects of the world are characterised by *annicca* (impermanence), *dukkha* (suffering) and *anatta* (having no permanent soul or substance).[4] If one by his *sādhanā* realises the true nature of *dhammas*, he will not make the mistake of developing attachment to and passion for the objects of the world and will be free from grasping (*upādāna*). It is the quantum of grasping that distinguishes a *puthujjana* (an average man) from an Arhat. The former has infinite grasping, the latter has none at all and a *sekkha* who comes in between is on his way to realize the true nature of *dhammas* and get rid of grasping.

Why is it that *a puthujjana* regards conventional symbols as ultimate truth ? It is because they are not thoroughly understood by him (*tassa apariññātattā*). Complete understanding or comprehension (*pariññā*) consists of three stages viz.: *ñāta pariññā, tīraṇa pariññā and pahāna pariññā; Ñāta pariññā*[5] is a stage at which one becomes thoroughly familiar with an object say, earth (*paṭhavī*) in terms of its characteristics (*lakkhaṇa*), its function (*rasa*), its immediate cause (*paccupaṭṭhāna*) and its source (*padaṭṭhāna*), i.e. one does not know only its characteristics but one also knows its immediate cause and the source from which it rises. *Tīraṇa pariññā*[5] is a higher state of comprehension at which one realizes that nothing is permanent. All that look permanent reveal their three characteristics of impermanence, suffering and substancelessness or no-soulness. This is a stage at which a *sādhaka* penetrates into *dhammas* and knows their true nature. *Pahāṇa pariññā* is the highest state at which one begins to practise what he knows i.e. one begins to live up to his knowledege. In other words, he gives up his attachment to worldly objects and becomes completely free from *rāga* or passion for them - the *rāga* that used to attract him powerfully and strongly.

A *puthujjana,* not recognizing the true nature of any *dhamma* or any element like *paṭhavī,* takes it to be real and identifies himself wrongly with it and rejoices in it.[6] As a result of this, *taṇhā* (desire) for it is developed which causes suffering. *Taṇhā* springs up only when one has ego. Egolessness is a *sine qua non* for attaining true knowledge.

A *sekkha* (learner) who has set out on his spiritual journey to attain perfection and strive for the incomparable security from bondage, intuitively knows the real nature of *dhammas* and of elements like *paṭhavī,* does not make the mistake of identifying himself with any one of them and does not like a *puthujjana* rejoice in it. It is true he has not yet become a *khīṇasava,* i.e. one whose *āsavas* (cankers) are annihilated but he is not like a *puthujjana* either who has immense craving for the objects of the world. As Ācariya Dhammapala says in his commentary on the

Majjhima Nikāya, he occupies a rank somewhere in between - far removed from a puthujjana, but yet not a perfect *khīṇāsava.*[7]

A *khīṇāsava* thoroughly understands the real nature of *dhammas,* makes no mistake of identifying himself with them and frees himself from all desires, passions and cravings, gets rid of *avijjā* (ignorance), attains prefection and begins to live a life unruffled by any desire.

Lord Buddha makes it abundantly clear that real knowledge can be attained only by a *khīṇāsava*. One becomes a *khīṇāsava* by destroying the four *āsavas* which are responsible for intoxicating and muddling the mind. Freedom from these *āsavas* constitues arhatship. A *khīṇāsava* destroys ten fetters and becomes what is called *prikkhiṇabhavasañyojana.*

An *arhat* does not rejoice in worldly objects owing to the waning of his attachment (*tassa vītarāgattā*), owing to the waning of aversion (*tassa vītadosattā*) and owing to the waning of ignorance (*tassa vītamohattā*).

From all this it is pretty clear that freedom from grasping or *upādāna* or destruction of all the cankers is a *sine qua non* for attaining real knowledge. By means of three kinds of *pariññā* he has penetrated into the real nature of *dhammas* and has known that delight is the root of suffering (*Nandī dukkhassa mūlaṃ ti*). Having realized this he becomes *a Tathāgata* - the fully self-awakened one.

From definitions of a *puthujjana,* à *sekkha,* and a *khīṇāsava* it is clear that whereas a *puthujjana* is under the complete grip of grasping, slackening of grasping takes place in the case of a *sekkha* and a *khīṇāsava* is completely free from it.

In the Gita[8] also a *sthitaprajña* (stable of mind) is described more or less in the same terms in which a *khīṇāsava* has been described. Like a *khiṇāsava, a sthitaprajña* has no thirst for pleasures. He is free from passion, fear and anger, and is unattached to everything. He neither rejoices nor recoils and he withdraws his senses from all sense objects. He, like a *khīṇāsava,* has thoroughly understood that desire (*taṇhā or tṛṣṇā*) springs from attachment for sense objects, which in turn gives rise to anger. Anger causes infatuation, which causes confusion of memory which results in loss of reason and leads a man to complete ruin and destruction. In spite of the difference in terminology both the Buddhists and the Gita give the same necessary conditions of attaining real knowledge or wisdom.

It is interestisng to compare what Buddha said with regard to the necessary conditions of getting real knowledge or wisdom with the conditions given by Schopenhauer - one of the great philosophers of modern times. He, in his book *The World as Will and Idea*, defines *will* in these words: "Under the conscious intellect is the conscious or unconscious *will*, a striving, persistent vital force, a spontaneous activity, a *will* of imperious desire"[9] Without going into detail it can be said that Schopenhauer's *will* is what Buddha calls *taṇhā* (desire). While elaborating *will*, Schopenhauer says at one place that the *will* of course, is a will to live, is a will to maximum life. Isn't it equivalent to Buddha's definition of *kāmataṇhā* and *bhava taṇhā* ? Then Schopenhauer goes on to say that if the world is will it must be a world of suffering. As Will Durant says, "*Will* indicates want and its grasp is very strong. Desire is infinite and fulfilment only limited". Schopenhauer characteristically says, "it is like the alms thrown to a beggar that keeps him alive today in order that his misery may be prolonged tomorrow... As long as our consciousness is filled by our will, so long as we are given up to the throng of desires with their constant hopes and fears, so long as we are subject to willing, we can never have lasting happiness or peace".[10] We desire for more and more, because we do not know the true nature of what we desire. If we knew their true nature, we would not have grasping for them. Desire, as a matter of fact, is insatiable and "the satisfied passion oftener leads to unhappiness than to happiness". Schopenhauer says, "of ten things that annoy us, nine would nrot be able to do so, if we understood them thorougly in their causes, and therefore knew their necessity and true nature...For what bridle and bit are to an unmanageable horse, the intellect is for the will in man".[11]

While defining genius Schopenhauer says that "man in

general is mostly will and little knowledge and genius is mostıy knowledge and little will".[12] Here man's nature has been very nicely and succinctly defined. This kind of philosophical understanding can purify the will. And philosophy Schopenhauer defines as experience and thought, the Buddhist equivalents of which are *bhāvanāmayīprajñā* and *cintāmayīprajñā*.

Lord Buddha's path consists of *samādhi* or practice of meditation which enables one to concentrate one's mind and know the real nature of things. The real knowledge thus attained is not only Schopenhauerean intellect but *prajñā*-intuitive knowledge or wisdom.

The *Mūlapariyāya sutta* categorically says that the real nature of *dhammas* can be known only by a *khīṇāsava* or what the Gita calls a *sthitaprajña* or by what Schopenhauer calls a man who has destroyed his will which is nothing but *taṇhā* or *tṛṣṇā*. Endowed with the intuitive knowledge of the highest kind one can penetrate into the real nature of *dhammas* which are characterised by impermanence, suffering and substancelessness or no-soulness. When one realizes this, one does not fall a victim to one's ego. His ego is annihilated and he rises above "this is me" and "this is mine".

Thus the *Mūlapariyāya sutta* is a treatise of epistemology and ontology inasmuch as it not only describes the nature of reality but also says how the real nature of *dhammas* can be known (which is real knowledge) and who can get it.

References

1. *Idamavoca Bhagavā, na te bhikkhu bhagavato bhāsitam abhinandun ti. cf. Attamanā te Bhikkhu Bhagavato bhāsitam abbinandum ti. - Sabbāsava sutta* M-N.1.
2. Ten *Sañyojanas* are : - *sakkāya diṭṭhi* (speculation as to the eternity or otherwise of one's own individuality), *vicikicchā* (doubts), *sīlabbata parāmāsa* (rituals), *kāmacchanda* (excitement of sexual pleasure), *Vyāpāda (ill-will)*, *rūparāga* (lust after birth in the *rūpa loka*), *Arūparāga* (lust after birth in

the *arūpa loka*), *māna* (pride), *uddhacca* (distraction, flurry) and *avijjā* (ignorance)

3. *Kāmāsava* (sensuality), *Bhavāsava* (rebirth), *diṭṭhāsava* (speculation) and *avijjāsava* (ignorance).
4. *Yaṁaniccam taṁ dukkhaṁ, yaṁ dukkhaṁ tadanattā.*
5. *Tattha katamā nāta pariñña? Pathavidhātuṁ parijānāti Ayaṁ paṭhavidhātu ajjhatikā, ayaṁ bāhirā, idamassā lakkhaṇam, imāni rasa-paccupaṭṭhāna-padaṭṭhānāniti ayaṁ ñātapariññā. Katamā tīraṇa pariññ‹ā? Evaṁ ñataṁ katvā pathavidhātuṁ tīreti aniccato dukkhato rogato ti dvācattātisāya ākārehi - ayaṁ tiranapariññā. Katamā pahānapariññā? Evaṁ tirayitvā aggamaggena pathavidhātuyā chandarāgam pajāhati - ayaṁ pahānapariññā.*
6. *Paṭhaviṁ pathavito sanjānāti; paṭhaviṁ paṭhavito saññatvā paṭhaviṁ maññati, paṭhaviyā maññati paṭhavito maññati, paṭhaviṁ me ti maññati, pathaviṁ abhinandati.* M.N.I.p.3.
7. *Sekhassa pana diṭṭhimaññana pahinā itarā pana tanubhāvam gatā, tena so maññati pi na vattabbo puṭhujjana viya, na maññati ti pi na vattabokhiṇāsavo viyā ti. Papañcasūdanī* (Nalanda Edition) p.55.
8. *The Bhagavadgita*, Ch. II (esp. verses 56-63). *Krodhādbhavati sammohah, sammohātsmṛti vibhramah.*
   Smṛtibhranshād buddhināsho buddhināshātpranaṣyati.
9. *The Story of Philosophy* by Will Durant, p.312.
10. *ibid.*, p.323 (quoted).
11. *ibid.*, p.331.
12. *The Story of Philosophy*, p.334.

Elements of Mahāyāna in the Sutta-Nipāta

In this paper I propose to examine if there are any elements of Mahāyāna in the *Sutta Nipāata*. This book of the *Khuddaka Nikāya* has been purposely chosen because it is now pretty well established that it contains some of the oldest teachings of Buddha. This book was held in such a high esteem that King Asoka took as many as three *suttas* out of seven which he got incised or engraved on the Bhabru rock edict. The *Moneyya sutta*, *Muni gāthā* and *Upatisapasane* are the same as the *Nālaka sutta*, *Muni sutta* and *Sāriputta sutta* respectively.[1] From the language point of view also it can be said without any doubt or hesitation that the *Sutta Nipata* is very old in so far as its language is very close to the language of the *Vedas*. Fausboll has very thoroughly examined the language, style and metre of the *gāthās* of the *Sutta-Nipata* and has rightly come to the conclusion that it has greater affinity with the *Vedas*[2].

If the *Sutta Nipata* is so old, the question is, does it contain some of the traces of Mahāyāna ? Are there some seeds of Mahāyāna in it which sprouted forth in later literature ? It can be said for sure that the rise of Mahāyāna was not sudden nor did it develop out of nothing. It did develop as other movements rise and develop in course of time. Many thinkers and philosophers make their contribution and in many cases it seems that the developed form of movements is far away from the original philosophy. From the philosophy of Buddha there developed other philosophy called the philosophy of the Buddhists and yet claimed identity with the philosophy of Buddha as A.K. Warder says in his article[3].

Out of the two sects viz. Hīnayāna and Mahāyāna, the latter claims superiority over the former because of its high ideals.

According to the Mahāyānists the aim of the Hīnayānists was to attain *Nibbāna* and their goal was arhathood. The aim of the Mahāyānists, on the other hand, was to become a Buddha. There are other difference too. The aspiration of the Hīnayānists is to have an insight into what is called *Pudgalanairātmya* or *Pudgalasūnyatā* but that of Mahāyānists is to have an insight into *Dharmanairātmya* or *Dharmaśūnyata* which according to them is the only means of the attainment of the highest knowledge.

Nagarjuna who is acclaimed as one of the great stalwarts of Mahāyāna by all its schools holds that in order to attain highest knowledge it is necessary to give up all points of view. Whatever point of view is held has its limitation and consequently it cannot help one in attaining the highest knowledge. Nagarjuna, as a matter of fact, was a Mahāyānist of a different kind. He did not, like other Mahāyānists, advocate a complete break with early Buddhism but in the words of Warder "his aim was to prevent a break, to reunite all Buddhists on the basis of the texts which all accepted, to restore the original Buddhism."[4]

Nagarjuna's express aim was to reject all views that had come to develop. In the Abhidhamma literature that developed following the *mahāparinibbāna* of the Master, *Citta*, *Cetasika*, *Rūpa* and *Nibbāna* were regarded as ultimate reals (*parmārthas*). In the post-canonical literature and commentaries *dharmas* were defined as something having *svabhāva* or their own nature.[5] These were views which Nagarjuna wanted to demolish and reject. A cursory glance at the *Mūlamādhyamikakārikā* - the *magnum opus* of Nagarjuna - will immediately reveal that Nagarjuna was against all kinds of views. It is for this reason that he ends this book with the following *kārikā* :

Sarvadṛṣṭiprahāṇāya yah saddharmamadesayat /
Anukampāmupādāya taṁ namasyāmi Gotamaṁ //

(To Him, possessing compassion, who taught the Real *Dharma* for the destruction of all views - to Him, Gotama, I humbly offer reverence. - translation by Inada, from *Fundamentals of the Middle Way*.) At another place Nagarjuna says that Buddha has preached voidness, i.e. refutation of all view points.

Śūnyatā sarvadṛṣṭiṇāṁ proktā nihśaraṇam Budheh /[6]

(Voidness is proclaimed by the Victorious One as the refutation of all points of view. Translation by Inada.)

What do all these statements made by Nagarjuna mean ? It is clear from them that Nagarjuna is not in favour of holding any point of view, nor does any point of view prove to be tenable. *Sassatavāda* (eternalism) and *Ucchedavāda* (annihilationism) tell only the half truths and they are not tenable. Buddha realised that all things, all *dharmas*, are in a constant state of flux and to hold that the soul and the world are eternal as the eternalists hold or the soul is annihilated after one's death as the annihilationalists hold are only wrong views. In the *Brahmajāla Sutta* Buddha has made it very clear and has said there in lucid language that he is free from all such views[7]. It has been possible for him to keep himself aloof from all such views because he had realised the *Dhamma* which was profound, deep, subtle, hard to understand, comprehended only by the wise...[8] Therefore he does not develop any *diṭṭhi*.

Nagarjuna's avowed aim in writing the *Mūlamādhyamika kārikā* is to steer clear of the two extreme views of *Sassatavāda* and *Ucchedavāda* and establish the untenability of any view. He has, therefore, gleaned all or practically all such passages from the *Tipitaka* he had before him to buttress up *diṭṭhisuññatā* as propounded by the Master. He set himself the task of refuting all the views which did not faithfully represent the view of the Master. For what he says in the *Mūlamādhyamika kārikā* he finds support in the *Tipiṭaka* from which he quotes with reverence. If from this point of view we examine the *Sutta Nipāta* we find that it contains the seeds of the refutation of all points of view and Nagarjuna must have laid his hands on this book and got inspiration from it to demolish all views and show their untenability. The *Aṭṭhaka vagga* and the *Pārāyaṇa vagga* of the *Sutta Nipāta* contain many such *gāthās* where *diṭṭhivāda* has been criticised. In the *Duṭṭhaṭṭhakasutta* of the *Aṭṭhaka vagga* it has been said that a real *muni* does not hold any view and consequently he does not develop narrow-mindedness.

Vadanti ve duṭṭhamanāpi eke, athopi ve saccamanā vadanti /
Vādañca jātaṁ munino upeyi, tasmā muni natthi khilo kuhiñci //[9]

Some persons speak with a wicked mind, some speak with a good mind, but a real *muni* does not hold any view i.e. he rises above all kinds of views and so he is not pegged and bolted by his *rāgas* or attachments. In other words, he keeps all the windows of his mind open. It has been further said in the same *sutta* that it is very difficult to give up a view which is held after long consideration or reflection, even though the view is imaginary, born out of desire (*taṇhā*) and complicated. One is attached to it without fully knowing about it. A man completely liberated has no imaginary point of view. As he is free from desires, so why should he hold any view or fall in its trap ?

Pakappitā saṁkhatā yassa dhammā, purekkhatā santi avīvadātā /
Yadattani passati ānisansaṁ taṁ nissito kuppaticca santi //
Diṭṭhi nivessā na hi svātivattā, dhammesu niccheyya samuggahīṭaṁ /
Tasmā naro tesu nivesanesu, nirassati ādiyaticcahammam //
Dhonassa hi natthi kuhiñci loke, pakappitā diṭṭhi bhavābhavesu /
Māyañca mānañca pahāya dhono sakena gaccheyya anūpayo so //
Upayo hi dhammesu upeti vādaṁ anupayaṁ kena katham vadeyya /
Attaṁ nirattaṁ na hi tassa atthi, adhosi so diṭṭhimidheve sabbaṁti //[10]

In the *Suddhaṭṭhakasutta* it has been said that salvation or *nibbāna* is not possible through mere knowledge born out of a point of view, but it is possible through non-attachment born out of *prajñā* or *paññā*. No point of view can lead one to liberation. It is a tragedy that one who holds a view superior to all regards it as the highest knowledge or *prajñā*, but he is not purified by it.

Passāmi suddhaṁ paramaṁ arogaṁ diṭṭhena suddhi narassa hoti /
Etābhijānaṁ paramaṁṭi ñatvā, suddhānupassīti pacceti ñaṇaṁ // [11]

It has been emphatically said in the same *sutta* that neither any view, nor the reading of scriptures, nor knowledge of moral precepts can drive out impurities and make one pure. Pure is he who keeps himself aloof from vice and virtue and from egoism and *saṁskāra*.

Na Brāhmaṇa aññato suddhimāhā, diṭṭhe sute sīlavate mute vā /
Puññe ca pāpe ca anūpalitto, attañjaho nayidha pakubbamāno //[12]

A view is necessarily born out of *taṇhā* and if one gives up one and takes up another, does so under its influence and pressure. One who does so is likened to a monkey who jumps from one branch of the tree to another. It is not for nothing that a man has been compared here with a monkey. A monkey has never been famous for his knowledge.

Purimaṁ pahāya aparaṁ sitāse, ejānugā te na taranti sangaṁ /
Te uggahāyanti nirassjanti, kapīva sākhaṁ pamukhaṁ gahāya// [13]

The true characteristics of a *mahāprajña* have been enumerated in the following *gāthā* :

Na kappayanti na purekkharonti, accantasuddhīti na te vadanti /
Ādānaganthaṃ gathitaṁ visajja, āsaṁ na kuhiñci loke //[14]

(Neither does he side with any point of view, nor does he highly praise it, nor does he call it the best and the purest view. He gives up his attachment to any point of view and keeps himself from all desires and gives up orthodoxy.)

One who has transcended all desires has no prejudice against or in favour of any view or for that matter any kind of knowledge. Not only is he attached to any kind of desire but he is not even attached to *vairāgya*, i.e. non-attachment. He has nothing left to learn.

Sīmātigo Brāhmaṇa tassa natthi, ñatvā'va disvā'va samuggahītaṁ/
Na rāgarāgī, napi rāgaratto, tassīdha natthi paramuggahītanti //[15]

In the *Paramaṭṭhakasutta* it has been asserted that truth is not dependent on any *diṭthi (view) but it is beyond it. He who has a diṭṭhi,* becomes argumentative, begins to think himself superior and others inferior and ultimately is held by *diṭṭhi* itself and becomes a slave to it. What is needed for liberation is giving up of egoism and all kinds of desires.

Paramanti diṭṭhīsu paribbasāno, yaduttariṁ kurute jantu loke /
Hīnāti aññe tato sabbamāha, tasmā vivādāni avītivatto //
Attaṁ pahāya anupādiyāno ñaṇepi so nissayaṁ na karoti /
Sa ve viyattesu na vaggasārī, diṭṭhiṁpi so na pacceti kiñci //[16]

In the *Jarāsutta* like the *Duṭṭhaṭṭhakasutta* the characteristics of a real *muni* are brought out. Just as the drops of water do not stay on lotus leaves, i.e. just as the latter do not get soiled similarly a real *muni* is above all views, is completely detached and remaining unattached he neither loves anybody nor feels jealous of him.

Udabindu yathāpi pokkhare, padume vāri yathā na lippati /
Evaṁ muni nopalippati, yadidaṁ diṭṭhaṁ sutaṁ mutesu vā //[17]

This can well be compared with what is said in the *Māgandiya Sutta.*

Yehi vivitto vicareyya loke, na tāṇi uggayha vadeyya nāgo /
Elaṁoujaṁ kaṇṭakaṁ vārijaṁ yathā, jalen pankena ca nūpalittaṁ //
Evaṁ munī santivādo agiddho, kāme ca loke anūpalitto //[18]

(To hold fast to any view, however efficacious one takes it to be, is still a kind of *taṇhā,* a prejudice).

Idheva suddhiṁ iti vādiyanti, nāññesu dhammesu visuddhimāhu /
Yaṁ nissitātattha subhaṁ vadānā,paccekasaccesu puthū niviṭṭhā//[19]

Those who take part in debates and fight for their view (*Pasūrasutta,*46.1) have been humorously compared to the wrestlers who feed on the food given by a king.

Sūro yathā rājakhādāya puṭṭho, abhigajjameti pātisūramicchaṁ /
Yeneva so tena palehi sūra, pubbeva natthi yadidaṁ yudhāya //[20]

The *Cūlaviyuhasutta* and the *Mahāviyuhasutta* are together a strong and forceful critique of all views. In the former Buddha asserts that he never says that 'this alone is truth' but he holds at the same time that Truth is one *'Ekaṁ hi saccaṁ na dutiyamatthi'*[21] and in the latter it has been categorically asserted that those who hold one view or other are not liberated. A seeker after truth has to give up all views in order to realize peace. Neither a view becomes true because somebody holds it nor does it become untrue because some others belittle it or speak against it.

Parassa ce vaṁbhayitena hīno, na koci dhammesu visesi assa /
Puthū hi aññassa vadanti dhammaṁ nihīnato samhi dalhaṁvadānā //
Saddhammapūjā ca panā tatheva yathā pasansanti sakāyanāni /
Sabbe pavādā tathivā bhaveyyuṁ, suddhi hi teasṁ paccattameva//[22]

Nagarjuna advocates the middle way which alone can lead one to quiescence of plurality (*prapañcopśama*). This has been described in the *Tuvaṭaka Sutta*. The root cause of *prapañca* is egoism which must be got rid of.

Mūlaṁ papancasaṁkhāyāṁ (ti Bhagavā), mantā asmīti sabbamuparundhe /
Yā kāci taṇhā ajjhatam. Tāsaṁ vinayā sadā sikkhe //[23]

In the *Pārāyaṇa vagga śūnyatā* has been explicitly and overtly mentioned. *Śūnyatā*, as a matter of fact, is one of the important elements of Mahāyāna. In the *Upasivamāṇavapucchā* Lord Buddha instructs Upasiva to cross the flooded river with the help of *śūnyatā*. He should be mindful and at the same time realize nothingness.

Ākincaññaṁ pekkhamānosatimā, natthīti nissāya tarassu oghaṁ /
Kāme pahāya virato kathāhi, taṇhakkhayaṁ rattamahābhipassa //[24]

In the *Mogharājamāṇava pucchā* Lord Buddha once again explicitly, while preaching Mogharaja, says that one who is mindful and looks at the world as 'void' i.e. empty-having nothing, is beyond the clutches of Death (*Maccurāja*).

Suññato lokaṁ avekkhasu mogharājā sadā sato /
Attānudiṭṭhiṁ ūhacca evaṁ maccutaro siyā /
Evaṁ lokaṁ avekkhantaṁ Maccurājā na passatīti //25

Buddhaghoṣa while commenting on this *gāthā* explains *suññato lokam avekkhasu* as *avasiyapavattasallakkhaṇavasena vā tucchasamkhāravasena vāti dvīhī karaṇehi suññato lokam passa*[26] which means that void can be interpreted by holding that the characteristics of any thing are not in one's control and can also be interpreted as viewing all *saṁkhāras* or *dhammas* as *tuccha* having no reality. One is immediately reminded of what is said in the *Dhammapada* :

Sabbe saṁkhārā aniccā ti yadā paññaya passati[27]
Sabbe dhammā anattā ti yadā paññaya passati.[28]

'Attānudiṭṭhiṁ uhaccāti' has been explained by Buddhaghoṣa as *'śakkāyaditthim uddharitvā*[29] which means that the view that there is a permanent soul should be given up. *Sūññatā* definitely means *pudgalaśūnyatā* and *dharmaśūnyatā* here. The same meaning is confirmed by what has been said in the *Posālamāṇava pucchā.*

Ajjhattaṁ ca bahiddhā ca natthi kiñcī ti passato.[30]

Void is realized both within and without.

From what has been said above it is clear that the seed of *suññatā* is found in the *Sutta Nipata* and Nagarjuna's logic and conviction to give up all views has been considerably inspired by it.

References

1. B.S. Upadhyaya, *Pāli Sāhitya kā Itihāsa*, p.235.
2. See Introduction to Fausboll's edition of *Sutta Nipata*.
3. Mervyn Sprung (ed.). *The Problem of Two Truths in Buddhism and Vedānta*, p.78.
4. *ibid.*, p.84.
5. *ibid.*, see pp.82-83.
6. Nagarjuna, *Mūlamādhyamika Kārika*, 13.8.
7. *Brahmajālasutta (Nalanda edition, p.34). "Tayidaṁ, Bhikkhave, Tathāgato pajānāti, 'Ime diṭṭhiṭṭhānā evaṁgahitā, evaṁparāmaṭṭhā, evaṁgatikā bhavanti, evaṁ samparāyā'ti'. Taṁ ca Tathāgato pajānāti, tato ca uttaritaraṁ pajānāti, taṁ ca pajānamaṁ na parāmasati. Evaṁ aparāmasato cassa paccattaññeva nibbati viditā, vedanānam samudayam ca, atthangamam ca assādam ca, ādinavam ca, nissaranam ca yathābhūtam viditvā anupāda vimutto, Bhikkhave, Tathāgato.*

8. T.W. Rhys Davids, *Dialouges of the Buddha*, Part I, see The *Brahmajālasutta*.
9. *Sutta Nipāta*, 41.1.
10. *ibid.*, 41.5, 6, 7 & 8.
11. *ibid.*, 42.1.
12. *ibid.*, 42.3.
13. *ibid.*, 42.4.
14. *ibid.*, 42.7.
15. *ibid.*, 42.8.
16. *ibid.*, 43.1 & 5.
17. *ibid.*, 44.9.
18. *ibid.*; 47.11.
19. *ibid.*, 46.1.
20. *ibid.*, 46.8.
21. *ibid.*, 50.7.
22. *ibid.*, 51, 11 & 12.
23. *ibid.*, 52.2.
24. *ibid.*, 61.2.
25. *ibid.*, 70.4.
26. Angraj Chaudhary (ed.) *Suttaṇipāta Aṭṭhakathā* (Nalanda edition), p.486.
27. S. Radhakrishnan (Tr.), The *Dhammapada*, p.146.
28. *ibid.*, p.146.
29. Angraj Chaudhary (ed.) *Suttäṇipāta Aṭṭhakathā* (Nalanda edition), p.486.
30. *Suttanipāta*, 69.2.

Ethical Teachings in the Dhammapada

The *Dhammapada* is very popular throughout the Buddhist world for containing ethical teachings which have bearing not only on individual life but also on social life. The well-being of individuals and society can be greatly achieved if we follow the teachings. *Dhammapada* means the path of virtue. Therefore, its main thesis is human conduct. Righteous behaviour, practising of meditation and keeping oneself from impurities of all kinds are more important than metaphysical speculations which, however subtle and deep, do not necessarily lead one to follow the path of virtue.

The ethical teachings in the *Dhammapada* are meant to ensure our physical as well as spiritual well-being. Lord Buddha, perhaps, more keenly than anybody else, observed the infinite miseries and suffering that the flesh is heir to. And like a benevolent and compassionate physician he found out the way to get rid of them. *Taṇhā* or craving according to him, is at the root of all our sufferings. We are born again and again and are bound to the wheel of existence because we have endless cravings for worldly pleasures. If we can put an end to all our hydra-headed desires, we can free ourselves from the cycle of birth and death. Even Lord Buddha had to run through a course of many births before he could get rid of all sufferings by annihilating all desires.

Taṇhā or craving is the builder of life and the cause of cycles of births and deaths. It has been expressed in the following words :

"I have run through a course of many births looking for

the maker of the dwelling and finding him not : painful is birth again and again".

"Now are you seen, O builder of the house, you will not build the house again. All your rafters are broken, your ridge-pole is destroyed, your mind set on the attainment of *nibbāna*, has attained the extinction of desires".[1]

Lord Buddha was a great psychologist. According to him mind is the spring of all actions good or bad. And what is mind? It is the whole content of consciousness, it is also the active thinking principle. Mind, therefore, plays a great part in shaping, our life. The first verse of the *Dhammapada* speaks of the pivotal role that it plays in our life.

"All that we are is the result of our thought. If a man speaks or acts with an evil thought, sorrow follows him (as a consequence) even as the wheel follows the foot of the drawer (the ox which draws the cart)".[2] If, on the other hand, he speaks or acts with a pure thought, happiness follows him like a shadow.[3] The influence of thought on our life is all-pervasive. If our thoughts are pure, our life can be happy and we can plant peace in our society. It is said in the *Dhammapada* that a wrongly directed mind can do us greater harm than an enemy can do to an enemy or a hater to a hater.[4] And if our mind is well directed it will do us greater service than our parents or relatives.[4] It is therefore, very necessary to cultivate pure thoughts and drive away impure ones. But mind is vey fickle. It is very difficult to corntrol it. But, howsoever difficult it may be to control it, we have to do so. Our mind will have to be disciplined. By filling our mind with pure thoughts, we can change our life and indirectly we change the character of our society and the world at large, because it is the purity of mind which causes our well-being.

What is needed in the world of today, which is torn by strife and hatred is to cherish noble and pious thoughts. We should, therefore, drive out all feelings of hatred and cultivate the feelings of love. The sublime teaching in the following verse of the *Dhammapada*, if put into practice, can go a long way in establishing the peace of mind and world peace :-

"Not at any time are enmities appeased here through enmity but they are appeased through non-enmity. This is the eternal law".[5]

Evil thoughts always have a tendency to prey upon us. It is, therefore, necessary to be always vigilant, so that no evil thought can pollute our mind. All moral actions are born of '*appamāda*' (vigilance). "Vigilance is the path to eternal life."[6] The importance of vigilance has been set forth in the most eloquent terms in the *Dhammapada*.

"Vigilance is like a fire which consumes every bond small or large. Higher quality of life depends on vigilance because it is the latter which makes one diligent".[7]

The *Dhammapada* teaches us to live a virtuous life and says the fragrance of the virtuous people, unlike the fragrance of flowers and sandal-wood, travels even against the wind.

Virtue, therefore, is to be assiduously cultivated. Only when a man can control his mind and five senses, he can attain what is called serenity of mind. He must be restrained in respect of three kinds of actions-mental, vocal and physical. "Even the gods envy him whose senses are controlled and subdued".[8]

Only a virtuous man can practise meditation and it is the power of meditation that leads one to attain what is called '*prajñā*' through which one is able to see the real nature of worldly objects to which we all cling due to ignorance.

In one of the verses of the *Dhammapada* it has been said that the opportunities offered by human life are indeed great. Therefore, the most important thing to do in life is to eschew all evils to perfect good deeds and to purify our mind.[9]

Some of the verses in the *Dhammapada* vividly describe the impermanence of our life. The world is perpetually changing and burning. This body of ours, of which we become so proud is nothing but a 'painted image, a body full of wounds, put together in which there is neither permanence nor stability'.[10] It has been compared with a citadel made of bones, 'plastered over with flesh and blood and in it dwell old age and death, pride and deceit'.[11]

What, therefore, is the good of being infatuated by this short-lived beauty ? What is the good of clinging to such sensual pleasures ?

We should, therefore, try to do good deeds and keep ourselves from sensual pleasures. Sensual pleasures are caused by attachment and there is no fire like attachment.

In the *Piyavagga*[12] of the *Dhammapada* it has been said that one should not cling to what is pleasant or unpleasant because both are painful. Our love of an object gives rise to grief and our affection for and enjoyment of it give rise to fear and grief. It is, therefore, necessary to be free from attachment and liking.

There are many teachings in the *Dhammapada* which may be called the gems of ethical teachings. "He who has a fool as his companion suffers greatly, but he who lives in the company of the noble enjoys infinite happiness."[13]

It has been said that anger is our great enemy. It must be put away. Pride and worldly attachments also should be avoided. Then only we can attain bliss.

"It always takes two to make a quarrel. Is it, therefore, not always good to overcome the angry by non-anger, evil by good, the miser by liberality and the liar by truth ?"[14]

In the *Mahābhārata* the same thing has been said.

It has been repeatedly said in the *Dhammapada* to speak the truth ('*saccan bhaṇe*') and to be watchful of 'bodily irritation' 'speech irritation' and 'mind irritation.'

Buddhism upholds the dignity of man and believes in his infinite capacity to ameliorate his lot. For his salvation a man need not go to any god. He can, if he wants to, work out his salvation by his own efforts. He is the lord.

Apart from these ethical teachings the *Dhammapada* has many verses which teach what is called social ethics. It is the instinct of man to love life and fear punishment. Therefore, we must have what Confucius calls consideration for the feelings of others. This is the basis of a good society. In the Bible also it has been said, "Therefore, all things whatsoever ye would that man should do to you, do you even so to them."[15]

In the *Gita* also it has been said that those who look upon others as they look upon themselves are real Pundits.[16] If we follow this teaching we can make the miserable world of ours a better world, a happier world.

There are many *gāthās* in the *Dhammapada* which teach us to develop our intrinsic quality. What matters most for our spiritual progress is our quality of inner life, our nobility and honesty. All outward signs of asceticism have been rejected in the *Dhammapada* and they have been pronounced as devices to earn livelihood. "Not nakedness, not matted hair, not dirt, not fasting, not lying on the ground, not rubbing with ashes, not sitting motionless purify a mortal who is not free from doubt."[17] Sant Kabir also stresses the purity of soul. Growing a beard and having a matted hair do not necessarily make a *sādhu*. The same idea is re-echoed in a saying by Lucius. "If you think that to grow a beard is to acquire wisdom, a goat is at once a complete Plato."

Thus we find that the ethical teachings in the *Dhammapada*, if they are followed, can go a long way in moulding our life. They have direct bearing on individual and society and they are true not only for one age but for all ages. They, therefore, are eternal. They are the key to a happy and peaceful life here as also the key to salvation, to *Nibbāna*.

References

1. *Dhammapada* XI, 8 & 9.
2. *Dhammapada* I, 1.
3. *ibid*., I, 2.
4. *ibid*., III, 11, 12.
5. *ibid*., I, 5.
6. *ibid*., II, 1.

7. *ibid.*, II, 11.
8. *ibid.*, VII, 5.
9. *ibid.*, XIV, 5.
10. *ibid.*, XI, 2.
11. *ibid.*, XI, 5.
12. *ibid.*, XVI, 2.
13. ibid., V, 415.
14. *ibid.*, XVII, 3.
15. See the *Bible*,
16. See the *Gita*.
17. *ibid.*, *Brāhmaṇavagga*.

Ethicization Makes Buddhism a World Religion

Buddhism like Christianity and Islam has spread in the greater part of the world. There are historical causes why Buddhsim once spread far beyond in other countries than in the country of its origin. Like Christianity it also received royal patronage in the beginning. Aśoka in the 3rd century B.C. and Kaniṣka in the Ist century A.D. are great names in history who took several unfailing measures to spread the message of the Master (Lord Buddha) in the length and breadth of their empires and even beyond them. The indefatigable zeal of the Buddhist Bhikkhus, their vast learning and profound erudition coupled with their unshakeable faith in the teachings of Lord Buddha and their purity of life went a long way not only in spreading the message but also in securely establishing it in the land of the half-civilized people as well as in the land of the highly civilized people. Wherever it went in its long and arduous journey it met people so sweetly and compassionately that the land of Confucius and Lao-Tse also offered no resistance in embracing it. We never hear of the role of sword, nor do we ever hear of any persecution in its name in the long history of its spread and development. Its power of tolerance and its catholic outlook in matters of food (even meat eating was not absolutely forbidden) contributed greatly to its spread. The great role of Nalanda Mahavihara, the only University in the world of that time, where several thousand students from a great part of the world taught by some finest minds lived harmoniously practising both *pariyatti* and *paṭipatti*, with 'more than negative tolerance, in the sense of an absence of intolerance of a differing point of view' cannot be exaggerated inasmuch as it was a living example of world Buddhism. *Snātakas* of this University acted as cultural ambassadors and forged the ties of friendship between Nalanda and their respective countries and widened the platform on which humanity from all over the world could sit together and discover those values which can save it in all ages of stife and strain.

In addition to all these causes there are yet some greater causes related to the intrinsic qualities of Buddhism, which helped in its spread and development. One such cause is that Lord Buddha ethicized religion. Let one be an atheist, he will have no difficulty in accepting Buddhism and one who is a theist will have no difficulty in looking upon Buddha as the embodiment of all the best qualities that he seeks to find in the God of his heart's desire. The Mahāyāna concept of Bodhisattva is almost the same as the concept of God according to the *Gita* at least in some respects. If one just utters the name of a Bodhisattva sincerely and faithfully, one is bound to cross the ocean of *sansāra*-the cycle of birth and death. It is true that thought development did take place in the course of the history of Buddhism but the tone set in early Buddhism i.e. *Theravāda* Buddhism continues to be there in all the phases of its development.

Lord Buddha's unique contribution is his ethicization of religion. Religion according to him is not a belief in certain rituals, nor does it mean worshipping certain deities and powers and gods and even God with a capital 'G' but it means purity of conduct i.e. purity of mental, vocal and physical actions. Purifying mind from all defiling factors is the quintessence of Buddhism. He also did not believe in or bank upon that philosophy that indulges in speculations which lead one no where and which can be rightly said to be intellectual exercises in futility. He propounded a philosophy that pertained to the real need of life. With his deep experience and profound insight he arrived at the conclusion that life is full of suffering of all kinds physical, mental and cosmic and our aim should be to put an end to them. He also explained the cause of suffering and said that it can be removed by annihilating *taṇhā* or *tṛṣṇā*. We are bound to the wheel of existence so long as our desires are not extinguished. If the aim of religion is to free oneself from the bondage of suffering, Buddha's ethicized religion is the only most effective and powerful religion. It is, in fact, the panacea for all evils.

What does this religion consist in ? It primarily consists in freeing one's mind from all polluting factors and eliminating desires. Buddha made a thorough study of mind and came to the conclusion that it is our mind that binds us to the wheel of existence and it is mind once again which can liberate us from this inexorable bondage.

Manopubbaṁ gamā dhammā mano seṭṭhā manomayā,
Manasā ce paduṭṭhena bhāsati vā karoti vā
Tato naṁ dukkhamanveti cakkaṁ va vahato padaṃ [1]

"(The mental) natures are the result of what we have thought, are chieftained by our thoughts, are made up of our thoughts. If a man speaks or acts with an evil thought, sorrow follows him (as a consequence even as the wheel follow the foot of the drawer) i.e. the ox which draws the cart [2]."

Our consciousness is the spring of all our actions good or bad. In the *gātha* that follows the above quoted *gātha* in the *Dhammapada* it is said that if we act or speak with pure thought happiness will come to us. It is clear from these *gāthā*s that our sorrow and happiness proceed from our mind. But the nature of mind is very unsteady and fickle, and it is very difficult to control it.

Phandanaṁ capalaṁ cittaṁ, durakkhaṁ dunnivārayaṁ [3]

It can, however be controlled by a wise man, in the way a fletcher makes straight his arrow.

Ujuṁ karoti medhāvī usukāro' va tejanaṃ [4]

Buddha ascribed the unsteadiness of mind to its being under the influence of desires. It roams in the world of desires. Infinite desires cause infinite *taṇhā* in us and we have to come to this world again and again till our desires are completely eliminated. How to control our desires from rising is the problem of all problems. In answering the 'how' of this problem Buddha makes a psychological study of mind and happily combines it with ethics. Buddha's *Abhidhamma* is a beautiful and subtle combination of both psychology and ethics. Mind works under the influence of six *hetus*, three of them namely *lobho*, *doso* and *moho* are *akusala hetus* and the rest three *alobho*, *adoso* and *amoho* are *kusala hetus*. In order to purify our mind it is essential to root out the *akusala* roots of actions. Another question arises here as to who will uproot these *akusala hetus*. Lord Buddha says that 'self is the lord of self, what higher self could there be ?"

Attā hi attano nātho ko hi nātho paro siyā.[5]

He says once again that our self is stained by our own evil actions and to purify our self is in our own hands.

Attanā va kataṁ pāpaṁ attanā saṁkilissati,
attanā akataṁ pāpaṁ attanā va visujjhati
Suddhi asuddhi paccataṁ nāñño aññaṁ visodhaye.[6]

Purity and impurity depend on one's own self. No man can purify another. Buddha says again and again that we can make or mar our own self. What we are today is because what we have done in the past. The resultants (*vipākas*) of our actions in the past lives follow us like our shadows. Our suffering, in the last analysis, is traced to *tṛṣṇā*-our desires which arise when our sense-organs come in contact with their respective objects and arouse in us sensations which we either relish or do not. Our sorrow is not caused by any outside agency such as a god or a supernatural power but we are ourselves responsible for it. It, therefore, follows from this that it is we who can eliminate our suffering. And we can do it by rooting out our desires. But how to do it ?

Mind can be controlled and desire can be eliminated by treading upon a path called the eightfold path which has been mapped out by Buddha on the basis of his experiences gained in his spiritual journey. This path comprises *sīla, samādhi and poññā*. By observing *sīla* one practises *samādhi* and attains *paṇṇā* (insight). The eightfold path is not an easy path but is a very difficult and steep one. The traveller who wishes to go along this requires to have a lot of patience and perseverance. one can only show the path to some one but he will have to walk along it himself in order to realise the *summum bonum* of life. Lord Buddha said to Bhikkhus, "Work out your own salvation with diligence" and "be island unto your own self". What does it mean ? It simply means that it is in our own hands to make our life. Thus Lord Buddha with his clarion call asserts that man is his own master. For his salvation he need not depend upon any outside agency. This, I think is, a great tribute to man and to his infinite capacity that lies in him.

Buddha's assertion that a man can put an end to his suffering and can free himself from the bondage of birth and death appeals to all men. Even confirmed atheists also have a lot of hope to achieve salvation without believing in God. Buddha has very clearly shown that our ethical nature is inseparably connected with our psychological one. The more we understand the nature of our mind and how it works the more are the chances of getting rid of the defilements that pollute it and the more is the possibility of eliminating desires that cause suffering. Steady journey along the arduous eightfold path is bound to result in annihilating desires and experiencing the supreme bliss.

Lord Buddha was the wisest and most rational philosopher that the world ever had. Like Plato he was completely shorn of all kinds of emotionalism. Swami Vivekanand says about Buddha, "And consider his marvellous brain. No emotionalism. That great brain was never supertitious." He further says, "See the sanity of the man. No gods, no angels, no demons, nobody. Nothing of the kind. Stern, sane, every brain cell perfect and complete, even at the moment of death"[7] He was so sane and perfect that he always advised his disciples not to follow him blindly nor to take for granted what he said without weighing the pros and cons of his words but he wanted their *śraddhā* in him illumined by *prajñā* (*Prajñānvayī śraddhā*). The *Dhamma* that he preached produces results in this very life here and now. He says "come and see" and if one begins to practise Buddhism one reaps fruits here and now and not in distant future.

Whereas ethicization, on the one hand, results in not necessarily believing in God for one's salvation, on the other hand, it results in a relentless belief in the results of *kamma* and consequently reward for good *kammas* and a stay in heaven after death or punishment for bad *kammas* and torture in hell after death. It is true that Buddhsim produces fear in man for his *akusala kammas.* Compared to the philosophical and ethical theories propounded by Buddha's contemporary thinkers like Pūraṇa Kassapa, Makkhali Gosāla, Ajita Kesakambali, Pakudha Kaccāyana and Sañjaya Velaṭṭhaputta who did not believe in the theory of *kamma* and rebirth according to one's actions but believed in what is called the helpless nature of man and in fatalism and who propounded no theory for man's pollution and purification, Buddha's ethical theory with a strong belief in man's capacity to make his own life better and free himself from the bondage of suffering is *par excellence.* None of those theories could satisfy the higher aspirations of man but Buddha's *Dhamma* superbly does it.

Buddha's teaching to practise non-violence is the crying need of the hour particularly in the world of today when the superpowers are amassing dangerous and deadly weapons in their arsenals. His instruction to insist on the purity of livelihood is more relevant today than ever. Hasn't Buddha expressly asked us to avoid earning livelihood by selling meat as also by selling weapons ? Buddha's teaching to avoid egoism is more relevant today than ever. If the super powers do not inculcate the discipline of controlling their ego, it may not take long for the world to be completely destroyed.

The *vipassanā* form of meditation which is an essential part of Buddhism is open to all. A theist or an atheist or a Christian or a Muslim can easily practise it as it is free from any bias in respect of god or in respect of the subjects of meditation. The four *Brahma vihāras* (sublime thoughts), viz. *mettā, karuṇā, muditā, and upekkhā* have a universal appeal. Who would not regard them as great qualities worth developing and practising ?

In the later phase of its development the concept of Bodhisattva came into being according to which each being has in him the seed of Bodhisattva which properly nurtured and cared for sprouts forth into the tree of *sambuddhatva*. This quite obviously holds out hope of salvation to all mankind.

Ethicization, therefore, makes Buddhism a world religion.

References

1. *Dhammapada.*
2. Trans, by S. Radhakrishnan
3. *Dhammapada 3,1.*
4. *Dhammapada 3. I.*
5. *ibid.,*
6. *ibid.,*
7. *Prabuddha Bhārata*, vol.88, quoted from an article entitled, *The Marvellous Brain Buddha*, p.187.

Buddha's Concept of Non-Violence in Proper Perspective

The principle of non-violence is not the be all and end all of Buddhist religion and philosophy as has been wrongly interpreted by some scholars. Those who regard Buddhism as a negative religion inasmuch as it teaches man to renounce the world and does not prepare him to face the problems of mundane life barely do justice to Buddhism and its great exponent Lord Buddha. The remark that it inculcates a weakening influence is not justified. In fact, interpreters of Buddhism have laid great emphasis on the principle of non-violence, which they regard as the central teaching of Lord Buddha. But, to my mind, they are mistaken in so far as they lay disproportionate quantum of emphasis on this principle. It does not actually deserve as much emphasis and the Master himself has not given so much emphasis. In actual fact, it is only one of the various *sīlas* to be observed by a Buddhist and *sīla* itself is only one of the three important mile-stones in the spiritual path mapped out by Lord Buddha in his endeavour to make a quest for spiritual attainment.

It is because of the wrong and unbalanced view taken by some scholars that the weakening of the nation as a whole is ascribed to Buddhism. It is said that Buddhism and particularly its principle of non-violence adopted as a way of life by kings and their subjects exercised a debilitating influence on the citizens so much so that the followers of the Buddha could not take up arms in their own defence against those who came to make a short work of them. The great University of Nalanda could not be saved by the monks living there and the people living in the vicinity of Nalanda also did not take up arms against the invaders. Perhaps they had been too much debilitated by the principle of non-violence as a way of life and, as a result, they had become incapable of countering the attack.

It is true that this is a recorded fact in history but is Buddhism to blame for it, or to be more precise, is Buddha's principle of non-violence to blame for the debility caused in the countrymen who fell an easy victim to foreign invaders and eventually lost their independence for several centuries together ?

My expressed object in this paper is to show the place of non-violence in the perspective of the teachings of Lord Buddha and also to show the quantum of emphasis laid by him on it. As I have said in the beginning, Buddha never regarded it as the most important of his teachings although this is the impression inevitably created by the *Sīle Patiṭṭhāya gāthā* in the *Visuddhimagga*[1] and many other passages in the *Nikāyas*[2] themselves where *Pāṇātipāta* (injury to creature) is enumerated first. It is quite natural that when one begins to speak glowingly about any thing the balance is tilted in its favour and the impression that it is the greatest and the best is not infrequently created, but this cannot be said to be true even of *sīla*, let alone of non-violence. It is, as I have said in the beginning, only one of the three mile-stones in the long, arduous and stupendous but splendid spiritual journey to attain the highest goal of human life.

Before making an assessment of what Lord Buddha said in the context of non-violence, it is indispensable to isolate the two broad views viz. mundane and supramundane. In the first place Lord Buddha's teachings are concerned primarily with our moral and spiritual life i.e., with the supramundane life. He had nothing to do with the logistics of war in order to defend himself from the attacks of enemies. According to him the greatest enemy of mankind is lust (*tṛṣṇā* or *taṇhā*) and all his moral teachings are geared to fight this enemy. Like a territorial king he did not concern himself with raising an army to fight and sugjugate his enemy.

It is true that his teachings do have a bearing on our

mundane life but to judge him by his successes and failures in aspects of life other than moral is to confuse the issue at hand. Lord Buddha should be judged in the context in which he gave his teachings. If we judge him out of context it will not be a real assessment of what he attained and what he contributed to our culture. Buddha was the most enlightened person of his time. He roared like a lion. Therefore, any principle that he taught could not have been a weak weapon.

It is possible that the weapon he wielded to annihilate lust (*tṛṣṇā*) became a weak weapon at the hands of his followers. But this is not his fault. A weapon's effectiveness depends not only on its quality but also on who uses it. If a man does not know how to use a sword while fighting an enemy he is most likely to injure himself grievously. As far as non-violence is concerned there is nothing intrinsically wrong in it but it is specially meant for improving one's moral life.

Buddha knew it well that his teachings are meant for improving one's moral life. He also knew it well that all persons of the world are not spiritually advanced to practise what he taught. They were meant specially for individuals who could apply themselves assiduously in order to rise higher and higher in the path of *sādhanā*. If after his *mahāparinirvāṇa* kings like Aśoka embraced Buddhism and asked their subjects to follow the principle of non-violence as a way of life, it is not Buddha's fault. During his time, he never asked kings to give up weapons. At that time warriors used to go forth among the monks. When Bimbisara reported this to Buddha he said, "Monks, one in a king's service should not be let go forth. Whoever should let (one such) go forth, there is an offence of wrong-doing".[3] Besides, there are many passages in the *Tipiṭaka* where Lord Buddha has explained elaborately the duties of a king. The principle of non-violence was to be practised rigorously by Buddhist monks and the laity were asked to practise it as much as it was possible and practicable for them. Lord Buddha did not lay as much emphasis on it as Lord Mahavira did.

There is another argument which proves conclusively that Buddhism, particularly its principle of non-violence, does not have any inherent drawback in it to weaken and debilitate a nation. Had it been so, all the nations where Buddhism spread would have been as weak as India. But this is not so. China and Japan have not been weak and if Tibet became weak and mild, it is because of some other causes. In other words, the weakness of India and Tibet can be set down to some other causes and not to Buddhism.

Buddha's aim was to eradicate all sufferings and achieve a state of desirelessness, so that the cycle of repeated existence is put an end to. The realm which he envisaged was quite different from the realm in which ordinary human beings move and the laws propounded by him are different from the laws that apply to this realm. We will be doing injustice to him if we apply the laws that are suitable for the higher realm to the realm in which we normally move about.

In order to assess the value of the principle of non-violence it is necessary for us to examine the perspective in which it is set. In the *Brahmajāla Sutta* of the *Dīgha Nikāya* Lord Buddha has made it abundantly clear that the *Dhamma* which he has realized is very subtle and deep.

"There are, brethren, other things, profound, difficult to realise, hard to understand, tranquillising, sweet, not to be grasped by mere logic, subtle, comprehensible only by the wise. These things the Tathāgata, having himself realised them and seen them face to face, hath set forth; and it is of them thet they, who would rightly praise the Tathāgata in accordance with the truth, should speak.'[4]

From the context it is clear that Lord Buddha asks the Bhikkhus not to be happy if one praises him, the *Dhamma* and the *Sangha* and also asks them not to bear malice if one speaks ill of them. He says that their happiness and anger would stand in the way of their spiritual progress and self-conquest. And then he goes on to say that many people praise him on the ground that he observes *sīla* whereas other monks do not. He says that this is not the proper yardstick by which he should be judged because *sīla* is just a matter of little value, a trifling thing.

"It is in respect only of trifling things, of matters of little value, of mere morality, that an unconverted man, when praising the Tathāgata, would speak."[5]

He says that he can be best appreciated by those who can realize the great achievement made by him along the spiritual path trodden by him-the path in which the important mile stones are *sīla, samādhi* and *paññā*. It is true that *sīla* is the foundation stone on which the superstructure of *samādhi* and *paññā* is constructed. The splendid edifice of *samādhi* cannot be constructed without observing *sīla*. As has been aptly and succintly said by Buddhaghoṣa one cannot concentrate one's mind and attain *Bodhi* without observing *sīla*. *Sīla* has its importance no doubt, but it should not be exaggerated. It should be put in the proper perspective. Buddha's teachings are too great to be explained in term only of *sīla*. As only a small part of ice is seen floating on the surface of water, and quite a great part of it remains submerged, so observance of *sīla* is only a small part of the great mass of spiritual achievement made by him. And the principle of non-violence or abstinence from injury to creature is only one of *sīlas*. Therefore, it will not be proper to say that Buddha would have regarded a man great if he practised only non-violence. It is true that he did expound its importance but the perspective in which he put this principle should not be lost sight of. He has explained at length in the *sutta* referred to above that *sīla* is only a small fraction of what people see in him and praise and those who praise him on this account have not actually gauged the depth of his attainment and have not measured the spiritual height he has reached. Besides, he was concerned with the uplift of moral life and if this principle did debilitate people, he is not to blame for it, because he was not principally concerned with mundane life.

References

1. *Sīle patiṭṭhāya naro sapañño, cittaṁ paññaṁ ca bhāvayaṁ*
2. *Ātāpi nipako Bhikkha, so imaṁ vijaṭaye jaṭaṁ ti.*
3. *The Book of the Discipline*, Vol.IV. Tr. by I.B. Horner, p.92.
4. *Dialogues of the Buddha* tr. by T.W. Rhys Davids, p.26.
5. *ibid.*, p.3.

Right Livelihood - its Significance in Modern Times

Right livelihood is one of the constituents of the noble eightfold path mapped out by Lord Buddha in his arduous spiritual journey to put an end to the cause of suffering and attain *nirvāṇa* (salvation). This is actually one of the *ādibrahmacariyaka sīla* (morality of genuine pure conduct) which consists of right speech, right physical action and right livelihood. These three come under *sīla* without observing which it is not possible to lead a spiritual life. The Buddhist *sādhanā* consists of sīla (virtue), *samādhi* (concentration) and *paññā* (insight). The latter two are not possible without the first one.

If we look at *sīla* a little closely we will immediately realise that it is the basis of spiritual life. How can we lead a spiritual life ? Only by avoiding evil and doing good. The quintessence of *sila* is the doing of all that is good and avoiding all that is evil. *sabba pāpassa akaraṇaṃ, kusalassa upasampadā*. Of the two kinds of *sīla* viz. *vāritra* and *cāritra*, the former is the practice of those ethical precepts which make a man good and which are primarily based on love and compassion towards all beings. This is *ahiṁsā*. The latter means good manners.

If we practise the two kinds of *sīla*, we do not only become individually good but we also become useful citizens and we help in the growth of social harmony and peace. Man lives in society and, therefore, what he does must be wholesome for it. *Sīla* pertains to both individual and social life. If the ethical precepts are observed, it does good to the individual and goes a long way in the purification of all the three kinds of actions, physical, vocal and mental. And also it does good to society in so far as it brings peace and harmony to the whole society. It is individuals who make a society and if individuals lead a pure life, live in peace and harmony, society will naturally be peaceful and harmonious.

Lord Buddha has asked us again and again to refrain from killing, stealing, sexual intercourse, lying, speaking harshly, making slanderous speech and talking uselessly as also from drinking liquors. If we can practise restraint with regard to these, our life will be happy. Abstinence from killing, stealing, sexual intercourse, telling lies and taking alcoholic drinks constitutes five precepts which must be observed. Right livelihood means earning livelihood without breaking the five precepts. For example, how can one's livelihood be regarded as pure if he earns it by killing human beings, say, by taking part in a war or by slaughtering animals and dealing in flesh ? How can his livelihood be regarded as pure if he earns it by selling arms, poison or liquor; for dealing in these things clearly violates some of the precepts mentioned above ?

For earning livelihood in the right manner it has been said by the Buddha that one should not indulge in five trades. "Monks, these five trades ought not to be plied by a lay disciple...Trade in weapons, trade in human beings, trade in flesh, trade in spirits (intoxicants) and trade in poison."[1] The list, however, is not exhaustive. It simply points to the possible trades which must never be indulged in in order to earn one's livelihood. As Lord Buddha was addressing the people who lived in the sixth century B.C. he mentioned the trades which were prevalent in those days. He also gave a list of other means of earning wrong livelihood.[2]

Man must live and the means of his livelihood are matters of his greatest concern. We know that a hungry man is an angry man because satisfying one's hunger is the basic need of life, even more basic than satisfying sexual desire. But we must earn our livelihood by right means so that peace and harmony can prevail in society. If we do not do so, we will disturb the peace and harmony of society. Our dishonest means of earning livelihood will be detrimental to the welfare of society. Right livelihood, therefore, is important both for the individual's spiritual journey as well as for the peace and prosperity of society in which we live.

If we look at the modern world, what Buddha said with regard to livelihood becomes more clear and we see its relevance in modern times more than ever. Right livelihood should not be earned only by individuals but it should be earned by the nations also so that the whole world may realize peace, prosperity and harmony. Lord Buddha did not mention only the right means of earning livelihood but he also listed several wrong means of earning it.

Lord Buddha laid a great stress on earning one's livelihood by honest means. The mode should be perfect and correct. And what he said with regard to it is very important and holds good for ever, more so in modern times. Take for example the case of trading in weapons. Individuals and nations trade in weapons today on a very large scale. The danger, therefore, of annihilation of mankind has become infinitely great. Today the world is sitting on the crater of a volcano and any moment the situation can be explosive so much so that the entire mankind and all glorious achievements made by man can be reduced to cinders. America and Russia are two powerful blocks of the world amassing deadly and dangerous weapons and filling their arsenals with nuclear, hydrogen and other powerful bombs. They do not only store them in their arsenals but sell them to the developing nations of the world. The result is the growing tension between one nation and the other and the cold war situation in the whole world. In such a situation how can the world live in peace ? Buddha expressly forbids us to make our living by means of trading in arms and weapons. His teaching, therefore, is nore relevant today than ever before.

Trading in human beings is also very bad. One who is devoid of love and compassion can indulge in such monstrous trade. Negroes from Africa were brought in America as slaves. The tension between the black and the white is still continuing.

Trading in flesh implies committing violence which means breaking the first precept. Slaughtering innocent animals and selling their meat are really the wrong means of earning one's livelihood. Besides, meat is a *tāmasika* food which produces indolence, that is *pramāda*. Lord Buddha has disapproved of *pramāda* in several of his *suttas*.

Trading in wine for one's livelihood is equally harmful. Wine is bad for health and if one is addicted to it he loses all his sense of responsibility and becomes a bad citizen. He spends all that he earns on it, indulges in wrong modes of earning money and deprives the members of his family of their right to enjoy his income. It is, therefore, harmful not only for oneself but for family and society.

The last trade Lord Buddha forbade was trade in poison. Poison takes life, so it is very dangerous and harmful. Now a days many kinds of weapons which are used in chemical warfare are prepared from poison. Chemical weapons can be as harmful as nuclear ones and in some cases, perhaps, more harmful. Their consequences can be disastrous. Where wars are fought with chemical weapons, people have greater chance of being afflicted with serious diseases that last for the whole life and in some cases they are carried from generation to generation. Knowing such dangerous consequences of poison Lord Buddha forbade us to earn our livelihood by dealing in poison. If poison can be used as a medicine, selling it is not forbidden . In that case it no longer remains a poison but it becomes a life saving drug.

In our effort to earn our livelihood we come in contact with our fellow beings and it is necessary, therefore, to earn our livelihood without hurting and injuring others. We must be honest so that our own members are not cheated by us. As time changes, there come into being a number of dishonest modes of earning one's livelihood. Blackmarketing, making adulteration in food, blackmailing, character assassination, yellow journalism, dishonest advertising and publicity. etc. are dishonest modes of earning livelihood. They must be avoided at all costs. If we do not indulge in the forbidden trades and if we do not use the above mentioned modes to earn our livelihood we shall live in peace. By adopting right means of earning our livelihood, we shall cut down our desires and, thus, we will be able to make progress in our spiritual journey. Right livelihood, thus, will secure our worldy and spiritual progress.

In modern times, thereofore, the importance of right livelihood is very great. If individuals and nations make it a point to earn their livelihood by honest and just means, we will not be ourselves peaceful but the whole human society, nay, the whole world will become an abode of peace.

References

1. A.N. Vol.III.p.
2. See *Brahmajālasutta* in The *Dīgha Nikāya* Vol.I.

Concept of Paccekabuddha

A Sammāsambuddha is a fully Enlightened one who is able to lead others on to the path of liberation. On the other hand, a Paccekabuddha is one who attains enlightenment through his own efforts but is not able to enlighten others.

The notion of Paccekabuddha is as old as the origin of Buddhism. In the earliest Pali canonical texts there are quite a few references to Paccekabuddha. In the *Isigili Sutta* of the *Majjhima Nikāya*[1] Lord Buddha has enumerated as many as one hundred and five of them while explaining to the Bhikkhus the origin of the name of the hill Isigili at Rajgir. In the *Anguttara Nikāya* two types of Buddhahood have been mentioned by Lord Buddha. In the *Apadāna* he says. "In the whole universe, there is except me only no one who is equal to the Paccekabuddha".[2] In the *Sutta Nipāta* which according to some scholars contains some of the oldest *suttas*, we find the characteristics of a Paccekabuddha set forth in detail.[3] *Puggalapaññati*[4] also includes Paccekabuddha as one of the innumerable types of persons. In the *Milindapañho*,[5] too, which comes under non-canonical literature, references to Paccekabuddha are found.

From these references, therefore, it can at once be concluded that not only the notion of Paccekabuddha is found in the early canonical and non-canonical texts, but also the notion is quite developed as the characteristics of a Paccekabuddha have been clearly mentioned. The last two books mentioned above have attempted to define a Paccekabuddha and thus implicitly brought out the differences between him and a Buddha. A Paccekabuddha, like a Sammāsambuddha, attains *bodhi* by his own efforts and not with the help of any teacher, but like the latter the former does not become omniscient and omnipotent.[6] *Milinda*

Pañho gives almost the same characteristics of a Paccekabuddha and adds that he wanders alone like the horn of a rhinoceros.[7]

We also find the concept of Paccekabuddha in the commentarial literature. In the commentary of the *Khaggavisāṇasutta* Buddhaghosa - the celebrated Pali commentator is seen quoting Lord Buddha's explanation of a Paccekabuddha in detail. He has incidentally brought out the differences between a Buddha, a Paccekabuddha and also between them and a Sāvaka in several respects namely, their *sampatti,*[8] their spiritual attainments, *kulas* they are born in as also in respect of the time of their birth.

All the three must have *patthanā* and *abhinihāra,* but they have them in different degrees. A Paccekabuddha practises his *pāramī* for at least two *asaṁkheyya* and hundred thousand *kappas*[9] from his resolution to the attainment of *bodhi,* but a Buddha practises his *pāramī* for any period from a minimum of four *asaṁkheyya* and hundred thousand *kappas* to a maximum of sixteen *asaṁkheyya* and hundred thousand *kappas* from his *abhinīhāra* to Buddhahood. Incidentally three types of Buddhas have been conceived here; one has more of *pañña* than *saddhā* and *viriya;* the second has more of *saddhā* and the third has more of *viriya.* A *Sāvaka,* however, does not have to devote such a long time to attain his goal. An *Aggasāvaka* has to devote one *asaṁkheyya* and hundred thousand *kappas* whereas a *Mahāsāvaka* devotes only hundred thousand *kappas.* Apart from these numerical differences, the major difference between a Buddha and a Paccekabuddha is in respect of spiritual attainments.

The former not only attains to supreme and perfect knowledge but he also proclaims it to the world and founds an Order, whereas the latter is enlightened like the former by his own efforts but he remains self-centred. He does not preach the *Dhamma* to others and that is why he is known as a 'silent Buddha'. A Peccekabuddha, however, does ordain others, admonish them in reference to good and proper conduct (*ābhisāmācārika*). His realization of the *Dhamma* is "like a dream seen by a deaf mute". "As a man from countryside cannot find words in praise of the delicious dishes he eats in a city, so a Paccekabuddha cannot explain it". Like a Buddha he does attain to all the *Iddhis.*[10] *samāpattis*[11] and *paṭisambhidās*[12] but in respect of other higher attainments he occupies a middle rank, the Buddha ranking above him and the *Sāvaka* ranking below.

All the three, namely a Buddha, a Paccekabuddha and a Sāvaka are born in the same *vivaṭṭamānakappa* but a Paccekabuddha never meets a Buddha face to face as they are not contemporary, whereas a *Sāvaka* lives contemporaneouly with a Buddha and learns the *Dhamma* from him. A layman also can become a Paccekabuddha, but the marks of a layman immediaitely disappear.[13]

The differences between a Buddha and a Paccekabuddha are shown in some other respects too, which to my mind, do not seem to be fundamental. A Buddha is said to be born in a Khattiya or a Brahmin family. So are the two *Aggasāvakas* said to be, but the case of a Paccekabuddha is different. He can be born in a family of *gahapati* as well.

There is no limit to the number of Paccekabuddhas who appear simultaneously. Their dwelling places are the three caves namely *Suvaṇṇaguhā, Maṇiguhā* and *Ratanaguhā* in the *Nandamūlakapabbhāra.* Paccekabuddhas hold their *uposatha* in the *Ratanamālaka* at the foot of the *Mañjūṣā* tree in Gandhamādana which is one of the five mountain ranges that encircle Anotatta. Whenever any Paccekabuddha appears in the world, his first concern is to find out *Ratanamālaka* where seats for Paccekabuddhas are appointed. All other Paccekabuddhas assemble there to know from him the circumstances which led to his enlightenment. They also assemble there when one of them dies.

Even a cursory glance at the distinctions shown above will reveal that while some of the differences shown between a Buddha and a Paccekabuddha are fundamental, others are only superficial. For example, how can Lord Buddha who always extolled *karmas* (action) in preference to *jāti* (caste) say that a Buddha is born in a family of Khattiya and Brahmin and a Paccekabuddha can be born in a family of *gahapati* as well and thereby show his superiority over a Paccekabuddha ? To me it seems that this statement has been put into the mouth of Lord

Buddha who is said to have brought out the distinctions in *Pubba Yogāvacara sutta*. That it has been done by the commentators is also borne out by the fact that the aforesaid *sutta* is not included in the canonical text. Bearing in mind the generous and compassionate nature of Lord Buddha, it does not seem to me proper to ascribe to him the statement given above.

In spite of shortcomings like this, the commentators have attempted to bring out the differences between a Buddha and a Paccekabuddha and between them and a *Sāvaka* in detail. Three categories seem to be well-established in the early canonical texts and in the *Sutta-Nipāta Aṭṭhakathā*. The pertinent question, therefore, is why such a distinction has been made at all ? Does it only speak of a hierarchy in the Buddhist spiritual world in keeping with the hierarchies found in other or does it have to say something of importance with regard to the psychology of Buddha, Paccekabuddha and Sāvaka ?

La Velle Poussin asserts in his excellent article on Pratyekabuddha in *Encylopaedia of Religion and Ethics* that this theory of the Pratyekabuddha, the hermit saint has arisen from acrtual fact as he is a Buddhist counterpart of the Upaniṣadic Ṛṣi. He says, "The Pratyekabuddha embodies the old ideal of a solitary and silent life - an ideal that was flourishing before Śakya Muni came. Śakyamuni did not favour it. He, indeed, condemned the vow of silence, and did his best to encourage spiritual exercises in common reading, teaching, and social activities of many kinds. But he was shrewd enough to leave some scope to the more ascetic tendencies of his countrymen. Accordingly after they had undergone some training (novitiate), monks were allowed to live in the forests, like the Ṛṣis of old".[14]

It is apparent from Poussin's comparison of the Pratyekabuddha with the Ṛṣi that he gives only a social explanation in that the notion of Pratyekbuddha was introduced into the Buddhist world in sheer imitation of the Vedic Ṛṣis.

Dr. Oldenberg has put forward a pragmatic theory of the notion of Paccekabuddha. According to him the notion of a Paccekabuddha seems to have been principally intended to imply that even in such periods (when there were no universal Buddha and no Orders) the door of deliverance is not shut against earnest and powerful effort.

But the explanations that the concept of Pratyekabuddha was introduced to continue the age-old tradition of Ṛṣis as put forward by Poussin and that it was introduced to encourage individual efforts (cf. Buddha's teaching : work out your own salvation) offered by Oldenberg tell only half truth.

Some sort of hierarchy is found practically in all the religious systems, let alone the governmental ones in a country and it is necessitated by the actual fact that the levels of consciousness found in men are different. The dictum that all men are born equal may well be valid in the political realm but in the spiritual realm it has hardly any relevance. In fact, it may be regarded as a myth. The dispositions of men are not the same; consequently, their attainments in the spiritual field must also be different.

A more satisfying and precise explanation of why there are three categories is found in Mahāyāna literature. It is not within the scope of my article to trace out the outlines of the development of Hīnayāna into Mahāyāna but it can safely be assumed that from Hīnayāna to Mahāyāna there has been a continuous growth of thought process and the two indicate only the two stages in what is called 'the great chain of ideas' with several intermediary stages. Mahāyāna with the developed concept of Bodhisattva who represents a much higher stage in the thought process than one represented by the early tradition, represents the later stage. In Mahāyāna literature the analysis of the term Pratyekabuddha adds a new dimension to the concept. A Pratyekabuddha is compared and contrasted with a Buddha and a Śrāvaka and differences between them are brought out not only in respect of their aspiration and their achievements, but also in respect of their subtle dispositions. Some of the superficial differences pointed out earlier in early Pali canonical texts and in commentarial literature are not mentioned at all. Instead, an attempt has been made to explore deeper psychology and subtler springs of actions found in the three categories of aspirants. One major point of difference between them is in respect of altruism each of them professes to have.

We also enter a new phase here in so far as we find a very subtle and clear analysis of their mental dispositions, which is more psychological than arbitrary. In the *'Saddharma Punḍarīka'*, it is said that the mental capacities of persons are different. This difference accounts for their classification into three categories. The *Sūtrālaṁkāra*[15] brings out the differences in respect of aspirations. It shows that a Buddha, a Pratyekabuddha and a Śrāvaka receive different instructions according to their capacities. Their exertions and consequently their fruitions are also different.

The *Sūtrālaṅkāra* holds that there are persons with high, moderate and low aspirations. In fact, there can be innumerable categories of men if the quantum of aspiration for *bodhi* found in different persons is taken into account. The *Sūtrālaṅkāra* broadly divides them into three categories. In the first category come all the three, Śrāvakas, Prateykabuddhas and Buddhas ; the second category comprises border cases and the third includes all those who will not attain it for the time being. The *Laṅkāvatāra* also treats of persons in terms of *gotrabheda*. According to it there are five *abhisamaya gotras* (classification of persons with reference to the attainment of enlightenment).

From these references it is clear that in Mahāyāna literature we get deeper analysis of the ingredients that go to make a Buddha, a Paccekabuddha and a Śrāvaka. Chandrakīrti in his *Madhayamakāvatāra* says :

"The name and the nature of a Buddha belong to three classes of persons ; the Śrāvakas, the Pratyekabuddhas and the incomparable perfect Buddhas. The name of Buddha, therefore, is suitable for the Pratyekabuddhas. These owing to their merits and knowledge, are greater than the Śrāvakas. But as they lack the equipment of merits and knowledge (of the perfect Buddha), the great compassion, the universal knowledge, they are inferior to perfect Buddhas. They are intermediary. And as knowledge (i.e. the knowledge that brings *nirvāṇa*) is born in them without a teacher, as they are Buddhas by themselves, isolated and acting for their own sake, they are Pratyekabuddhas".[16]

A Pratyekabuddha falls short of a Buddha. He lacks the great compassion and the universal knowledge which a Buddha develops by virtue of his incessant and untiring efforts coupled with lofty aspirations for a far longer period than a Pratyakabuddha. The absence of these two qualities and also the special nature of his training[17] are ultimately responsible for his incapacity to teach the *Dhamma* and work for pulling people out of suffering in the world. Consequently they have lesser degree of altruism.

Both a Buddha and a Paccekabuddha begin their strenuous journey as Bodhisattvas,[18] but the latter due to some inherent weakness breaks his journey somewhere in the way out of sheer annoyance at what he sees in the world. The *Kanakāvarṇāvadāna Sutta* has a story which throws sufficient light on why a Bodhisattva abandons his career, and becomes a Pratyekabuddha in order to achieve *nirvāṇa*.

The forbearance (*kṣānti*) needed for continuing uphill journey and compassion (*karuṇā*) for suffering humanity are not found in some Bodhisattvas. As a result, their growth into perfect Buddhas is retarded.

In the successive periods of the growth of Buddhism an in-depth analysis was brought to bear upon the three concepts of Buddha, Paccekabuddha and Sāvaka and the differences, though primarily psychological, were brought out in technical terms. Thus the possession of five *balas*[19] and the four *vaiśāradyas*[20] distinguish a Pratyekabuddha from a Śṛāvaka and the possession of omniscience, omnipotence and infinite compassion distinguish a Buddha from a Pratyekabuddha. Not only that, the attainment of these qualities was set down to the stages where the three reached in their spiritual journey. Asaṅga gives a beautiful account of it in the *Dasabhūmika Sutra*[21]

Later on the indissolubility and the inseparability of the psychological and the technical explanation was neglected. The technical side became so prominent that in Tibet a Paccekabuddha became known as Pratītyabuddha, (ṛten brel bsgon) as he was supposed to understand only the *Pratityasamutpāda*.

As men's dispositions, capacities and aspirations for spiritual attainments are different, so all who try to become perfect Buddha cannot be so at least in the same *kalpa*. There will be different categories of people. The concepts of Buddha, Paccekabuddha and Sāvaka, therefore, show a real hierarchy based on a sound psychological analysis of men's innate dispositions.

References

1. *M.N.* Vol.III, pp.133-34 : also see *Apadāna Aṭṭhakathā* Vol.1,p.143 (Burmese edition) where sixty two paccekabuddhas are mentioned by name. In the *Aṭṭhakaṭhā* of the *Khaggavisāna Sutta* also Paccekabuddhas are menetioned by name.
2. *A.N.* Vol.1 p.72; *Apadāana*, Vol.1,p.9.
3. See *Khaggaviṣāṇasutta*.
4. *Puggalapaññati*-p.23,p.110.
5. *Milindapañho* (ed.by R.D. Vedekar) p.108,
6. *Puggalapaññati*-p.23,110.
7. *Milindapañho*, 108.
8. *Samāpatti* has been translated as 'excellency' or 'magnificence' by T.W. Rhys Davids. But it seems to connote the requisites necessary for a Buddha and a Paccekabuddha. See S.N.A. Vol.I, pp.60,63.
9. By '*Kappa*' is meant an infinitely long period of time. It is said that if one keeps on taking out a seed every after hundred years from a *yojana* cubic box filled with mustard seeds, the box will be emptied sooner than one *Kappa*. See S.N.II, p.154.
   At another place it has been explained by another simile. It is said that if a solid rock one *Yojana* in length, breadth and height is rubbed with a piece of fine Kashi cloth, the rock will wear out sooner than one *kappa*. See S.N.II, pp.153-154.

10. *Iddhis* (psychic powers) are ten, viz. the power to project mind-made images of oneself; to become invisible; to pass through solid things such as a wall, to penetrate solid ground as if it were water, to walk on water, to fly through the air, to touch the sun and the moon and to ascend into the highest heavens.
11. *Samāpattis* (attainments) are eight : four *rūpa jhānas* and four *arūpa jhānas*.
12. *Paṭisambhidas* are four viz. attha (analysis of meanings "in cxtension"), Dhamma (of reasons, condittions or casual relations), Nirutti (of meanings "in intension" as given in definition), and Paṭibhāna (of intellect to which things knowable by the foregoing processes are presented).
13. *S.N.A.*, p.78.
14. Vol.X, p.153.
15. *Sūtrālaṅkāra*, p.4.
16. Quoted from E.R.E. Vol.X, p.153.
17. From the *Khaggavisāṇasutta* it is clear that a Paccekabuddha wanders alone like the horn of a rhinoceros for years. He does not live in the company of laymen, monks or Paccekabuddha for a long time. He does not receive training from a teacher. Therefore he naturally develops a distaste for human contact.
18. According to the *Saddharma Puṇḍarika* a Śrāvaka also begins his journey as a Bodhisattva because there is only one vehicle. *Prajñāpāramitā*, on the contrary, believes in the three vehicles. It clearly says that what is necessary for becoming a Śrāvaka or a Paccekabuddha is the realisation of voidness.
19. There are five *balas*, viz. *Saddhā, Vīriya, Sati, Samādhi and Paññā*.
20. *Antarāyika-dhamma-jānanam, Niyyānikadhamma-passanaṁ, Kilesādīnaṁ hananaṁ, and Sammā sāmaṁ ca sabba-dhammānaṁ bojjhanaṁ*. D.N.A.I., p.57.
21. Sammāsambuddhahood is achieved only after making a strenuous journey and keeping a lofty ideal in one's mind. Asanga has enumerated the ten stages, namely *Pramuditā, Vimalā, Prabhākarī, Arcismatī, Sudurjayā, Abhimukhā, Dūrangamā, Acalā, Sādhumatī and Dharmameghā*, which a

Bodhisattva-to-be has to pass before he mounts upon the summit and sits upon a luminous seat. There he is consecrated by the Buddhas in Supreme enlightenment. A Pratyekabubbha does not continue to aspire after the Supreme status, so he ranks but second to the Sammāsaṁbuddha. For detail see Asanga's *Dasabhūmikasūtra*.

The Altruistic Motive and the Changing Ideals of Bodhisattva as Revealed from the Dāna Pāramitā

The concept of Bodhisattva has evolved over the ages. In early Buddhism Bodhisattva was the name given to Siddhārtha who ultimately became Buddha. In other words, Siddhāratha is called Bodhisattva till he attained *nirvāṇa*. This was the name given to him in his several previous lives in which he perfected several *pāramitās* in order to enable him to attain *nirvāṇa*.

But the concept underwent changes and when Mahāyāna Buddhism came into being, it was fully crystallised. We find the full-fledged form of the concept of Bodhisattva in *Laṅkāvatāra* and *Sikṣā Samuccaya*. In the *Laṅkāvatāra Sūtra* Bodhisattva says that he will not enter into final *nirvāṇa* till all beings have been liberated. In the *Sikṣā Samuccaya* by Śāntideva more or less the same thing has been repeated. "I must lead all beings to liberation. I will stay here till the end, even for the sake of one living soul".

These vows and declarations of Bodhisattva immediately make it clear that he has become fully compassionate to all living beings. The concept of Bodhisattva is an important Mahāyāna ideal which represents the warm sunshine as opposed to cold *arhatship* of early Buddhism. The *arhats* were no doubt very austere, saintly, self-restrained and meditative ascetics but at the same time they were rather frigid and self-centered. When the Mahāyānists propounded their theory, they levelled the charges of selfishness and egotism against the *arhat* ideal of early Buddhism. An *arhat* makes all his efforts to achieve his own liberation from the sufferings of the world. He does not work for the liberation and happiness of other beings. The Mahāyānists prove this by quoting from the *Vinaya Piṭaka* where it is said that Buddha after attaining *nirvāṇa* was hesitant and reluctant to preach to the people the way out of suffering. As against this ideal which is regarded as inferior, the Mahāyānists put forward the ideal of Bodhisattva. The ideal of Bodhisattva is the highest good for himself as also for suffering beings. An *arhat* was regarded as a self-complascent, self-centered and unsocial recluse but a Bodhisattva, on the contrary, thinks not of himself only but also of others, even of birds and beasts and other lower creatures. In short, the ideal of an *arhat* is narrow and mean; he promotes only his own interests, but the ideal of a Bodhisattva is characterized by nobility and generosity. He rises above *svārtha* (selfishness) and thinks of *parārtha* (doing good to others).

It is clear from what has been said above that Bodhisattva has altruistic motives. His altruism does not concern itself with only helping others to attain *nirvāṇa* but also with helping others to obtain material happiness and welfare in the world. The motive of Bodhisattva has become more human.

One of the definitions of Bodhisattva is that he has the seeds of enlightenment which he developes over the aeons. Mahāyāna believes that every body has the seed of enlightenment and if he nurtures and waters it with care and sincerity he is sure to attain *nirvāṇa*. Thus, we see that the concept of Bodhisattva happily combines humanistic attitude and a belief in the strength and prowess of man and his altruistic ideals to serve others.

The ideals of Bodhisattva which are really great did not grow all at a time. They grew slowly and steadily till they became crystallised. The milieu of a particular period is not less responsible for the growth of the Bodhisattva ideal. As Buddhist writers and philosophers thought more keenly and subtly on the high ideals of Bodhisattva, they came out with higher and subtler ideals. One can very well examine a particular Mahāyāna book depicting the ideals of a Bodhisattva and relate them to the prevailing social, economic, and religious conditions of the society of that time. But this is not the subject of my paper. In the present paper I am going to deal with *Dāna pāramitā-one of the pāramitās* which a Bodhisattva must practise in order to attain enlightenment. *Pāramitā* means highest perfection and a Bodhisattva must have the highest perfection with regard to six or ten *pāramitās*. These *pāramitās* provide a Bodhisattva with the essential qualifications of being able to walk along the road to perfect enlightenment. Actually this is known as *saṁbhāra* (requisite ingredients) which is of two types. *Puṇya saṁbhāra* and *jñāna saṁbhāra*. The former is a means to the latter and consists of those meritorious actions which help one in the attainment of *prajñā*. In the early texts of Mahāyāna only six *pāramitas* have been enumerated. They are *Dāna, Sīla, Kṣānti, Vīrya, Dhyāna* and *Prajñā*. *Prajña pāramitaā* occupies a place of supreme importance as it means real knowledge. One cannot put an end to the rounds of birth and death unless one attains highest knowledge and the highest knowledge can be achieved only when the other *pāramitās* are practised to higher perfection. The first five *pāramitās* are subsumed under *pūṇya saṁbhāra* and the last is called *jñāna saṁbhāra*. In order that the first five *pāramitās* become perfect, they must be accompanied by *prajñā*. In other words, if we practise the five *pāramitās* without an element of *prajñā* they will not help us attain Buddhahood, but if they are practised with *prajñā* they are sure to help us attain Buddhahood.

Dāna pāramitaā is the first *pāramitā*. It implies *dāna* (charity) *dātā* (giver) and the person to be given. Therefore it essentially implies altruism. Unless there are persons other than oneself, the question of giving charity will become absurd. Besides, the fact that one wishes to give to others clearly brings out one's fellow feeling. A gives charity to B. It means that A recognises the existence of B, sees at the same time his need and expresses his willingness to part with some thing of his own, even valuable things, to him. If a man is self-centered, he will not be inclined to think of others. The act of giving, therefore, implies altruism which is one of the important characteristics of Bodhisattva. *Sīla* like *Dāna*, too, implies altruism.

If we read literature dealing with *Dāna pāramitā*, we shall be able to pin-point several stages in its growth as a concept. It has undergone changes over the periods. What to give, how to give and whom to give are some of the questions which have been thoroughly examined. If we analyse the 'motive, method and merits' of "giving" we shall know how the concept of *Dāna pāramitā* grew over the different periods and how the motive became exalting. The ideal of *Dāna* was developed in five ways by the Mahayanists. In the words of Haradayala, "They coloured it with the avarice and selfishness of a mendicant monastic Order. They extended its scope and included life and limb among the objects which should be sacrificed for others. They introduced a spirit of exaggerated sentimentality by praising imaginary men and women who sacrificed themselves for the protection of animals. They gradually eliminated the noble self regarding motive of attaining *nirvāṇa* or *Bodhi* and taught that *Dāna* should be based solely on the feeling of mercy and compassion. They evolved the new and revolutionary idea of the 'gift of merit' by which a Bodhisattva could save all sinners from punishment or bestow undeserved happiness on all creatures". (Haradayal, p.170)

The idea of the gift of merit is really revolutionary and is further away from the spirit of early Buddhism where a man is exhorted to work out his own salvation and where it is said again and again that what a man reaps accords with what he sows. Nobody else can make or mar his life. He alone is responsible for it. Lord Buddha has said that he is to show one the path but unless he himself walks along it, his salvation cannot be guaranteed. He should be ready to work out his own salvation. The Mahāyāna concept of *Dāna* encompasses the gift of merit also.

In the *Bodhisattvabhūmi* nine kinds of *Dāna* have been described. One of them is *vighatārthika Dānam*-the *dāna* which prevents other persons from being hostile and converts them into suppliants. Incidentally I may bring out the importance of *Vighatārthika dānam* and show its great relevance in modern times. The world today is more or less sharply divided into two classes-the haves and the have-nots. The people of the third world are living a substandard life. The people of the U.S.A.

and of U.S.S.R. live a life of higher standard and of more comfort but the government of these two nations never think of sharing their wealth with the poor people of the third world. It is possible that in the U.N.O. a resolution may be passed by the members of the third world who outnumber the representatives of the capitalist and socialist countries. In the beginning it may be in the name of humanity but gradually it may take the form of a right. I, therefore, think that the rich countries should always extend their helping hand to the poor countries and practise *Vighatārthika dānam* by renouncing a part of their wealth. If this sort of *Dāna* is practised, the world will be a happy place to live in. This ideal of a Bodhisattva, if practised by rich nations, can go a long way in ameliorating the conditions of the poor people.

There are other points which must be examined thoroughly before gifts are made. Who should be helped ? The persons who deserve help are divided into three categories. According to the *Jātakamālā, Śikṣāsamuccaya* and *Bodhisattvabhūmi* a Bodhisattva should give gifts to his friends and relatives. In the *Divyāvadāna* and *Mahāyāna Sūtrālaṅkāra* another category of people has been mentioned. They are the needy, the poor, the sick, the afflicted and the helpless. According to the *Jātakamālā* and the *Avadāna śataka* the persons to be given gifts include *Śramaṇas* and Brāhmaṇas. Thus we see that gradually the persons to be bestowed gifts are not only the friends and relatives of a Bodhisattva whom he will be naturally inclined to help but they include the needy and the poor as well as the *Śramaṇas* and the Brahamaṇas. One will not have to go deep into it in order to understand the growth of the altruistic motive of a Bodhisattva.

In this connection an important question is raised. What objects should be given in charity ? In answer to this it is said categorically that a Bodhisattva should give all that he has. He should not only part with his wealth but also should be ready to give his limbs and sacrifice even his life. He should also give his earned merit to others to save them from going to hell. What Boddhisattva gives should not be beneficial only to one to whom it is given, but it should be beneficial to others also. In this respect a Bodhisattva is required to exercise his discretion in the choice of gifts. In the *Boddhisattva Bhūmi* it is said that a Bodhisattva should not give anything which may be used to cause injury to others. And again it is mentioned here that any thing that gratifies sensual appetites and passions should never be given. Further it has been said here that poisons, weapons, intoxicating liquors and nets for capturing animals should not be given. It is also said that a plot of land should not be bestowed where, it is feared, that animals may be hunted or killed. A Bodhisattva should never give instruments of torture and instruments for committing suicide and the wealth that he gives must be earned by honest, righteous and peaceful means. Even if he has something very rare which he has got with difficulty, he must not refuse to part with it. If he is sure that poisons will be properly used be may give them to others.

In the *Prajñāpāramitā Śatasāhasrikā* it is said that a Bodhisattva should sacrifice even his limbs for the good of others, but this sort of sacrifice is not judicious. Bodhisattvas are full of altruistic motives and are indeed very rare. If they end their lives like this, the world will suffer a great loss. This ideal of Bodhisattva was not considered a good one and, therefore, the author of the *Bodhisattva Bhūmi* says that if the mind of a Bodhisattva is pure he need not give away his life and limb. However, he can become a servant or a slave for the sake of others.

A lot of thinking has gone into the question of how to give. While giving, a Bodhisattva must be all courtesy, should be respectful towards whom he gives. When he gives away something to somebody he must be happy and joyful. He should be even happier than one to whom he gives. In the *Bodhisattva Bhūmi* it is specially mentioned that he should not repent of his generosity nor should he talk of his charity. While giving he should make no distinction between friends and foes. He should give to the deserving and the undeserving, the wicked and the righteous everywhere and all times but he should not lose the sense of measures and proportions in his charity. It is true that he has mercy but it must be combined with wisdom. In other words, he must not sacrifice himself for trivial causes.

A Bodhisattva should also know why he should give. We must know that charity makes one earn merit. It also ensures rebirth in heaven. It also affords protection against premature death and is the source of power, long life, welfare and prosperity. The *Avadāna śataka* is full of stories where it is narrated how charity brings him rewards. A Bodhisattva, however, must practise charity without the thought of reward. He should give without any hope of gaining any selfish end.

Thus we see how the ideals of a Bodhisattva have changed with the passage of time in respect of only one *pāramitā*. The Buddhist writers have analysed *Dānapāramitā* in depth and have described the ideals of a Bodhisattva in respect of *Dānapāramīta*.

Jain Culture and Śramaṇa Tradition in the Pāli Tipiṭaka

Śramaṇa tradition is as old as Brāhmaṇa tradition and has been in existence since time immemorial. Some scholars are of the opinion that the former is older than the latter.[1] They see it in the Indus valley civilization which flourished long before the arrival of the Aryans[1]who were primarily responsible for the Vedic and what later came to be known as Brāhmaṇa culture and civilization. As time rolled on, the latter changed and came to be associated fundamentally with sacrifice which became cruder and cruder and meant killing animals. The ideals of Upaniṣads which we find embodied in the seminal reflections like 'know thyself' and 'Thou art He' i.e. the individual soul was regarded as the spark of the Absolute Brahma, were completely forgotten and the merit gained by performing sacrifice slaughtering animals was considered the only passport to heaven.

Śramaṇa tradition, on the contrary, did not believe in the creator God and, therefore, did not regard the *Vedas* as His authoritative words, raised its voice against killing of innocent animals in the name of sacrifice and stressed the need for penance (*tapas*) for cleansing oneself from the impurities that gathered layer after layer due to immoral actions performed under the influence of *lobho, doso* and *moho*-the three fundamental roots of *karma* as the Buddhist holds.

Brāhmaṇa tradition is succintly characterised by what Lord Sri Krishna says in the Gītā, "Come to my refuge, I will absolve you from all sins". The sublime Śramaṇa tradition like the Jain and the Buddhist, on the other hand, says unequivocally that man is supreme. He is the centre and circumference of the universe as the Greeks held. There is no other power greater than and outside of man. Immense power exists in him potentially and if he exerts he cannot only do good to himself but to others also. He can free himself from all sufferings and miseries that he is heir to and attain the *summum bonum* by his own efforts without depending upon any other power. Thus the sublime Śramaṇa tradition is man-centered. Man, according to it, is responsible for his good as he is equally responsible for his own harm. This sublime Śramana tradition, therefore, is humanistic. The spirit of this tradition is beautifully epitomized by what Chandidas says later.

'Sabār ūpara mānusa satta tāhār ūpara nei.

Man is the measure of all things in the universe. That the sublime *Śramaṇa* tradition held all these is clear from its etymology. The word *Śramaṇa* is derived from the root *śram* which means to exert, to labour hard. This means that *tapa* is the primary pre-occupation of a *Śramaṇa* who by dint of his *tapa* or austerity cleanses himself from all impurities. Here also the Jains and the Buddhists differ. The former lay more quantum of stress on *tapa* than the latter. Buddha's view of *tapa* is moderate but it is a sort of exertion none the less. His concept of eightfold path brings out its meaning clearly. To walk along the eightfold path is an uphill task and only those who can exert themselves assiduously can reach the goal.

There is another meaning of the word *śramaṇa*. This is derived from its *Prākrit* equivalent. *Śramaṇa* (Bsk) becomes *samana* in Prākrit, of course *samaṇa* in Pali and *śamaṇa* in Ardhamāgadhī. One who extinguishes all kinds of fire in him and attains that mental condition in which he lives in peace is a *samana*. Fire is a very seminal and significant symbol not only in Indian religious tradition but in all the religious traditions of the world. What does fire do ? It burns. So different kinds of fire like *rāga, dveṣa* and *moha* also burn a man. If these extraordinary fires can be put out one will enjoy heavenly peace. But putting out these fires means a lot of physical and mental exertions because as has been said above they are not ordinary fires. One kind of it (*rāgaggi* [2]) feeds on desires and desires are infinite. Desires have to be curbed, have to be reduced in number and have to be ultimately annihilated if one is to get rid of fire born out of attachment. In this way other fires can be extinguished. A *śramaṇa* works hard in order to keep himself away from it. Hence he is a *śramana* and as he puts it out eventually or is in the process of doing it, so he is a *samana*. A *śramaṇa* or *samana* ordinarily is a wanderer, a recluse or religieux,[3] according to T.W. Rhys Davids (See his Pali Eng. Dictionary).

The use of *samaṇa Brāhmaṇā* (leaders in religious life) in the sense mentioned above is clearly seen in practically all the *suttas* of the *Ṭipitakas*. The phrase *samaṇa Brāhmaṇā* refers to the two traditions of the *Śramaṇa* and Brāhmaṇa existing together and running side by side. Their religious and philosophical views are mentioned in the *Brahmajāla sutta* and the *Sāmaññaphala sutta* as also in other *suttas*. But Śramaṇa Gotama propounds a view peculiar to all. His philosophy is superior to all in that whereas other philosophical views are only false views (*micchā diṭṭhis*) his is the real one which can help one realise the goal of religious and spiritual life.

Lord Buddha is addressed a *samaṇa (samaṇo Gotamo)* in *Soṇadaṇḍa sutta* and in the *Mahāsīhanāda sutta*. In the *Saṅgīti sutta* Lord Buddha is called a *samaṇa* who is (*samaṇamacalo*) - a *samaṇa* who never wavers and tends to fall, he is like a lotus among *samaṇas* (*samaṇa padumo, samaṇa puṇdariko*) i.e. the purest of all *samaṇas* the whiteness of lotus symbolising purity. He is also called the *samaṇa* of all *samaṇas* (*samaṇa samaṇā*)[4]

All these titles point out the high esteem and reverence in which Lord Buddha was held by his followers. At the same time they also speak of the followers', unwavering faith in him.

In the Pali non-canonical literature *samaṇa* refers to a non-Buddhist *tāpasa*.[5]

There is another edifying etymology of the word. This it came to acquire in course of time. In the *Dhammapadaṭṭhakathā*[6] it has been defined as *samita-pāpattā* i.e. a *samaṇa* is a *samaṇa* by virtue of his having absolved himself from all sins. He is also a *samaṇa* because all his sins are gone (*samita pāpānaṃ samaṇo*).[7] Lord Buddha is often mentioned and addressed as *samaṇa* by non-Buddhists.[8] It is interesting to note here that even non-Buddhists call Buddha a *samaṇa* i.e. not only Brāhmins but also *Samaṇas* other than Buddhist call him a *samaṇa*, This fact is really very important in so far as the word *samaṇa* refers to the external signs as well as the internal qualities of a *samaṇa* at the same time. At one place *samaṇa* is defined as one who is ordained i.e. all those who have left home for good in order to lead a homeless life as also, perhaps, as one who has his hair and beard shaved and wears a robe of a particular colour, yellow or saffron. But these external signs cannot make one a real *samaṇa*[9]. In order to be a real *samaṇa* one has to have inner qualities, one has to be pure in respect of all actions mental, vocal and physical. If we look at from this point of view then the meaning of even *sâmaṇas* respecting the Buddha and addressing him as *samaṇa* would be clear. Buddha was a *samaṇa* in the true sense of the term. He had developed all those qualities-inner qualities which are the hallmarks of a *samaṇa*.

External signs cannot make one a *samaṇa*. So long as one has desires, one acts under the influence of greed, he cannot be a true *samaṇa* howevermuch he may look like one with the help of external signs. Voices were raised against fake *samaṇa*.

Na muṇdakena samaṇo abbato alikaṃ bhaṇaṃ.
Icchālobhasamāpanno, samaṇo kiṃ bhavissati.[10]

There is a third sense in which the term *śamaṇa* is used. In this sense it refers to all who are ordained *pabbajūpagatabhāvena samaṇa*.[11] Even those who were Brāhmins by birth are *samaṇas*. Brāhmins are called so by virtue of being born as Brāhmins - *jātiya* Brāhmaṇā [12]. They are also so called because they address one another as *bho* (*ye keci bhovādikā*)[13]. *Ye keci ito bahiddhā pabbajūpagatā paribbājakā samāpannā* [14].

Looked at from the point of view of inner qualities a Brāhmin is not different from a *samaṇa* or a *bhikkhu*. Any one who is quiet, whose sense-organs are well controlled, who lives a life of celibacy and who is kind to all creatures is a true Brāhmin or a *samaṇa* or a *bhikkhu*.

Alaṁkato ce pi samaṃ careyya, santo danto nivato
Brahmacāri

Sabbesu bhūtesu nidhāya daṇḍaṃ so Brāhmano, so samaṇo so bhikkhu.[15]

The *Brāhmana vagga* of the *Dhammapada* brings out the salient qualities of a Brāhmaṇa.

We have seen above the fundamental differences between a Brāhmin and a *Śramaṇa*. But there are differences between one sect of *samaṇa* and another. One group of *samaṇas* differs from another group in respect of some points, say, in respect of the quantum of exertion they make and severe penance that they take upon themselves. The Jains for example lay great stress on doing *tapa* i.e, lay emphasis on leading a life of penance and austerity whereas the Buddhists do not lay as much stress. In fact, Lord Buddha saw severe penance as useless, doing more harm and damage to the body than good. He regarded it as one of the two extremes and asked his followers to avoid it meticulously.[16]

In the *Samaṇa sutta* of the *Anguṭara nikāya*[17] Lord Buddha has said that a monk has three pursuits viz., training in the higher morality, higher thought and higher insight i.e. he observes *sīla*, practises meditation and attains insight. *Sīla sāmādhi* and *paññā* are the three milestones in the path of *sādhanā*. The path is long and arduous but a *samaṇa* exerts along the path to develop himself spiritually and free himself from the cycle of birth and death.

In the *Anguttara nikāya* four kinds of *samaṇas* are mentioned viz. *sotāpatti, sakadāgāmī, aṇāgāmī and arhat. Sotāpatti* has just entered the stream which flows towards *nibbāna*. *Sakadāgamī* is a monk who will be born only once to attain *nibbāna*. *Anāgāmī* will not be born into this world but will achieve *nibbāna* in some other *deva* world and *Arhat* is one who has realised and seen *nibbāna*. His is a mental state where there is peace and tranquillity. He achieves it by putting an end to all desires. It is from this point of view that it is said that the state of a *samaṇa* is attended by eight blisses.[18]

Some of the characteristics of *samaṇa* are given in the *Uttarādhyayana sūtra, Anuyogadvāra sūtra* and *Uttaradhyayana cūrṇi*. It is clearly said that shaving one's hair and beard does not make one a *samaṇa*, nor uttering the word *Om* makes one a Brahmin, nor living in forest makes one a *muni*, nor wearing *kusa* cloth makes one a *tāpasa*.[19] Whether one is a *samaṇa* or not is judged by his internal achievement of purity and peace. *Uttarādhyayana sūtra* says that one who develops *samatā bhāva* (equanimity) i.e. one who develops the quality of looking at all things alike, looking at grass and gold with indifference is a real *samaṇa* and a Brahmin is one who observes celibacy i.e., one who falls in love with his own soul. One becomes a *muni* by virtue of attaining knowledge, a *tāpasa* is one who does austere penances.[20] One of the most important characteristics of a *samaṇa* is that he should put out all fires of desires and should be rid of greed, jealousy and ignorance.[21] He should never boast and think much of himself.[22] To be conceited is against all canons or manners of a *samaṇa*.

If a *samaṇa* has these qualities in him then Nigaṇṭha Nātaputta is not a *samaṇa*. This is the impression that we gather from a perusal of the *Tipiṭaka*. In the Pali *Tipiṭaka* there are several references to Nigaṇṭha Nātaputta who is Lord Mahavira himself. Muni Sri Nagaraja ji has culled fifty one references from canonical, non-canonical, Aṭṭhakathā and Mahāyāna literature as against eleven[23] collected by H. Jacobi in his *Introduction to the Jain Sutras*. In his significant and monumental research work Muni Sri Nagaraja ji has shown on the basis of references to Niganha Nātaputta how he has been treated by the Buddhists.

From a perusal of the *Sāmaññaphala sutta* it is clear that besides the view of Lord Buddha, other six views have been mentioned. They include the view of Nigaṇṭha Nātaputta. All these views have been presented here in a disparaging light and one is immediately compelled to observe that the views of the contemporary thinkers of Buddha have not been presented here objectively. They have been quoted here in a way which puts Buddhism at an advantage. Buddha is shown pronouncing these views as *micchādiṭṭhis* because they are not satisfying ethically, are in fact not sublime and edifying and do not help one achieve *nibbāna*. These heretical thinkers (they are called so in Pali literature) are also called *samaṇas* as is clear from the

Sāmaññaphala sutta.[24] But there is a world of diffrence between the view held by the Buddha and the views shown to have been held by others. Pūraṇa Kassapa's view is known as *Akiriyāvāda.* According to him there is neither merit (*puṇya*) nor sin (*pāpa*). Even if one were to kill all the people of the world with a sharp weapon and make a mountain-like heap of dead bodies he would commit no sin. And if one were to perform *tapa,* give *dāna* and live a celibate life he would earn no merit. Makkhaali Gosāla was a fatalist. In his view there is no cause of the suffering of beings. They become purified also without any cause. They become polluted also without any cause. Man is helpless and can do nothing. He has no power and no energy. Ajita Kesakambali believed in annihilationism. Everything ultimately is annihilated and there is nothing which is permament. Pakudha Kaccāyana held that there are seven elements which are permanet and uncreated. They are earth, water, fire, air, *sukha, dukha* and life. So he would conclude that there is neither a killer nor a killed, neither a hearer nor one who would make him hear. Sañjaya Velaṭṭhiputta's view is known as *Aniscitatāvāda* for he would neither affirm any thing nor not affirm (deny) it. For he said how could he say when he was himself not sure about it. *Evaṃ ti pi me .no. Tathā ti pi me no, Aññathā ti pi me no. No ti pi me no. No no ti pi me no.*[25]

Nigaṇṭha Nātaputta's four kinds of restraints (*saṁvara*) are mentioned here. A Nigaṇṭha is restrained as regards all cold water, restrained as regards all evils, all evils has he washed away and he lives suffused with the sense of evil held at bay.[26] The four restraints are *sabba vāri vārito, sabhavāriyutto, sabbavāridhuto, and sabbavāri phuṭo.* Out of these six heretical thinkers it is Nigaṇṭha Nātaputta's view which seems to be ethically viable. He talks here of bonds and liberation. A Nigaṇṭha has been defined as one who is free from all bonds (sources of suffering), all *ganthis* (knots) and all *palibandhas* (obstructions). *Sutta vibhanga* defines it as *amhākaṁ ganthanakileso, palibandhanakileso natthi, kilesaganthararahitā* mayaṃ ti *evaṃ vaditāya laddhanāmavasena nigantho.*[27] A Nigaṇṭha is one who is free from all bonds. He is so by virtue of attaining his goal (*gatattā*), by virtue of his being one whose heart is under command (*yatattā*) and by virtue of being one whose heart is fixed and steadfast (*ṭhitattā*).

In the *Sāmaññaphalasutta* Jain religion is represented through its propounder, Nigaṇṭha Nātaputta whose four restraints are the ones propounded by Pārśvanatha. Had Lord Mahavira's view been represented here it would have proved more satisfying to Ajātsatru. His religion as has been said above is definitely satisfying and edifying from the ethical point of view. It is very difficult to see the ground on which king Ajātsatru found it unsatisfying, and consequently rejected it. One can very well understand his outright rejection and disapproval of the five other views held by Pūraṇa Kassapa, Makkhali Gosāla and others because they are definitely not ethically satisfying, morally elevating and spiritually ennobling. But why is it that King Ajātsatru rejcts the view of Nigaṇṭha Nātaputta ? Perhaps the disciples of Buddha in their religious overenthusiasm and zeal to paint Buddha a taller religious leader than Nigaṇṭha Nātaputta very conveniently and deliberately omitted that part of Nigaṇṭha Nātaputta's teaching which, if explained at length, might have given solace and satisfaction to the repentent king Ajātsatru. Had his view been presented in detail, perhaps Ajatsatru would not have found it so unsatisfying and would have been satisfied with it. The disciples of Buddha who were responsible for collecting these *suttas* tried deliberately to put their adversaries at a disadvantage by describing their views in a partisan manner and unfavourable light. In the *Sāmaññaphala Sutta* Buddha's view is explained at length i.e. more space has been alloted to Buddha than to Nigaṇṭha Nātaputta and others and perhaps rightly but their views are not represented correctly. Had Nigaṇṭha Nātaputta been allotted more space, he would have definitely won the king to his side, for does he not talk of keeping himself from all sins and does he not talk of the way to cleanse himself from all sins ?

The tone nd tenor that we find in the *Sāmaññaphala Sutta* runs throughout the *Tipiṭaka*. Wherever Nigaṇṭha Nātaputta's view has been described, the attitude to look down upon it and the tone of derision and caricature is there. At all the places in the *Tipiṭaka* the professed aim of the Buddha's disciples has been to misrepresent the view of Nigaṇṭha Nātaputta or describe it in a disparaging manner. Very often they present his view in such a manner that the readers who are quite unaware of Jain religion cannot help laughing at his view because it has been presented ridiculously. This is clear from the *Uposatha sutta* in the *Anguttaranikāya*. Of the three kinds of *uposatha* described here viz. *Gopāla, Nirgrantha* and *ārya*, the last is regarded as the best and the first two have been looked down upon.

Buddha says that although the followers of Nigantha take upon themselves the *uposatha vata* they do not do so in the right spirit. They do so only in name. They say that they give up the use of servants and maid servants, but as soon as their *vrata* is over (and they eagerly wait for it) they begin to take their services and also begin to use all the material wealth they possessed. In this way they tell a lie as also they take what is not given to them. Thus, their *vrata* is polluted. Here we find Buddha laying some charges at the door of the followers of Nigaṇṭha but as has been very ably shown by Muni Nagaraja ji that these charges can be laid at the door of the Buddhists as well, for don't they observe *uposatha vrata* for a day and behave in the same manner, as they used to do before. Thus Buddha's interpretation of Jain *uposatha* is erroneous. It is definitely not an interpretation, but a misinterpretation, not a representation, but a misrepresentation. The logic put forward by Muni Nagaraja ji is sound.

From a perusal of the *Tipiṭaka* we find that invariably the disciples of Nigaṇṭha Nātaputta go to Lord Buddha and become so much impressed by him that they become converted and embrace Buddhism. This is always the case. We never find any disciple of Buddha going to Nigaṇṭha Nātaputta and embracing his faith. Sīha Senāpati, Dīrgha Tapasvi and Upāli are all converted. In the context of Sīha Senāpati, we find Nigaṇṭha Nātāputta as very ungenerous. He has been shown as boasting of his religion but when the truth that Sīha went to the refuge of Lord Buddha "dawned upon him he was shocked, vomitted hot blood and had to be carried in a litter". In the light of this description Nigaṇṭha Nātaputta seems to be an ordinary religious teacher. He is shown as boastful, too much involved and attached and not generous at all.

From all this it seems that the only preoccupation of the collectors of these *Suttas* was to make Buddha a taller, nobler and more majestic religious leader than Nigaṇṭha Nātaputta.

Apart from this, we do not find these descriptions historically correct and satisfying. As Muni Nagaraja jee says that Upāli in whose mouth the view of Nigaṇṭha Nātaputta is put, is not a historical figure. His name does not appear in the Jaina Āgama. So is the case with Sīha Senāpati and others. This shows that the disciples of Buddha wove imaginary stories around fictitious names and belittled the view propounded by Nigaṇṭha Nātaputta.

From the *Abhaya Thera Apadānam* we get a picture of Nigaṇṭha Nātaputta, which definitely shows the Buddhist disciples' prejudice against him. N. Nātaputta asks Abhaya Rajkumar to go to Buddha and enter into polemics. He also tells him how to put questions to Buddha so that he might find it difficult to answer.

From the *Upāli sutta* (*Majjhima Nikāya*) it is clear that Nigaṭha Nātaputta's view has not been presented correctly. As Muni Nagaraja jee says *Mano daṇḍa* and *kāya daṇḍa* are synonymous. If Lord Buddha regards *cetanā* as *kamma* (*cetanāhaṃ, Bhikkheva, Kammaṃ vadāmi*) Nigaṇṭha Nātaputta also holds the same view. What he says here is that *Kāya daṇḍa* is a *pāpa bandha*.

There is one *Saccaka sutta* in the *Majjhima Nikāya* where Saccaka has been shown impressed by the answers given by Buddha to his knotty questions, but there is nobody of this name in the Jaina tradition as has been pointed out by Muni Nagaraja jee.

That the Buddhist tradition is aware of the two sects of Jaina viz. *Sacelak* and *Acelaka* is clear from the *Dhammapadaṭṭhakathā*.

That Buddha also learnt a lot from Ālāra Kalām and Uddaka Ramaputta is evident from *Mahāvastu* where *jina-srāvaka* has been used for Ālāra Kalām, Uddaka Ramaputta and their followers. It can be said that Buddha found something worthwhile in the teachings of Nigaṇṭha Nātaputta. This should be regarded as Buddha's tribute to Nigaṇṭha Nātaputta.

References

1. See G.C. Pandey
2. *Rāgaggi, dosaggi, mohaggi*
3. See A.N.I.67, D III 16, 95 sq 130sq. S.145. Dh.184.
4. *See Sangīti sutta, Cūla assapura sutta, Abhayarāja Kumār Sutta, Mahasakuladāyī Sutta,*
5. Dh A III.84.
6. Dh A 2.65.61. DI 4.87. Sn P.91 & 95. Vin.I8.350
7. ibid.,
8. ibid.,
9. Ākāsena padam natthi, samano natthi bāhire
   Samkhārā sassatā natthi, natthi Buddha namajjitam
10. *Dhammapada*
11. *Sutta Vibhanga* I.87.
12. *ibid.*, I.121
13. *Culla Niddesa* 122,124,126.
14. *Ibid.*,
15. *Dhammapada.*
16. *Dve antā vajjitabbā, Kāmesu kāma sukkhallikānuyogo attakilamathānu yogo.*
17. A I 229.
18. A II 238.
19. *Na vi mundisaṇa samaṇo, na omkāreṇa vambhaṇo.*
    Na muni raññavāseṇaṃ, kusacīreṇa na tāvaso.

    Uttarādhyayanasutta 25/31.
20. *Saṃayoye Samano hoi, Bambhacereṇa Bambhaṇo,*
    Nāṇeṇa ya munī hoi, taveṇa hoi tāpaso. ibid., 25/32.
21. *uva samasāraṃ khu sāmaṇnam samo sabsatta maṇo jassa bhavati sa samaṇo. Sabbatthesu samaṃ care.*
22. *Na hu kaitabe samano.*

23. *Introduction to The Jain Sūtras by H. Jacobi.*
24. *Sāmaññaphalasutta.*
25. *ibid.,*
26. *ibid.,* See The Eng. Version of the *Sāmaññaphala Sutta.*
27. *Sutta vibhanga.*

Nature in The Theragāthā

'Solitude in the sense of being often alone,' says John Stuart Mill, 'is essential to any depth of meditation or character.' This reflection came from a mind agonised a monstrous deal by disastrous results that followed in the wake of the great phenomenon in England known popularly as the Industrial Revolution. The philosophers of the Victorian age which was characterised by 'its sick hurry, its divided aims'[1] sought refuge in the healing solitude of Nature. Mill was long ago anticipated by Lord Buddha who, seeing sufferings and miseries in the world which is in constant flux and where there is nothing permanent, made Arhatship as his ideal and betrayed a predilection for solitude, "and that not within walls, but away in the forest." 'Formerly I did not live at ease, being troubled by those litigious, contentious, quarrelsome, disputatious Bhikkhus of Kosambī, the constant raisers of questions before the Saṃgha. But now being alone and without a companion I live pleasantly and at ease remote from those litigious, contentious, quarrelsome disputatious Bhikkhus of Kosambi, the constant raisers of questions before the Saṃgha".[2] And 'thus the noble one and the noble, the elephant tusked with tusks like cart poles (and the noble one among men) the mind of the one and the mind of the other harmonise in this, that they take delight in dwelling alone in the forest'.[3] *Suttanta* also bears out that the members of the Order were advised to cultivate the art of solitude. 'If a Bhikkhu should desire, Brethren, by the complete destruction of the three Bonds to become converted, to be no longer liable to be reborn in a state of suffering, and to be assured of final salvation, let him then fulfil all righteousness, let him be devoted to that quietude of heart which springs from within, let him not drive back the ecstasy of contemplation, let him look through things, let him be much alone.'[4] The founder of the Monastic Order had tasted the advantages of solitude and on more than one occasion explained them to the Bhikkhus and warned them. 'Now have I made this clear to you. Here, Bhikkhus, are the roots of trees, here are empty places. Meditate, be earnest lest hereafter ye regret.'[5]

It is, therefore, quite natural that the members of the Order too, should betray the same predilection. In the *Theragāthā* which is a collection of the psalms of the Brethren as the *Therigāthā* is of the sisters, a number of *Theras* have sung the praises of solitude.

Delightful are the forests, where no crowd
Doth come to take its pleasure; there will they
Who are released from passions find there joy.
Not seekers they for sense-satiety.[6]

They realised that many were the distracting elements in the mundane life and they would not let them concentrate their mind and meditate and achieve the tranquillity of mind and serenity of soul.

Therefore what was utterly needed was to go far away from the madding crowd, because it was only solitude which would provide the most congenial atmosphere for practising meditation. Tissa-Kumāra, the youngest brother of the king Dhammāsoka was fed up with the court life. He disliked the sycophants, courtiers and the soldiers and longed to be rid of them. One day he saw the Greek *Thera*, Mahā Dhamma Rakkhita seated under a tree and was so impressed that his longing to live in the forest multiplied several times. This story is told in the *Mahāvaṃsa*. Longing for the happiness of the recluse, he uttered the following *gāthā*.

'If there be none in front, nor none behind
Be found, is one alone in the woods
Exceeding pleasant doth his life become.'[7]

But one thing is of vast importance to notice here. Did the Exalted One advise all to retire into solitude ? Did he prescribe even to the novice to cultivate the art of living in solitude ? No, in fact, only the Arhat is pronounced to be really fit to dwell in such solitudes. The Master knew that in the Order there were persons of various temperaments and solitude could not be prescribed to all. Subhūti says :-

'When lustful thoughts arise within my heart,
Examining myself alone I beat them down.
Thou who art by lust excited, who by things
That give offence, allowest of offence,
Feeling bewildered when strange things occur,
Thou shouldst retire far from the lonely woods.
For they are the dwelling place of men made pure
Austere in life, free from the stains of sin
Defile not that pure place, leave thou the Woods.'[8]

Subhūti seems to say here categorically that the woods are not for one who has not achieved self-control. Only he can live in the woods whose heart is 'thoroughly purged and well-composed.'

'But they who in the bosom of the hills
Sit with heart thoroughly purged and well-composed,
Like to so many lions crouching still,
Are vanquishers over the creeping dread,
White-minded, pure, serene and undefiled.[9]

What I have said above will serve as necessary prolegomena to what I shall say in the following pages. That the members of the Order loved Nature is evinced by the utterances of a large number of *theras*. The *Theragāthā* is a collection of such utterances and, therefore, it is a supreme record of the feelings, emotions, the thrilling sensations of joy which they derived from solitude and from the hundred thousand objects of Nature, while they practised meditation.

Primarily, the *Theragāthā* is a monumental work in the whole of Pāli literature as it is a record of the psalms of the Brethren who had broken the ten fetters[10], who had become thoroughly purged from every kind of taint, who enjoyed the tranquillity of mind and finally, who had realised *Nibbāna*, the ultimate goal and the *summum bonum* of life according to Buddhist Ethics. But it is not only this. It is a *tour de force* from yet another point of view which is literary and aesthetic. The spiritual songs which are undoubtedly superb also record the *theras'* love of and admiration for Nature. They have, not perhaps incidentally, described the sights and sounds of Nature very feelingly and so Winternitz is perfectly right in saying that the *gāthās* are the real gems of Indian lyric poetry[11]. Some of the *theras* are evidently gifted with poetic talent and among the motives urging them to seek solitude, a poetic gift may very well have counted.[12] And that is why even if they renounced the world, they could not afford to be aesthetically insensitive and unresponsive towards Nature. They sat in the lap of Nature, drank deep its beauty and experienced the myriad sensations coming from different objects of Nature. But it is very important to note that their love of Nature is not like that of Keats. These *thera* poets would not have agreed with John Cowper Powys who says, "One ought to touch it, to taste it, to embrace it, to eat it, to drink it, to make love to it"[13]. And by 'it' he means Nature.

These *thera* poets did not solely cultivate the art of self-expression. It will be far from truth to say that they practised art for art's sake. On the other hand, they made it subservient to the great theme of their life-the realisation of *Nibbāna*. No doubt, they had the capacity to appreciate the beauties of Nature but they never forgot that happiness which was yielded by 'beholding the Norm' far excelled any derived from natural scenery.

Not music's fivefold wedded sounds can yield
Such charm as comes over him who with a heart
Intent and calm rightly beholds the Norm.[14]

But yet the *Theragāthā* remains a unique literary work in the entire extant Pāli literature.

Although the love of Nature and, therefore, the description thereof is scattered in Pāli literature, the *Theragāthā* is the only book wherein we get it in abundance. Among the *Jātakas*, the *Vessantara Jātaka* is important for the realistic descriptions of Nature. Here the flora and fauna of Himvanta region have been described at length.

When you shall hear the rivers roar, the fairy creatures sing
Believe me, you will clean forget that ever you were king.

Rhinoceros and buffalo, that make the woodland ring
Lion and Tiger-You'II forget that ever you were king.
When on the mountain top you see the peacock dance and spring
Before the pea-hens, you'II forget that ever you were king.
When in the winter you behold the trees all flowering.
Waft their sweet odours, you'II forget that ever you were king
When in the winter you behold the plants all flowering
The bimbajāla, kūṭaja and lotus, scattering
Abroad their obours, you'll......[15]

The description of Nature here is realistic and it is not this kind of treatment of Nature which the *Theragātha* is important for. As a matter of fact, it stands supreme from all in that kind of description of Nature which Ruskin calls the Pathetic fallacy. The poet *theras* credit Nature with their emotions. When the peacocks call, it seems to Cittaka that they wake him from his noonday sleep to set himself to thought profound and religious.

Peacocks of sapphire neck and comely crest
Calling, calling in Kāraṃviya woods ;
By cool and humid winds made musical :
They wake the thinker from his noonday sleep.[16]

Such descriptions and the like are characteristics of the *Theragātha* and this excellent merit of the book earns for it a place supremely important in all the literature of the world, more so in Pali literature where there is much of philosophy and ethics. Even if the *Theragātha* be regarded as a collection of the spiritual songs, it will, nevertheless, ever remain a unique literary feat wherein the *theras* have recorded their asethetic feelings and vibrations of the fine chords of their heart. It will not be an exaggeration to say that the *Theragātha*, the *Therīgātha*, and perhaps a few other books, are the only oases in the vast dry land of Pali literature. And this quality of the *theras* that they had a love of Nature and they expressed it adds to rather than detracts from the spiritual and literary merits of Pali literature.

This quality of the *Theragātha* takes us back to the pre-historic days when the hymns of the *Vedas* were composed and shows that the tradition of describing Nature in Indian literature remained uninterrupted. In the *Vedas* which are regarded by Winternitz 'as the oldest Indian and, at the same time the oldest Indo-European literary monument',[17] Nature has been described at length, although quite differently. This difference is due to different attitude. In the Vedic age the philosophical speculation had just begun and the people who interpreted every phenomenon of Nature in terms of anger and pleasure of gods had to glorify, worship, invoke and above all propitiate them. They worshipped the starry sky of night, the roaring storms, the flowing water of rivers and the clouds. They addressed hymns to them.

Some of the hymns in the *Ṛgveda* which have been addressed to Dawn or to Vāta or to Savitā will ever be valued as works of poetic art. These are really the ' pearls of lyric poetry which appeal to us as much through their fine comprehension of the beauties of Nature as through their flowery language'.[17] Magnificent metaphors have been brought in to depict the splendour of the rising Dawn.

"The radiant Dawns have risen up for glory in their white splendour like the waves of waters

She maketh paths all easy, fair to travel, and, rich, hath shown herself benign and friendly.

We see that thou art good : far shines thy lustre ; thy beams

thy splendours have flown up to heaven

Decking thyself, thou makest bare thy bosom, shining in majesty,

thou Goddess Morning.[18]

The method in such descriptions is to personify Nature, as Dawn has been personified here. Homer and Shakespeare, too, have adopted the same method. We shall do well to compare the above description of the Dawn with that of Shakespeare. Nowhere in the literature of the world such magnificent and splendorous description of Dawn can be seen.

But, look, the morn, in russet mantle clad
Walks over the dew of yon high eastward hill [19].

The psalms of the *Theragāthā* were composed at too later a date and the *theras* do not exhibit that kind of curiosity as we find in the hymns of the *Vedas*. And this is quite natural. These *theras* made Arhatship the ideal of their life and it would have been a sheer waste of time and energy and poetic talent to indulge in such descriptions. Such descriptions, therefore, are almost absent in the *Theragāthā*. It will not be out of place to point out here that no *thera* has written anything about the 'Dawn'. The *Brahmavelā* has been glorified by all and sundry as the most suitable time for spiritual practice. Even Henry David Thoreau, the Amercian philosopher speaks in praise of it. Then wasn't it a congenial time for the Buddhist monks to practise meditation ? Or why is it that the glorious and splendorous Dawns have not attracted them ? I think, if some of the *theras* would have noticed the beauty of the Dawn and would have been attracted by it as they were by the dancing and springing peacocks of variegated plumes and by the graceful sailing of the clouds in the sky there would have been some more aesthetically superb lyrics in the collection.

But there is no denying that the *theras* were deeply associated with Nature. They reveal a remarkable love for hills and caves, for rivers and groves and for forests. And naturally, therefore, 'they delight in lingering over the descriptions of the forest and mountain scenery in the midst of which the solitary sage pursues his meditation.'[20] In course of their practising meditation either in a well-roofed hut or in a hut without a roof over it they directly experienced the change of season. Moreover, the magnificent landscapes formed by the change of colour in the sky filled their hearts with immense pleasure. And they garbed their reactions to these myriad forms of Nature in words. There are several descriptions of this kind in the *Theragāthā*. It is raining without and the Bhikkhu is sitting within. He utters the following *gāthā*.

Well-roofed and pleasant is my little hut, And screened
from winds. Rain, at thy will, thou god !
My heart is well-composed, my heart is free
And ardent is my mood, Now rain, god rain.[21]

He is not afraid of the rains, nor does he regard them as distracting. He is calm and tranquil within. The rains outside can do him no harm, now that he has withdrawn himself to contemplation. Girimānanda expresses this feeling in more beautiful words.

God rains as't were a melody most sweet.
Snug is my little hut, sheltered, well-roofed.
Therein I dwell, my heart serene and calm.
Now an it pleaseth thee to rain, god, rain.[22]

The falling rains have been compared here with a sweet melody. This is a beautiful simile and a marvellous achievement of the *thera* in matters of verbal expression. He lives in a hut roofed over, probably, with straw, so the falling rains cant make any harsh sound and the comparison of the rains with a melody is an apt one. And yet how closely observed and realised this simile is ! This *gāthā* can very well be compared with some of the modern poems.[23]

The rainy season provides the most congenial atmosphere for practising meditation. The graceful sailing of the clouds in the sky, the rolling of the thunder, the falling rains, the calling of the peacocks etc. help create a suitable atmosphere for meditation. It is here that we find a striking difference of attitude between the Sanskrit poets headed by Vālmīki and Kālidāsa and these *theras*. With the advent of the rainy season the Yakṣa finds it very difficult to bear the pangs of separation and so he requests the cloud to be his messenger. Vālmīki, too, describes the agitated state of Rāma who is separated from Sītā. That the rains and the clouds stimulate erotic passion has more or less become a poetic convention and they have been described in that light by many.[24] Even Tulasidasa could not help expressing this very idea.[25]

There arises then a very important question. Why do the *theras* describe the rainy season in an unconventional way ? No doubt, there are many charming descriptions of Nature in their *gāthās* but why are they largely instrumental in serving an altogether different purpose from what they do in Sanskrit works of art ? The answer can be found by analysing the predilections of the Sanskrit poets and the Buddhist brethren. Vālmīki and Kālidāsa were primarily poets; these *theras* had taken orders and their supreme object in life was to behold the Norm and realise

Nibbāna. And so the rainy season which served the purpose of stimulating the erotic passions of the lover and the beloved and increased their pangs of separation, inspired the *Theras* to practise contemplation.

Hark ! how the peacocks make the welkin ring,
Fair-crested, fine their plumes and azure throat,
Graceful in shape and pleasant in their cry.
And see how the broad landscape watered well
Lies verdure-clad beneath the dappled sky !
. . . .
Where dying cometh not, ineffable.[26]

The peacocks call. The vast earth is verdure-clad. The sky is filled with the rain-laden black clouds. There is mirth and gaiety in Nature, there is unflagging zeal everywhere. So the Bhikkhus, too, are fully awake in their mind. This inspires them to realize the subtly deep and the ineffable *Nibbāna*. The *theras* were not like the Yakṣa and they had an altogether different predilection. It is this predilection which gives spiritual tinge to the descriptions of Nature in the *Theragāthā*. This quality of the *gāthās* is unique and such charming and sublime descriptions of Nature are very rare. Besides, the alliteration here makes this lyric a real artistic achievement.

The *theras* had established a relationship with Nature which is almost Wordsworthian. Suppaka declares his love of retirement by praise of his dwelling-place. He says :-

'Whenever I see the crane, her clear bright wings
Outstretched in fear to flee the black stormcloud,
A shelter seeking, to safe shelter borne
Then doth the river Ajakarṇī
Give joy to me....
. . . .
She brings us luck. Here is it good to be'.[27]

On the one hand the above mentioned *gāthās* astonishingly reveal the *theras*' capacity to observe Nature and describe her as she is and on the other hand they express a profound love of Nature. 'Not from the mountain- streams is it time to-day to flit.[28] is an expression of that deep and profound love of Nature which is rare. In addition to these, they also show how the beauty of the rains inspires the *theras* for the great task they have set themselves to.

Unlike the Georgian poets[29] who left only on the week-end to observe and enjoy Nature, these *theras* sat in the lap of Nature and observed and enjoyed her protean moods from very close quarters. They did not enjoy the rains from a distance. The rains came to them with all their charms, attractions as also with fears. John Cowper Powys says 'No, the real Nature lover does not think primarily about the beauty of Nature ; he thinks about her life., whether at the particular moment she is looking lovely or sinister, cheerful, peaceful or tragic, he loves her for herself.'[30] Even when there is storm-cloud towering high in the heavens, emitting roars of thunders Sambula Kaccāna fearlessly sits in his dreadful cave and meditates. He is not in the least frightened by these fearsome clouds and lightning.

God's rain pours down, ay, and God's rain roars down,
And I alone in fearsome hollow dwell.
Yet dwelling so in fearsome rocky dell
To me no fear comes nigh, no creeping dread,
No quailing (of my soul).[31]

This reveals his absolute love of Nature and his immense fearlessness which is a fruit of his meditative exercise. He is firm and immovable like a rock. Bhūta declares emphatically that the pleasure derived from meditating lonely in the midst of natural beauties is greater than any.

When in the lowering sky thunders the storm-cloud's drum,
And all the pathways of the birds are thick with rain,
The brother sits within the hollow of the hills,.
Rapt in an ecstasy of thought no higher bliss is given to men than this.[32]

This and a few subsequent *gāthās* are really the marvellous achievement of the *theras*. Each *gāthā* presents before us a landscape and the descriptions of the sights and sounds of Nature are done in a few chosen words. How great is the economy, and how captivating the result ! Just a few strokes of pen and a landscape floats before our mind.

'The pathways of the birds are thick with rain' is an

altogether novel method of expressing that it is raining in torrents. And when it rains so heavily, the Bhikkhu hears the thunder and is rapt is an ecstasy of thought. It will not be too much to say that 'they present a unique blend of religious maturity, primeval shyness and aesthetic sensitiveness.'[33] Eka Vihari expresses his ardent love of solitude and his longing to go to a region remarkable for scenic beauties is expressed in these *gāthās*.

Yea, swiftly and alone, bound to my quest,
I'll to the jungle that I love the haunt
Of wanton elephants, the source and means
Of thrilling zest to each ascetic soul.
In Cool Wood's flowery glades cool waters lie,
Within the hollows of the hills ; and there
I'll bathe my limbs when hot and tired, and there
At large in ample solitude I'll roam.[34]

'Cool woods', 'flowery glades (सुपुप्फिते सीतवने) and 'cool waters' are the tactual and visual images which are sensuous enough to be Keatsean. But lest the meditator should indulge in them he immediately thinks of the ample solitude where he meditates. Nor are the auditory images absent from the *gāthās*. The *theras* not only hear the roarings of the clouds but they hear the melodious cries of peacocks and the trumpetings of the elephants. 'Of forest freshened by new rain' is a supreme example of visual image.

That the *theras* were poets and some of them were of the first rank is borne out by the verses uttered by Tālapuṭa. He expresses a longing for dwelling in the mountain caves and for the fresh torrents which would drench his raiment in the woods. Not only this but it is a great poetry in so far as it is born out of intense suffering.

O when shall I, who see and know that this
My person, nest of dying and disease
Oppressed by age and death,
Is all impermanent,
Dwell free from fear lonely within the woods-
Yea, when shall these things be.[35]

'Feeling such as lives in these verses, is conceivable only

in the growth of a culture that has won its way through much suffering. And to give expression to it as Tālapuṭa has done, could only be done by a poet.' This remark of Dr. Oldenberg about this poem is just.

Here is an admonitory verse from the Exalted One.

Nay, not for this that thou mayest slumber long
Cometh the night in starry garlands wreathed
For vigil by the wise this night is here.[36]

How beautiful is this visual image, 'Night in starry garlands wreathed.'

The sky seems to be rain washed and the stars are twinkling with added lustre and glory. This is the most congenial atmosphere to practise meditation. In the *Gītā* Śrī Kṛṣṇa has expressed the same idea.[37]

The *theras* besides describidng the rains and the landscapes of this season have described the winter season too. The Master asks Mogharājan :

Well, Mogharājan, thou skin-sufferer,
Thou blest of heart and constantly serene,
Cometh the time when winter nights are cold,
And thou a brother poor-how wilt thou fare ?[38]

and thereupon he replies

My little straw built canopy doth please
Better than other's way of finding ease.

Mogharājan's is a bold reply which clearly shows that he did not in the least mind to face the unpropitious weathers and forces of Nature for he knew his task was great and his aim was high.

On reading the *Theragāthā* one is immediately struck with two things. The first is the abundant descriptions of the rains and the sights and sounds of this season. The second is paucity of the descriptions of other seasons, particularly of the spring which has been magnificently and splenderously described in other Sanskrit works of art. And naturally, therefore, the question arises what made the *theras* love the rainy season so much and why there is a plethora of beautiful landscapes related to this season ? The key to this question lies, I think, in the Vinaya rules. It was inevitable on the part of the *theras* to spend the rainy season, which lasted for three months either from the first of *Āṣāḍha* to the end of *Bhādrapada* or from the beginning of *Śrāvaṇa* to the end of *Āśvina* [39]) in a place away from the villages or towns. In the rest of the year they were busy in their duty towards others. During the rainy season when they observed *Vassāvāsa* Retreat, they withdrew themselves from the world and engaged themselves in meditative practices. They had leisure enough to observe the beautiful landscapes which inspired them for winning Arhatship and realising *Nibbāna*. These landscapes were tinged with sublime beauty. They were rain-washed and pure and had almost the virginal lustre. We shall do well to notice here one thing and it is this that the descriptions of the rains in the *Theragāthā* are typically the descriptions of the rains in North India after the monsoon breaks out in the beginning or in the middle of June.

"When in the lowering sky thunders the storm clouds' drum
"And all the pathways of the birds are thick with rain."
or *"When at dead of night in lonely wood god rains"*
or *"Or in fair open glade, or in the depths of forest, freshened by new rain."*
or *"Hark, how the peacocks make the welkin ring,*
Fair-crested, fine their plumes and azure throat."
or *"And see how this broad landscape watered well*
Lies verdure-clad beneath the dappled sky"
or *"Whenever I see the crane, her clear bright wings*
Outstretched in fear to flee the black storm-cloud"[40]

These and many others are the landscapes which prove beyond any doubt that the rains which have been described in the *gāthās* are the rains after the monsoon breaks out. They further prove that these are the elaborate descriptions of the sky and the vegetational region in June,July and August in which the *theras* observed *Vassāvasa* Retreat.

'Depths of forest' clearly indicates that the trees in the forest have put forth new leaves and that is why the forest is dense. 'Freshened by new rain' proves it almost conclusively that it is the description of the rains. 'The landscape is verdant' leaves no room for any doubt.

That it is a description of North India can be proved topographically. The rivers - Ajakarṇi, Nerañjarā[41] etc. and the hills Vebhāra, Pāṇḍava,[42] Vulture's peak and the mountain Himalaya[43] are in North India.

Among the fauna described here are the peacocks, swan, crane, elephants, frogs, deer etc. Any ornithologist can say that they are seen in plenty only in the rainy season. The peacock is very much associated with it and so are swans and cranes.

The spring is not described elaborately by the *theras* because they were busy doing their duties in that season. But there may be another reason also. The spring with all its flowers, blossoms, and gorgeous wealth of colours was to the Sanskrit poets generally a time when the erotic passions were inflamed. The *theras* had no such business and hence they gave it up. But it is not altogether absent.

Now crimson glow the tress, dear Lord, and cast
Their ancient foliage in quest of fruit.
Like crests of flame they shine irradiant,
And rich in hope, great Hero, is the hour.
Verdure and blossom time in every tree,
Wherever we look delightful to the eye,
And every quarter breathing fragrant airs,
While petals falling, yearning comes for fruit :-
Tis time, O Hero, that we set out hence.[44]

This is a beautiful description of Nature. The trees casting their ancient foliage in quest of fruit is a picture original enough to be compared with such description in any other world literature. And this glowing season inspires the *theras* to contemplate. This is the hour when they too should gird up their loins to make a quest of the Great Fruit. This is the finest example of pathetic fallacy. 'Like crests of flame they shine irradiant'... ... ... is an excellent simile based on the clear visual perception.

Such are the descriptions of Nature in the *Theragāthā*. But my dissertation will not be complete if I do not point out the significance of moon in the *gāthās* and in the lives of the *theras.*

The moon is very dear to the romantics. When she sheds her lustre on fullmoon days, an enchanting atmosphere is created - a bewitching atmosphere, extremely appealing to them. But in the *Theragthā* there is an altogether different use made of the moon.

They have closely observed the waxing and waning of the moon. To them, therefore, a person who is free from ill- will, free from ten fetters and who has attained perfect equanimity is 'even as the moon of fifteenth day, sails clear in sky without a stain.'

He who in former days a wastrel living
In later no more so spends his time
He goeth over the world a radiance shedding
As when the moon comes, free in clouded sky.[45]

A Brother who has destroyed all cankers, who is sane and immune from all impurities is like a full moon[46]. Sometimes a man who by self-control has brought to perfection the breathing exercise casts a radiant sheen as is done by the full moon.[47]

All these go to prove that Nature has been described in the *Theragāthā* in a sublime manner with her beauty and awe and this induced the *theras* to engage themselves in meditation in order to enjoy the *dhyāna-sukha* and ultimately realise the Great Fruit i.e. Nibbāna.

References

1. Matthew Arnold - *The Scholar Gypsy.*
2. *Vinay Texts (Scard Books of the East* - Max Muller), Part II p.312.
3. *ibid.* 313-14.
4. *Ākaṅkheyyasutta* : *Sacred Books of the East.* Ed. Max Muller Vol.XI.
5. *Majjhima* 1, 118.

6. *Ramaṇīya araññāni, yattha na ramati jano /*
Vītarāgā ramissanti na te kāmagavesino //

7. पुरतो पच्छतो वापि अपरो चे न विज्जति,
अतीव फासु भवति एकस्म वसतो बने ।

8. रागूपरसहितं चित्तं यदा प्रज्जते मम,
सयमेव पच्चवेक्खित्वा एकको तं दमेम, हं ।।
रजते रजनीयेसु दुस्सनीयेसु दुस्सति,
मुयूहते मोहनीयेसु निक्खमस्सु बना तुरं ।।
विसुद्धानं अयं वासो निम्लानं तपस्सनं,
मा खो विसुद्धं दूसेसि निक्खमस्सु वना तुरंगति ।। दी. नि. महासमयसुत्त

9. ये सिता गिरिगब्भरं, पहितत्ता समाहिता ।
पुथूसीहाव सल्लीना, लोमहंसाभिसम्भुनो
ओदातमनसा सुद्धा, विप्पसन्नमनाविला ।।दौधनिकाय महासमयसुत्तं १९०

10. कामराग, भवराग, पटिध, मान, दिट्ठि, सीलब्बतपरामास, विचिक्छा, इस्सा, मच्छरिय, अविजा ।

11. Winternitz : *History of Indian Literature* Vol.II.

12. C.A.F. Rhys Davids : *Introduction to The Psalms of the Brethren.*

13. J.C. Powys : *Culture and Nature*

14. पञ्चङ्गिकेन तुरियेन न रति होति तादिसी ।
यथा एकग्गचित्तस्स सम्मा धम्मं विपस्सतो ति ।।

15. यदा सोस्ससि निगघोसं सन्दमानाय सिंधुया।
गीतं किम्पुरिसानञ्च न रजस्स सरिस्ससि।।
यदा सीहस्स व्यग्घस्स खगस्स गवयस्स च ।
वने सोस्ससि वालानं न रजस्स सरिस्ससि ।।
यदा मोरीहि परिकिण्णं वरिहिनं मत्थकासिनं ।
मोरं दक्खिसि नच्चन्तं न रज्जस्म सरिस्मसि ।।
यदा दक्खिसि हेमन्ते पुप्फिते धरनीरुहे ।
सुरभिसम्पवायन्ते न रजस्स सरिस्ससि ।।
यदा हेमन्तिके मासे हरितं दक्खिसिमेदिनिं ।
इन्दगोपकसंच्छन्नं न रजस्स सरिससिस ।।

16. नीला सुगीवा सिखिनो, मोरा कारंवियं अभिनदन्ति,
ते सीतवातकीलिता, सुत्तं झायं निबोधेन्ती ति ।।

17. Winternitz : *History of Indian Literature,* Vol.1,p.91.

18. उदु श्रिय उषसो रोचमाना अस्थुरपां नोर्मयो रुशन्तः
कृणोति विश्वो सुपथो सुगान्यभूदु वस्वी दक्षिणा मघोनी।

19. Shakespeare : *Hamlet.*
20. Winternitz, *History of Indian Literature,* vol.II,p.107.
21. छन्ना मे कुटिका सुखा निवाता, वस्स देव यथासुखं
    चित्तं मे सुसमाहितं विमुत्तं, आतापी विहरामि वस्स देवाति ।।

22. वस्सति देवो यथा सुगीतं, छन्ना मे कुटिका सुखा निवाता ।
    तस्सं विहरामि वूपसन्तो, अथ चे पत्थयसि पवस्स देव।।

23. O God, make it rain !
    Loose the soft silver passion of the rain !
    Send swiftly from above
    This clear token of the love,
    Make it rain !
    Prayer for rain : Herbert Palmer.

24. स्निग्ध श्यामलकान्तिलिप्तबियतो वेलद्बलाका घनाः ।
    वाताः शीकरिणः पयोदसुहृदामानन्दकेकाः कलाः ।
    कामं सन्तु दृढं कठोरहृदयो रामोऽस्मि सर्वं सहे।
    वैदेही तु कथं भविष्यति हहा हा देवि धीरा भव।।

25. घनघमंड गरजत नभघोरा । पियाहीन डरपत मन मोरा ।।
26. नदन्ति मोरा सुसिखा सुपेखुणा, सुनीलगीवा सुमुखा सुगज्जिनो,
    सुसद्दला चापि महामही अयं, सुव्यापितम्बू सुबलाहकं नभं ।।
    कुल्लरूपो सुमनस्स झायतं, सुनिक्खमो साधु सुबुद्धसासने,
    सुसुक्कसुक्कं निपुणं सुदुद्दसं, फुसाहि तं उत्तममच्चुतं पदं ति ।।
27. यदा बलाका सुचि पण्डरच्छदा, कालस मेघस्स भयेन तज्जिता
    पलेहिति आलयमालयेसिनी, तदा नदी अजकरणी रमेति मं ।
    यदा बालाका सुविसुद्धपण्डरा कालस मेघस्म भयेन तज्जिता
    परियेसति लेणमलेणदस्सिनी, तदा नदी अजरकरणी रमेति मं ।
28. नाज्ज गिरि नदीहि विप्पवाससमयो, खेमा अजकरणी सिवा सुरम्मा ति ।
29. W.H. Davies : *In the Snow.*
30. *Culture and Nature* : John Cowper Powys.
31. देवो च वस्सति देवो च गळगळायति,
    एको चाहंभेरवे बिले बिहरामि।
    तस्म मय्हं एककस्म भेरवे बिले बिहरतो
    नत्थि भयं वा छम्भितत्तं वा लोमहंसो वा ।।
32. यदा नभे गज्जति मेघदुन्दुभि, धाराकुला विहंगपथे समन्ततो
    भिक्खु च पब्भारगतो व झायति, ततो रतिं परमतरं न विन्दति ।

33. C.A.F. Rhys Davids : *Introduction to The Psalms of the Brethren.*

34. योगीपीतिकरं रम्मं, मत्तकुञ्जरसेवितं
एको अत्तवसी खिप्पं, पविसिस्सामि काननं
सुपुप्फिते सीतवने, सीतले गिरकन्दरे
गत्तानि परिसिञ्चित्वा चङ्कमिस्सामि एकको ।

35. कदा अनिच्चे बधरोगनीळं, कायं इमं मच्चुजरायुपद्दुतं
विपस्समानो वीतभयो विहस्सं, एको बने तं नु कदा भविस्सति ।

36. न ताव सुपितुं होति, रत्ति नक्खत्तमालिनी
पटिजग्गितुमेवेसा, रत्ति होति विजानता ।।

37. या निशा सर्वभूतानां तस्या जागर्ति संयमी ।
यस्या जाग्रति भूतानि सा निशा पश्यतो मुनेः ।।

38. छविपापक चित्तभद्दक, मोघराज सततं समाहितो,
हेमन्तिकसीतकालरत्तियो, भिक्खु त्वंसि कथं करिस्ससि ।

39. मासगताय आसालिहया पच्छिमिका उपगन्तब्बा इमा खो, भिक्खवे
द्वे वस्सूपनायिकाति। मबावग्गपालि

40. See above

41. अत्थाय वत मे बुद्धो, नदिं नेरञ्जरं अगा ।
यस्साहं धम्मं सुत्वान, मिच्छादिट्ठिं विवज्जयिं ।

42. वित्ररमनुपतन्ति विज्जुता, वेभारस्स च परण्डवस्स च ।

43. स वे अरुचि नागो, हिमवावञ्जे सिलुच्चये ।

44. अङ्गारिनो दानि दुमा भदन्ते, फलेसिनो छदनं विप्पहाय ।
ते अच्चिमन्तो व पभासयन्ति, समयो महावीर भागी रसानं
दुमानि फुल्लानि मनोरमानि, समन्ततो सब्बदिसा पवन्ति ।
पत्तं पहाय फलमाससना,कालो इतो पक्कमनाय वीर ।।

45. यो पुब्बे पमज्जित्वान, पच्छा सो नप्पमज्जित ।
सोमं लोकं पभासेति, अब्भामुत्तो व चन्दिमा ।

46. सोहं परिपुण्णसंकप्पो, चन्दो पन्नरसो यथा
सब्बासवपरिक्खीणो, नत्थि दानि पुनब्भवो ति ।

47. अनुपुब्बं परिचिता, यथा बुद्धेन दे.सिता
सो मं लोवं पभासेति, अब्मामुत्तो व चन्दिमा ।

Similes in the Sāmaññaphalasutta

The *Suttapiṭaka* which is a collection of the discourses of Lord Buddha abounds in similes, metaphors and parables. In this respect it is like the Bible where Jesus Christ explained his teachings to the people with the help of parables. *The Parable of the Sower* and *the Parable of Good Samaritan* can be cited as examples. Lord Buddha also explained his teachings with the help of similes and parables.

It was a part of the teaching method of Lord Buddha to convince his audience by means of similes and parables. A parable or a simile is not a logical argument but it has a great effect on the mind and even on the intellect of the hearer. Where arguments fail, similes can convince the audience.

It is for this reason that we find a plethora of similes in the *Suttapiṭaka*, which have literary value.

Lord Buddha's *Dhamma* was "profound, difficult to realise, hard to understand, tranquillising, sweet, not to be grasped by mere logic, subtle and comprehensible only by the wise". How could he make it simple and understandable to the common people whom he preached his *Dhamma* ? He, therefore, thought it necessary to interlard his teachings with parables and spice them with homely similes so that the masses might not have any difficulty in understanding the meaning of his teachings.

The similes used by Lord Buddha are important not only from the religious point of view but also from the literary point of view.

There are some similes which may be called Buddhistic and there are others which can be traced back to the Vedic Literature which occur *mutatis mutandis* to suit different contexts.

A simile serves many functions. Broadly speaking one of the functions of a simile is to make a little-known and unfamiliar object more known and familiar, for generally a concrete object is made the *upamāna* of an unfamiliar abstract object. *Upamānas* thus presented sometimes illuminate and beautify the object to be compared, and sometimes vividly present before us the unfamiliar. In short, we can say that similies concretise the most abstract things.

The *Sāmaññaphulasutta* sets forth the fruits of the life of a recluse. It also treats of the highest goal of a Buddhist monk and naturally, therefore, the subject is very difficult. Lord Buddha had to explain it to the common people and, therefore, he employed homely similes to serve the great purpose of making his teachings crystal clear to them. When he comes to the *jhāna* (meditation) stage, his language becomes rich in similes and glows with a beauty which is remarkable not only from the religious point of view but also from the aesthetic view point. Such passages become magnificent in their poetic grandeur and may aptly be called the gems of Pali literature. For the similes used here do not only simplify the profound matter but also explain its sublime nature. Out of the twentyone similes, five or so are the most sublime and they explain the true nature of the fruits of the life of a Buddhist monk. Moreover, the similes seem to be spontaneous and not *laboured* . This also proves beyond doubt that these passages are the utterances of a man who had himself attained the *summum bonum* and enjoyed the fuits of the life of a recluse.

The nature of similes throws a flood of light upon the mind which used them, for it reflects a clear realisation and profound insight into the fruits that come to a Buddhist monk. The sublime nature of the fruits and their clear realisation are highlighted by the analysis of these similes.

The subject that the *Sāṁaññaphalasutta* deals with is characterized by sublimity. Therefore, all the similes seem to take on a glorious and spiritual character. As I have said above, five or so are the similes which are soaked in sublime beauty. They relate to the five *Jhāna* stages when joy springs up as a result of meditation and the monk is filled with it, suffused with it and permeated with it. The paragraphs describing these stages of meditation are, in the words of T.W. Rhys Davids "of much eloquence and force in the Pali".[1] Such paragraphs evince that the sensation that Lord Buddha or a Buddhist monk felt was bodied forth into these apt similes.

Not only in this *sutta* but in others also these similes occur. In the *Mahāsappurisa sutta* of the *Majjhima Nikāya* all the similes except the first five have been used in the same context. *Majjhima and Saṁyutta Nikāya*s show a predilection for these similes either in the same context or in different contexts. I shall show below where and in what context these similes occur.

There are twentyone similes, all told, in this *sutta*. The first five relate to five hindrances, four are concerned with the four *Jhānas* and the remaining explain the *Paññā, Iddhi, Dibbasota, Dibbacakkhu* etc. The similes relating to the hindrances speak of great freedom. In short, we can say that they elaborate the great and important theme of freedom. They echo and re-echo it. The Buddhist monk after gaining mastery over the minor moralities feels and enjoys an indescribable freedom. He does not feel like a man in debt, not does he feel like a man suffering from disease, nor does he feel like a man in prison, nor is he a slave to anything, nor does he feel lost in a vast sandy desert, but on the other hand, he feels freedom from debt and disease. He feels to be at liberty and is no longer a slave. Nor is he assailed by doubt and perplexity. These similes, I think, do not point to physical states only but to spiritual states also. In the spiritual realm also he is free from debt, from disease, from slavery, and preplexity etc. To explain this spiritual advancement of a Buddhist monk to the people, Lord Buddha used these homely and familiar similes.

The question then is how do we account for the justification or aptness of these similes T.W.Rhys Davids says that the five similes relate to the five hindrances and they should be taken in order. The five hindrances in order are *kāmacchanda, vyāpāda, thīnamiddha, uddhaccakukucca and vicikicchā.*

Lord Buddha has compared a man suffering from *kāmachhanda* with a man who has contracted a loan but has not been able to pay it off. How then *Kāmacchanda* (excitement of sensual pleasure) is compared to a loan ? What is the point of similarity here ? Buddhaghoṣa, the celebrated commentator, says that as a debtor has to endure all the harsh words that his creditor speaks to him when he has not paid off the loan, so a man, slave to sensual pleasure, becomes shameless and has to endure all sorts of harsh words for his shameless behaviour. A debtor is morally degraded and so is the case with the man who has burning passions for sensual pleasure.[2]

I think this can be explained in another way also. As a debtor does not have any capital to set on foot a business of his own, so a Buddhist Bhikkhu burning with passions for sensual pleasure is not fit to make progress in the spiritual realm. He is morally bankrupt as the debtor is financially. And moral bankruptcy caused by sensuality is a great hindrance. As a man, who clears up the debt and has something more to his credit, no longer has to suffer harsh words and can himself run a business, so a man who has suppressed the first hindrance of *kāmacchanda* can make himself fit for spiritual progress.

In the second simile a man with *vyāpāda* (ill-will) has been compared with a man who is diseased, in pain, who has no strength left in him and who cannot digest his food. Buddhaghoṣa says that as a diseased man cannot make distinction between sweet and sour and as all *rasas* are sour to him, so a mind, the ruling passion of which is ill-will, cannot understand what is good and what is not good for him. His teacher may take pains to bring him to the right path, but what the right path is he does not understand. He is full of anger and, therefore, no reason is left in him. This simile is meaningful not only on the physical plane as Buddhaghoṣa explains, it becomes more meaningful on the spiritual plane. As a diseased person is physically unfit to perform any work of importance and as his life becomes a burden to him, so a man with ill-will can never exercise his reason properly and is spiritually unfit to perform the stages of *Jhāna* which are like the rungs of a ladder leading to *Nibbāna*. But as a man free from disease can tell sweet from sour, so a man who is free from ill-will can know what at the root of all evils is and can apply his mind to meditation.[3]

The third simile explains the third hindrance, namely *thīnamiddha*. As a man who is in prison is silent when some body relates to him the programme of a certain festive occasion, so a Bhikkhu suffering from torpor of mind or body or both cannot say the beginning, the middle and the end of the *Dhamma* preached.[4] What is this due to ? This is due to carelessness. This carelessness causes him to suffer in prison and, therefore, he cannot enjoy the festive occasion. So a Bhikkhu cannot enjoy the *Dhamma* when he is in torpor of mind or body. *Thīnamiddha* is a great hindrance. Only when the Bhikkhu comes to learn it as a hindrance, he can weaken it or suppress it and can get rid of it.

The fourth simile, besides explaining what *uddhacca kukucca* is, shows that there was slavery system in India during the time of Lord Buddha. As a slave is not master of his own self, as he cannot do what he wishes to, because he has to obey his master and even when he is not willing to work, he has to obey him, so a man subject to flurry and worry has to remain exactly like a slave.[5] A slave can buy back his freedom from his master. He can pay off what he owes to him and then he can be as free as the mountain wind. A Bhikkhu also can set himself free by suppressing the flurry and worry-the fourth hindrance.

The fifth simile reads like the first simile in 'The Divine Comedy' by Dante, the famous Italian poet. He writes that he was benighted. In this simile also is described the state of a rich and prosperous man who finds himself on a long road, in a desert, 'where no food was, but much danger'. "*Vicikicchā* is doubt and perplexity. And a man tormented by perplexity is like a man lost on a long road. His path is beset with danger and he has to suffer much.[6] However advanced a Bhikkhu may be on the road to spiritual progress, he feels a set-back if the storm of doubt rages in his heart and mind. But if he gets rid of this doubt, he will feel as if he has arrived safe on the border of his village. He will experience peace and security.

All the five foregoing similes have freedom as their main subject. Freedom, as I have said above, is the keynote; freedom on both the planes - physical and spiritual, is compared to freedom from debt, from disease, from prison-house, from slavery and from doubt. This may be called the *leit motif* of this *sutta*.

The joy that springs from freedom becomes the main theme of the four similes relating to the *Jhānas*. How logically Lord Buddha proceeds to show that immense and boundless joy springs up when the five hindrances are put away! Suppressing and weakening the five hindrances mean freedom which brings in its train a sense of peace and calmness.

"Then estranged from lusts, aloof from evil dispositions he enters into and remains in the first rapture - a state of joy and ease born of detachment, reasoning and investigation going on the while"[7]. The joy that thus springs up does not stop at one place. He fills his whole body with it, he pervades and permeates his person with the joy and ease born of detachment.

The four similes about the four *Jhānas* have pervading and permeating joy as their theme. The Bhikkhu has put away the five hindrances. What does he get now ? Joy and supreme joy undisturbed, pure and serene. The first simile explains how a Bhikkhu, like a skilful bathman or his apprentice, permeates with joy his body within and without. As a matter of fact, the way how a Bhikkhu drenches his body with joy is compared here with the art of the bathman who by sprinkling water drop by drop converts perfumed soap powder into a ball of lather. The fact that has been concretely explained here is that the perfumed soap powder takes up the unctuous moisture, is converted into a ball of lather but the water does not leak. Similarly the Bhikkhu's whole person is filled with joy and is drenched with it.

In the second simile the *karaja-kāya* (impure body) is compared with *rahado* (pool of water) and the joy that the Bhikkhu experiences in the second *jhāna* is compared with water. As the Bhikkhu gets rid of *vitakka* and *vicāra* which are disturbing and agitating factors, so he enjoys undisturbed joy which like the water of a pool comes from within and is calm and without any agitation. Rain water causes bubbles and the water of deluge is full of old leaves, grasses, woods etc.[8] Buddhaghoṣa explains it in the way adverted to above. Buddha takes this *upamāna* in order to convey concretely the nature of joy that the Bhikkhu experiences.

The third simile also carries the idea of permeation further. The Bhikkhu gradually fills himself more and more with joy. He is like the lotus flowers red or white or blue which are born in water, grow up in water and are pervaded, drenched, permeated and suffused with cool moisture thereof 'from their very tips down to their roots'.

The fourth simile explains that not only is he filled with joy but he is filled with a sense of purification, of translucence. Joy marked by sublimity and purity is the theme of the fourth *jhāna*. Buddhaghoṣa gives a good simile to explain it. As a piece of clean cloth reflects heat, so the body of a *Bhikkhu* reflects the joy that he feels. Dirty clothes donot reflect, so the Yogāvacara having impurity of mind cannot irradiate the boundless bliss that he may otherwise enjoy in the fourth *Jhāna*. Here the body of a good *Bhikkhu* is compared with a piece of clean cloth.'[9]

What is most important in the four similes explained above is that they convey a sense of immense and undisturbed joy experienced by the Bhikkhu, which ultimately is characterised by sublimity and purity. Whereas, on the one hand, unqualified joy is symbolized by the water springing from within, purity, on the other hand, is suggested by perfumed soap powder, lotus, white, red or blue and clean-white robes. Besides, it has been emphasized in each simile thast there is not even a small part of the body which is not suffused with joy. Let me mention here in passing that according to the poetic convention lotus stands for purity. The three colours white, red and blue also suggest purity and sublimity.

With his heart thus serene, made pure, translucent, cultured, devoid of evil, supple, ready to act, firm and imperturbable, he applies and bends down his mind to that insight that comes from knowledge.[10]

The Bhikkhu with the help of the insight grasps the fact that "this body of mine has form, it is built up of the four elements, it springs from father and mother, it is continually nourished by so much boiled rice and juicy food, its very nature is impermanence.;[11] This idea is concretely conveyed by the *veluriya* gem simile. As a man with eyes can easily see threads passing through a *veluriya* gem, so a Bhikkhu having *Vipassanā* (insight) can realize the true nature of the body.

In the next stage the Bhikkhu calls up a mental image of himself which exactly corresponds to his body. Buddhaghoṣa explains that if the Bhikkhu has unpierced ears, so will the image have and so on.[12]

The idea that Bhikkhu calls up another *monomaya* body from his body has been made clear with the help of the three very homely similes. The first is the reed and sheath simile, the second is the snake and slough one, and the third is the sword and scabbard one. As a man pulls out a reed from its sheath and then he would tell the reed from the sheath, so a Bhikkhu can tell the *manomaya* body from the body with the help of psychic power. As a snake can be taken out of its slough and a sword can be drawn from its scabbard, so a *manomaya* body can be called up from the body. These three similes are quite exact in point of similarity. The reed and sheath simile occurs in the *Satapatha Brāhmaṇa.*[13]

If *karanda* is rendered as basket, the simile will not be appropriate. *Karanda* also means *Ahi-kañcuka*. Therefore, Buddhaghoṣa is quite correct in rendering it as slough. One cannot take a snake out of its slough but one can do so in imagination.

In this way the Bhikkhu has prepared and made his body quite fit and supple. His mind is serene, pure, translucent. He developes power to perform psychic phenomena. This state of the mind of the Bhikkhu has been compared with the clay kneaded well by the potter. As the potter can mould the clay in any way he likes, as he can shape it into any pot he likes, so the Bhikkhu can become many or having become many he can become one, he can become visible or invisible, he can travel cross-legged in the sky, like the birds on wing. As an ivory carver carves out of ivory image of any shape he wants or a goldsmith does out of gold, so does the Bhikkhu. Here the specially prepared mind is compared with clay, ivory or gold and the Bhikkhu is like the potter, the ivory carver and the goldsmith. These similes are homely and reflect incidentally that during the time of Lord Buddha the crafts of ivory carving, making ornaments of different shape and size out of gold were quite popular.

He then applies his mind to the heavenly ear. As a man on the high road hears sounds of kettle drum, tabor or chank horns etc. and can tell one from the other, so the Bhikkhu with his heavenly ear can hear different sounds and make difference between them. According to Buddhaghoṣa the point of comparison is that if he is in trouble and has lost his way in a desert or jungle he might be in doubt and cannot be sure of the sound. But if he is calm and serene which a man can be when he is on a high road, he will have no doubt and he can tell the difference.[14]

He does not rest here on the road to spiritual progress. But he knows the minds of others by penetrating into their minds with his own. This has been made clear with the help of a very apt simile. The Bhikkhu knows the mind of others as clearly as a man or a woman or a lad sees his oswn face reflected in a mirror or in a vessel of clear water. What can be more appropriate and homely simile than these ?

Then he directs his mind to the knowledge of the memory of his previous births. He recalls to mind his various births. This he does as easily as a man remembers that from this village he went to that and there he stood like this and from there he came back home again.

The last but one simile explains how he knows the rise and

fall of beings. He knows it as easily as a man on the upper terrace of a house in the midst of a place where four roads meet, sees man entering or coming out of it.

The goal of the Buddhist monk is to achieve *Nibbāna*. Before enjoying this last fruit, he enjoys several fruits which lead up to the last one. Finally he reaches this stage too. He applies his mind to the destruction of the deadly floods. He has the knowledge of suffering, the origin of suffering, the cessation of suffering, and of the path leading to the cessation of suffering. He is thus set free from the deadly floods, from the deadly taints of lusts. He has the knowledge of his emancipation and he knows that he has destroyed his rebirth.

In the last simile the knowledge of the four noble truths has been explained. As a man standing on the bank of a pool of water perceives the oysters and shells, gravel and the pebbles and the shoals of fish in the clear, translucent and serene water, so he knows the four noble truths.

Thus going through the above-mentioned stages, the life of a Buddhist monk becomes pure. He accomplishes all that he has to do. His life becomes sweet and rich. The spiritual richness of his life is suggested by several similes adverted to above. Gold and ivory do not suggest material richness but spiritual richness.

Thus we see that not only from the view point of the religious teachings the *Sāmaññaphala Sutta* is important but it is also important for its similes which are aesthetically gratifying, rich and suggestive and which point to spiritual wealth.

The words like serene, calm, translucent, pure, freedom, excellent, lotus, ivory all indicate the life that a monk leads in order to reach the goal. The similes explained above are very beautiful and most of them are very important for their suggestiveness. It is due to this that they have been used in the *Tipiṭaka* many a time to explain the same thing as has been done above or in different contexts. It will not be out of place here to mention where they occur and in what contexts. Except the first five similes concerned with the *Nīvaraṇas*, all the similes are repeated in the *Mahāssapura sutta*[15] in the same context. The four similes relating to the *Jhānas* occur in the *Kāyagatāsasti sutta.*[16] The *veluriya* gem simile occurs in the *Acchariya-Abbhuta sutta*[17] *Sūsīma sutta*[18], and in *Samkhārupapattisutta*[19] in different contexts. The simile of the lotus occurs in the *Puppha sutta*[20] in different contexts. The simile of the woman or man or lad occurs many a time in the *suttas* like *Anumāna sutta.*[21]

In the *Mahāsakuludāyi sutta* as mentioned above all the similes occur as if they have been lifted bodily from the *Sāmaññaphala sutta*[22] and placed there. Reference my also be made to *Subha sutta*[23] for these similes. This explains how important these similes are for the understanding of the abstract ideas through these concrete similes.

References

1. Quoted from the footnote on page 84 of *Scared Books of the Buddhist* Vol.II.
2. *Sumangala Vilāsini* p.213.
3. *Sumangalaviliāsinī* p.213.
4. *ibid.*, pp.213-214.
5. *ibid.*, p.214.
6. *ibid.*, pp.214-215.
7. *So vivicca eva kāmehi vivicca akusalehi dhammehi savitakkaṃ savicāram vivekajam pītisukham paṭhamajjhānam upasampajja viharati. The Dīgha Nikāya* (PTS.Edition, p.75).
8. *Sumangalaviḷāsinī* p.218.
9. *Sumangalavilāsini.* p.219.
10. *'So evaṃ samāhite citte parisuddhe pariyodate anangaṇe, vigatūpakkilese, mudubhūte kammaniye ṭhite aneñjappatte ñāṇa-dassanāya cittaṃ abhinīharati abhininnāmeti. Dīgha Nikāya* PTS.p.76.
11. *The Sacred Books of the Buddhists* Vol.II Ed. by Max Müller. p.86.
12. Quoted from the footnote on p.88 in *The Sacred Books of the Buddhists* Vol.II Ed. by Max Müller. *'Sace aviddha-kṇṇo taṃ pi aviddhakaṇṇam ti evaṃ sabbākārehi tena sadisam evashoti.'*

13. *śatapatha-Brāhmaṇa* IV,3,3,16.
14. See footnote on p.89 in The *Sacred Books of the Buddhists.* Vol.II Ed. by Max Müller.
15. *The Middle Length Sayings-Majjhima Nikāya* Vol.I p.329. Tr. by I.B. Horner., (T.T.S.)
16. *ibid.*, Vol. III. p.132-134.
17. *ibid.*, Vol. III. p.167.
18. *D.T.P.D.* 2.29.43.
19. *The Middle Length Sayings* III.I.B. Horner p.141.
20. D.T.P.D. 22-94-103.
21. *The Middle Length Sayings* Vol.I. Tr. by I.B.Horner. p.131.
22. *The Middle Length Sayings* Vol.II. I.B. Horner p.215.
23. *The Sacred Books of the Buddhists* Vol.II. Edited by Max Müller. p.268.

Contribution of Buddhism in the Field of Rasa (Aesthetic Sentiments)

Of the two important branches of *Śramaṇa* culture, Buddhism with its great emphasis on withdrawal from the world of pleasures as also on the attainment of a state of desirelessness has contributed largely in the field of aesthetic sentiments inasmuch as it gave rise to a literature in which the *rasa* that is primarily delineated is *śānta* (quietistic sentiment). Not that it was unknown prior to the rise of Buddhism, but as there was not much literature delineating it, it was not as popular as the other eight *rasas* were. Bharata in his *Nāṭya-Śāstra* which represents the flowering up of a long and rich dramatic tradition, mentions only eight *rasas.*[1] It is clear from the *Nāṭya-Śāstra* that he had a remarkable insight into the human psychology and there are verses in it which amply prove his awareness of the quietistic sentiment.[2] He must not have regarded only the three *puruṣārthas* as the be-all and end-all of life but was also aware of *mokṣa*-the fourth *puruṣārtha*. But he did not mention it explicitly because there was not, perhaps, much of literature delineating *Śānta-rasa* and also because he thought that person embodying it could hardly be enacted on the stage. In another recension of the *Nāṭya-śāstra* there are verses which mention *Śānta-rasa*, but they are said to be interpolations made by Udbhaṭa who explicitly mentions it in his *Kavyālaṅkārasaṅgraha* as is pointed out by Abhinavagupta in his *Abhinavabhāratī* where he explains *rasa*, particularly *śānta-rasa* at length.[3]

Buddhism broke new grounds. Buddha had shown that man has infinite spiritual potentiality which should not be called in question. It is true he suffers on account of *avidyā* (ignorance), but it is also equally true that he alone can rend the veil of *avidyā* and can go beyond the enveloping darkness to the land of light and liberation. After attaining enlightenment Buddha preached to the masses for long fortyfive years and amply illustrated the fact that the achievement of the mental state called *śama* does not mean absence of feelings and activities. Instead, it means that one who has attained the mental state of *śama* is full of sublime feelings like *mettā, karuṇā, muditā* and *upekkhā* and best actions. Such persons do live in the world but do not cling to it and remain unaffected like a lotus leaf in water.

Tṛṣṇā, according to Buddha, is at the root of all our sufferings, physical, mental and cosmic and to achieve a state of desirelessness is the greatest human aspiration. This state can be achieved by treading on the eightfold path comprising *sīla, samādhi* and *paññā*. He had himself gone along the path and tasted the *nibbāna-rasa*. In all his discourses, therefore, he spoke at length about the cause of suffering and the way to get rid of it. He talked of *tṛṣṇā*, its cause as also of how to annihilate it. All his discourses explain the way to put an end to suffering by observing *sīla* (virtue), practising *samādhi* (meditation) and attaining *paññā* (insight). He also talked of the ineffable bliss that follows annihilation of desires. Thus the subject matter of his discourses is sublime.

The subject matter of Buddhist literature is different from other secular literature. Here the theme is not love, nor ambition, but it is spiritual progress, and purification of mind from all kinds of defilements and breaking of fetters that bind man to the wheel of birth and death. It is, in short, *tṛṣṇā-kṣaya* and the light and liberation that follow it. The first words that fell from the lips of Buddha after he had attained enlightenment embody the quintessence of his long quest and ultimate achievement in life :

Anekajātisansāraṃ sandhāvissaṃ anibbisaṃ
Gahakārakaṃ gavesanto dukkhā jāti punappunam/
Gahakāra diṭṭhosi puna gehaṃ no kāhasi
Sabbā te phāsukā bhaggā visakūṭam visankhatan
Visamkhāragataṃ cittaṃ taṇhānaṃ khayamajjhagā //[4]

(Through a round of countless births have I passed fruitlessly in search of the maker of this tabernacle and painful is the round of births. But now, the builder of the tabernacle, I have seen thee; never again shalt thou build me a house. All the rafters are broken and the ridge-pole is broken asunder; and the mind at rest in *Nibbāna* has passed beyond grasping desires).

Desires are insatiable and the more we try to satisfy them, the more they increase in number. Buddha, therefore, geared all his discourses to inculcating in us an innate love for leading an ethically noble life and for developing insight into the nature of things so that one does not always remain a slave to one's desires. His discourses, therefore, form a kind of literature whose precise function is to drive home the great value of annihilating desires and enable us to experience the bliss of living in the land of light and liberation.

The similes and metaphors used by Buddha to convey his glorious message are also sublime. They are not used to arouse erotic feelings, nor are they used to pander to other baser emotions but their express purpose is to arouse exalting emotions and enthuse us to work out our salvation.

When a man is rid of the five hindrances (*nīvaraṇas*) viz. *kāmacchanda, vyāpāda, thīnamiddha, udhaccakukucca* and *vicikicchā,* he feels as happy as a man feels when he has paid up the debt or like a man who has recovered from some serious disease, or like a man who has come out of a prison, or like a slave who has been emancipated or like a man who returned home after he had lost his way, respectively. The *jhāna sukha* pervades, fills, permeates and suffuses him just as a pool is done by the rising up of cool waters. His mind becomes supple and serene, translucent and cultured and there is not a spot left in his body which is devoid of the *jhāna sukha*. Such similes can be multiplied *ad infinitum*. In his discourse with Kasibhāradvāja he explains his spiritual agriculture at length. 'Faith is his seed, penance is rain and insight is his yoke.' *saddhā bījaṃ topo vuṭṭhi, paññā me yuganaṅgalaṃ*. The harvest that follows is *Nibbāna*.

Thus we find the theme of the discourses is very sublime and is connected with the spiritual life of man. Very sublime similes and metaphors are also used to explain our spiritual achievements in life.

If we have a look at the verses in the *Theragāthā* and *Therīgāthā* their sublime nature will become at once clear. The *theras* and *therīs* sing out their release from worldly sufferings of various kinds as also the infinite bliss which is consequent upon the release from suffering, mental, moral, domestic and social. Release from some situation that has become intolerable is also hymned in the verses.[5] Sometimes the *theras* and *theris* hymn their mental illumination-the light and insight that they experience, sometimes their cool, calm states of feeling and also the feeling of content. They also feel exalted when they achieve self-mastery over them. They also sing out their release from greed, ill-will and dullness and their keen experience of freedom, comfort, rest and their end of craving. They also sing out the fact that have realised the truth and have attained arhatship by realizing the six kinds of *Abhiññā* (higher knowledge).

The verses ascribed to Ambapāli embody the feelings of disenchantment and disillusion in her life. She was proud of her beauty and in her snares of love came princes just as moths come to a burning lamp. But time passed, her hair greyed and became like hemp. Her teeth decayed and the tautness and strength that she felt in the prime of her life gave way to looseness and lack of strength. She realized impermanence in life and instead of developing a pessimistic outlook she directed all her endeavours to realise a mental state of peace, poise and tranquillity. Her verses which express *tṛṣṇā kṣaya* and the ineffable joy that follows it, are, therefore, an example of great poetry.

There are other *therīs* who feel depression and disappointment in life but these do not dampen their spirit. They go along the spiritual path with renewed energy, gain insight into the real nature of things, come to know the temporary pleasures of senses and attain arhatship. The subject matter of their verses is the breaking of ten fetters that bind man to the wheel of life and death, practising meditation, beholding the Norm (*Dhamma*) and realisation of *Nibbāna*.

Thera Tālapuṭa in his verses utters such feelings poetically which as Oldenberg says show 'the growth of a culture that has won its way through much suffering.'

O, when shall I, who see and know that this
My person, nest of dying and disease oppressed by age and death is all impermanent
Dwell free from fear lonely within the woods
Yea, when shall these things be.[6]

If we analyse the use of objects of Nature made by the *theras* and *therīs*, it will be evident that the spring season, the sailing clouds and the moon do not arouse the kind of feelings they do in Romantic literature but they help them to practise meditation and purge them of all impurities to shine like the full moon. Such is the theme of the *Udāna, Itivuttaka* and the *Jātaka* stories.

The atmosphere in which the value of higher spiritual life could be appreciated was created by the preachings of Buddha and his disciples and it continued for a long time. The foundations of literature delineating *Śānta-rasa* were laid. It was in this atmosphere that the first ever dramatist and poet Aśvaghoṣa wrote *Sāriputraprakaraṇa, Saundarananda* and *Buddhacarita*. The *Buddhacarita* is an epic dealing with the theme of Buddha's great Renunciation, his ascetic practices, his battle with *Māra* and the attainment of Buddhahood. From the theme itself it becomes at once obvious that this work of art takes off from where other secular works of art land. Love - the most ubiquitous of all human feelings is not the theme here. In short, what constitutes the theme of this epic is liberation-the last of the *puruṣārthas*.

Siddhārtha sees great dangers in the objects of the senses : "For I am not so afraid of venomous snakes or of thunderbolts that fall from the sky or of fire allied with the wind as I fear the objects of the senses." Describing passions he says, "For the passions are ephemeral, robbers of the treasury of good, empty like the will-o-the wisps in the world. The mere expectation of them deludes man's minds, how much more can their actual possession ?" He further says that it is impossible to get satiety from passions. "For the lustful man can no more win satiety from the passions than a fire companioned by the wind can from fuel."

The thirteenth chapter of the *Buddhacarita* is entitled *Māra-vijaya*. *Māra* symbolises the forces of lustful passions. Siddhārtha's victory over him means rising above all evils and becoming able to realize *Nibbāna*. In the end Siddhārtha attains *Bodhi* and becomes the Buddha. The theme of *Saundarananda* and *Sāriputraprakaraṇa* also is similar to this-realisation of the impermanent nature of sensual pleasures and making endeavours to attain *Nibbāna*.

Thus we find that the enormous impact of Buddhism that it had on the masses made the rather difficult theme of the quest for peace and *Nibbāna* popular and the poets and dramatists began to write epics and dramas which delineate *Śānta-rasa*. This, to my mind, is a distinct contribution of Buddhism in the field of *Rasa* (Aesthetic sentiments).

References

1. *Śṛṅgāra hāsya karuṇa raudra vīra bhayānakaḥ /*
   Bibhatsādbhuta sanjñā cetyaṣṭau rasāḥ smṛtāḥ //
   Nāṭya-śāstra, VI,15-16.
2. *kvacciddharmah kvacit krīḍa kvacidarthah kvacit śamaḥ /*
   Dukkhārtānām śramārtānām śokārtānam tapasvinām //
   ibid., I,106.
3. V.Raghavan, *The Number of Rasas*, p.13.
4. *Dhammapada*, XI, 8 & 9.
5. C.A.F. Rhys Davids, *Psalms of the Sister*, Intro. p.xxiv.10
6. Aśvaghoṣa, *Buddhacarita*, Canto XI, 8 & 9,
   Nāśīviṣebhyo hi tathā bibhemi naivāśanibhyo gaganācutebhyah /
   Na pāvakebhyo' nilasanhitebhyo yathā bhayaṁ me viṣayebhya eva /
   Kāmā hyanityāh kusalārtha caurā riktāśca māyāsadṛśāsca loke / Āśāsyamānā api mohayanti cittaṁ nṛṇāṁ kiṁ punarātmasansthāh //

Buddha's View of Beauty

Whenever people think of beauty, they think mostly of physical beauty which is born out of proportion, symmetry and harmony. But even the physical concept of beauty which is most obvious is not universal. What is beautiful to an Indian, may not be beautiful to an African. Besides, physical beauty is not something which lasts for ever. It is transitory. Therefore, there have been serious thinkers who have shifted their attention from physical beauty to other kinds of beauty which are lasting. Plato's concept of beauty is 'the idea of Beauty', like his 'other ideas'. Buddha's concept of beauty is quite different from other concepts in so far as he conceives it in terms of moral well-being of a man. What is man's physical beauty in comparison to beauty born out of his moral well-being ? An analysis of Buddha's concept of beauty will reveal that he has added moral and ethical dimension to his concept of beauty and has made the concept universal.

Buddha did not put a premium on physical beauty, as he knew with his three kinds of *pariññā*[1] (understanding) that things that look beautiful only appear so. In reality they are characterised by *anicca* (impermanence). And as they are in a constant state of flux, they are the sources of sufferings.[2] At one place Buddha says, "Beauty is nothing to me, neither the beauty of the body nor that that comes of dress."[3] How can an object which is transitory and short-lived give pleasure ? Physical beauty and beauty got from Beauty-Culture are short-lived and they are not to be proud of.

There are many references in the *Tipiṭaka* where Lord Buddha has revealed his attitude towards physical beauty. To Abhirūpanandā, who was infatuated with her physical beauty characterised by perfect form and who would not go to Buddha even when he wanted her to come for instruction, out of pride, he proved the transitoriness of physical beauty by conjuring up a more beautiful woman and showing her becoming aged and fading. The sight caused anguish in the mind of Abhirūpanandā and she became disillusioned. Addhakāsī like, Abhirūpanandā was proud of her beauty, but when she attained real knowledge, physical beauty had no importance for her.

But irksome now is all my loveliness;
I weary of it, disillusionized.[4]

Vimala [5], too, was proud of her perfect form and being conscious of 'the bloom of her beauty, remained intoxicated but for a short time. When truth dawned upon her, she realized the real nature of physical beauty and applied herself assiduously to attaining the ineffable *nibbāna*. What Lord Buddha says to Sundarīnandā with regard to this body, reveals once and for all his attitude to physical beauty :

Behold, Nandā, the foul compound, diseased,
Impure ! Compel thy heart to contemplate
What is not fair to view. So steel thyself
And concentrate the well-composed mind.[6]

Disillusion about her beauty dawns upon Khemā when she sees Buddha surrounded by a celestial nymph, far more beautiful than she was. Buddha with his mystic power showed her that even celestial beauty passes from youth to old age and as a result, the nymph came to have broken teeth, grey hair and a face full of wrinkles. If celestial beauty were so transitory, what to speak of the physical beauty of the world. She soon realizes that the body is vile, a 'foul seat of disease and corruption.'[7]

From the verses uttered by Sujātā we get an idea of the means of beautification used in those days :

Adorned in finery, in raiment fair,
In garlands wreathed powdered with sandalwood,
Bedecked with all my jewellery...[8]

Ambapālī[9]-this once famous Thais of India-contemplates her wasted charms in her poem. It not only epitomizes her beauty, grace and charm but it also expresses powerfully her painful realization of their transitoriness :

Glossy and black, as the down of the bee my curls once clustered.

They with the waste of the years are liker to hempen or bark cloth.

Fragant as casket of perfumes, as full of sweet blossoms the hair of me.

All with the waste of the years now rank as odour of hare's fur.

....

Wrought as by sculptor's craft the brows of me shone, finely pencilled.

They with the waste of the years are seamed with wrinkles, overhanging.

Beauteous the arms of me once shone like twin pillars cylindrical.

They with the waste of the years hang feeble as withering branches.

Like to the coils of a snake the full beauty of yore of the thighs of me.

They with the waste of the years are even as stems of the bamboo.

The description of physical beauty is so powerfully and glowingly done here that it can compare with the description of beauty given by any great poet of any literature of the world. But Ambapālī at the same time expresses her tragic feelings of her 'wasted charms' very poignantly. In her we find the mood of disenchantment and disillusionment. Had Ambapālī only spoken of this waste, it would have been only a tragic poem, though a powerful one, but she goes beyond and studies the law of impermanence as illustrated in her own ageing body. She develops what is called *nirveda* as a result of *tattvajñāna* and all her painful feelings bring in their wake a mood of quietude-a mood of desirelessness. This gives rise to a different kind of aesthetic and spiritual joy called *Śāntarasa* with which I shall deal later in detail.

The way Buddha has described human body makes his attitude towards it pretty clear and produces in us the feeling of *jugupsā*. In Buddhist literature we find descriptions of physically beautiful things from two points of view. The first is empirical. Our experience proves beyond any doubt that what we call beauty is very short-lived and it dies out with the passage of time. The grace and charm of youth give way to the wrinkles of old age. Related to this empirical description is another description of human body in terms of its constituents. The *Satīpaṭṭhāna sutta* presents such a description. It is so disgusting that it produces in us a nauseating effect. The body is 'encased in skin and full of impurities, from the soles of the feet up and from the crown of the head down. There is connected with this body hair of the head, hair of the body, nails, teeth, skin, flesh, sinews, bones, marrow, kidneys, heart, liver membrances, spleen, lungs, intestines, mesentery, stomach, excrement, bile, phlegm, pus, blood, sweat. fat, tears, serum, saliva, mucus synovic fluid, urine'[10]. At another place, Buddha says that if what is within our body were without, we would always have to guard ourselves from jackals and vultures. Can such descriptions ever make us regard our body as beautiful ? They give rise to the feeling of loathsomeness. Reflecting on this aspect of body, one developes non-attachment to it and meditating on it becomes free from grasping (*upādāna*) which binds man to the cycle of birth and death.

If at all physical beauty has been praised[11] it has been done so only in the case of Buddha whose mortal frame, completely purified, shines more splendorously inasmuch as he had driven out all impurities from him. The calmness and serenity that Buddha achieved after his enlightenment shines through his face. The achievement of this calmness and serenity made his physical beauty more effulgent and beautiful. Here physical beauty has gained in moral and spiritual dimension. As far as Buddha's physical beauty is concerned, it answers to the definition of beauty given by Aristotle in terms of 'symmetry, order and definition'.

There is another point of view from which Buddha describes physical beauty. This point of view is characterised by higher wisdom and intutive knowledge which are born out of practising meditation. This kind of knowledge enables man to see things as they are i.e. objects of the world as characterised by *anicca* (impermanence), *dukkha* (suffering) and *anatta* (substanceless-ness). Therefore, Buddha in the famous fire sermon said to the Bhikkhus :-

"Everything O disciples, is in flames. And what everything, O disciples, is in flames ? The eye, O disciples, is in flames, the visible is in flames, the knowledge of the visible is in flames, the contact with the visible is in flames, the feeling which arises from contact with the visible is in flames, be it pleasure, be it pain, be it neither pleasure nor pain, this also is in flames. By what fire is it kindled ? By the fire of desire, by the fire of hate, by the fire of fascination, it is kindled ; by birth, old age, death, pain, lamentation, sorrow, grief, despair-it is kindled; thus I say the ear is in flames, the audible is in flames, the knowledge of the audible is in flames, the contact with the audible is in flames, the feeling which arises from contact with the audible is in flames, be it pleasure, be it pain, be it neither pleasure nor pain, this also is in flames. By what fire is it kindled ?......

Knowing this, O disciples, a wise noble hearer of the word becomes wearied of the eye, he becomes wearied of the visible, he becomes wearied of contact with the visible, he becomes wearied of the feeling which arises from contact with the visible, be it pleasure, be it pain, be it neither pleasure nor pain.....

While he becomes wearied thereof, he becomes free from desire; free from desire, he becomes delivered; in the delivered arises the knowledge; I am delivered; rebirth is at an end, perfected is holiness, duty done; there is no more returning to this world; he knows this"[12].

Buddha in his first sermon explained what suffering is and proved in the end that five aggregates of clinging are painful. The body cannot be permanent for it tends towards destruction. Consciousness also is not permanent inasmuch as it is transitory, it changes. And that which is transitory is definitely painful. Therefore about that which is impermanent, full of suffering and liable to change it cannot be said that "this is mine, this am I and this is my created soul. How can one, therefore, who has developed such an insight into the real nature of things regard this body as beautiful ? Therefore, Buddha and after him a whole host of his followers do not give importance to physical beauty.

Buddha, like Plato, is not concerned with the transcendental concept of beauty. According to Plato there is a world of 'Ideas'. Absolute beauty is also an Idea. All the beautiful objects of the world, according to Plato, lead us to Absolute beauty. In the *Phaedrus* and in the *Symposium* Plato discovers Absolute beauty through the beautiful objects of the world. He proceeds from bodily beauty to ideal beauty and goes even beyond this to beautiful forms, beautiful practices and beautiful notions and ultimately he contemplates 'the vast sea of beauty'. Buddha never talks of metaphysical or transcendental beauty.

His concept of beauty like that of Thomas Aquinas is not different from his ideal of the highest good. According to him he is beautiful who achieves the *summum bonum* of life. Who, therefore, can be more beautiful than the Buddha or Tāthagata? *Śivam* and *sundaram* are not inseparable from his point of view. Thus Lord Buddha has given a moral dimension to beauty. What is morally and ethically good is beautiful.

His philosophy consisted in analysing the cause of *dukkha* and finding a way out to put an end to it. So he propounded the philosophy of action and not simply of passive contemplation. He showed the path (the eightfold path) by treading along which man can achieve *nirvāṇa* or a state of desirelessness. The import of most of the teachings of Lord Buddha is that a man goaded by ill-will and anger, ruffled and disturbed by infinite sensuous desires is the most ugly to look at. He may be physically beautiful to look at but so long as he is a slave to *rāga, doṣa* and *moha,* he is not really beautiful. As Shakespear truly remarks-

For sweetest things turn sourest by their deeds,
Lilies that fester smell far worse than weeds.

Real beauty comes to a man when he destroys *rāga, doṣa* and *moha* and annihilates his protean sensuous desires. To Buddha, one who observes *śila* (virtue) practises *samādhi* (medittion) and attains *paññā* (wisdom) with which he attains *tattvajñāna* and keeps himself away from attachment is really beautiful.

Apart from this moral and ethical concept of beauty there is another which may be called aesthetic. This kind of beauty is found in Buddhist literature. Although Buddha was against dance, drama and music-vocal or instrumental-inasmuch as they pampered baser passions of man and instead of elevating him degrade him, he seems to have approved of one kind of poetry which delineated *Śānta rasa*-the supreme of all *rasas*. In many of his *udānas* he has given expression to his spiritual ideas and high thoughts. Plato believed that poetry waters emotions. Tragedy and comedy popular during his time simply "nourish and water our emotions when we ought to dry them up". It is pretty clear that Plato disapproved of that kind of literature which pampered baser emotions. Buddha, too, like Plato disapproves such poetry and art. According to him, these arts give sensuous pleasures which are appetitive and induce sensual, misanthropic and mentally confused states, which are bad. To *Tālapuṭa* who was an actor and who was sure to be reborn in the world of gods of laughter because he entertained people, Buddha said that such arts are of no use and those who practise them are sure to be reborn as an animal. At this *Tāla-puṭa* realized his mistake and in his fiftyfive verses he expressed in detail how he restrained and chastened his heart to deeper understanding.

Plato in his *Republic* approved of hymns to gods in the name of poetry. Buddha also approves of that kind of poetry which expresses higher understanding and produces calmness of mind and desirelessness.

If we make an analysis of the verses uttered by the *theras* and *therīs*, it becomes clear that although they express their sufferings poignantly, they also delineate that state of their mind which may be called the state of *nirveda*. They seem to learn the law of impermanence from their short-lived beauty. Ambapālī gives powerful poetic expression of the tragic realization that dawns upon her when she sees 'the deep trenches dug by her old age in her beauty's field'. But this is not her final realization.

She goes beyond this and soon learns the law of impermanence from this devastating realization, changes the course of her life and tries to attain salvation-a state of desirelessness. Up till now she had tried her best to achieve only two *puruṣārthas* viz. *artha* (wealth) and *kāma* (sensuous pleasure); this tragic realization sparked off in her an energy with which to work tirelessly for drying up all her passions with the fire of wisdom and attain *arhatship*.

Such verses are, therefore, beautiful, inasmuch as they express not only the transitoriness of the so-called beautiful things of the world but also as they express higher understanding of the real nature of things i.e. *tattvajṇāna*. Such verses, therefore, embody *Śānta rasa*. Sculptors and painters also later on depicted the supreme serenity and profound calmness on Buddha's face which in turn evoke *Śānta rasa*.

Ambapālī's verses contain great tragic experiences but she does not stop at expressing them. She delves deep and expresses the bliss that she gets after knowing the real nature of worldly pleasures. She developes *nirveda* and experiences the bliss of desirelessness. Other *therīs* also do not only keenly feel the sufferings that come to them but they also go beyond and meditating on their sufferings they gain insight into the true nature of things. They experience that kind of peace which no amount of wealth, nor physical beauty nor indulgence in sensuous pleasures can give. Lord Buddha himself has given vent to that experience in these words :

Anekajāti sasṁsāraṁ, sandhāvissaṁ anibbisaṁ
gahakārakaṁ gavesanto, dukkhā jāti punappunaṁ
gahakāraka diṭṭhosi, puna gehaṁ na kāhasi
Sabbā te phāsuka bhaggā, gahakūṭaṁ visankataṁ
visankhāra gattaṁ cittaṁ, taṇhānaṁ khayamajjhagā.

(I hàve run through a course of many births looking for the maker of this dwelling and finding him not, painful is birth again and again. Now are you seen, O, builder of the house, you will not build the house again. All your rafters are broken. Your ridge-pole is destroyed, your mind, set on the attainment of *Nirvāṇa*, has attained the extinction of desires).

Here Lord Buddha expresses the unworldly and spiritual pleasure that he gets from his knowledge that dawns upon him after all his desires are annihilated. This is called *tṛṣṇākṣaya sukhajñana*. He has risen above hopes and despairs and above worldly loss and gain, advantages and disadvantages. It is this kind of attitude which is reflected when he says *upasantaṁ sukhaṁ seti, hitvā jaya parājayaṁ*.

Most of the verses contained in the *Theragāthā* and *Therīgāthā* are sublime expressions of the mental state of desirelessness of the *theras* and *therīs*. It is clear from them that these *theras* and *therīs* in spite of their various kinds of sufferings or perhaps because of them, meditated and discovered the sources of ineffable bliss. This they called *amataṁ padaṁ* or *nibbāṇa*- state where they felt that they have become cool (*sīti bhūto*), free from the eleven kinds of fire which used to burn them before they realized this state. In these two books mentioned above, *Śānta rasa* has been delineated.

Śānta rasa is the supreme of all *rasas*. Whereas the first eight *rasas* are worldly, *Śānta* may be called supramundane. A great part of human psychology is covered by the eight *sthāyins* which are inborn in us due to *rāga, doṣa* and *moha* but the *sthāyī* of *Śānta rasa* is *śama* or *tṛṣṇākṣayasulhajñāna* and it comes into being only when all desires and *rāga, doṣa* and *moha* are destroyed.

There have been a lot of discussions about the *sthāyī* of *Śānta*. It appears from their discussions that *śama* is really the *sthāyī bhāva* of *Śānta rasa*. Namisadhu says *Samyagjñāna* or *tattvajñāna* is *the sthāyī* of *Śānta*.[13]

"Samyagjñānam sthāyibhāvaḥ. Vibhāvastu śabdādi viṣayasvarūpaṁ. Anubhāvojanmāditrāsadayaḥ".

Rudraṭa also agrees with him. Ānandavardhana gives *tṛṣṇākṣayasukhajñāna* and Mammaṭa gives *nirveda* as its *sthāyibhāva*.

Without going into detail as to what exactly is the *sthāyī* of *Śānta rasa* it can be said that *tattvajñāna* and *vairāgya* are the *vibhāvas* (*sthāyī bhāvas*) of *Śānta rasa*. Each of these helps the other and shades off into the other. Abhinavagupta says that in *Śānta* one can see and enjoy the *anubhāvas* viz. the slow disappearance of *kāma, krodha* and other evils and though the whole world of *bhāvas* becomes *vyabhicārins* for *Śānta*, such *bhāvas* like *nirveda* and *jugupsā* for worldly objects....and *śraddhā* will stand out prominently, as more intimate accessories, *abhyantara aṅgas*"[14]. *Śānta rasa* is born out of a state which is characterised by the absence of *dukkha, sukha, dveṣa* and *rāga* :

Na yatra dukkhaṁ na sukhaṁ na cintā na dvesȧ rāgo no ca kācidicchā,

Rasastu śāntaḥ kathiteṣu, munīndraiḥ sarveṣu bhāveṣu śamapradhānaḥ.

This mental state, hard to acquire, gives rise to inner harmony which is called beautiful.

From a study of the *Theragāthā* it is clear that the *theras* have treated the objects of Nature in a sublime way. The sailing clouds in the sky, the verderous woods and the graceful peacock instead of arousing passions help them sit in deep meditation and attain wisdom. In Kālidāsa's *Meghadūtam* a Yakṣa separated from his beloved requests the clouds to be his messenger and carry his words to her. In the case of these *theras* it creates a suitable atmosphere for meditation. These objects and the broad landscape inspire them to attain the supreme goal of life. Even the moon which plays a significant role in romantic literature plays a different role here. A Bhikkhu who has attained perfect equanimity is "even as the moon on the fifteenth day sails clear in the sky without a stain"[15] One who has destroyed all cankers and who is free from all impurities is like the full moon.

This kind of use of the object of Nature gives rise to sublimity. How Nature has been treated in the *Theragāthā* has been dealt with in "*Nature in the Theragāthā*".

From what has been said above it is clear that Buddha's concept of the beautiful is neither physical nor metaphysical nor transcendental but it is moral, ethical and spiritual. The delineation of *Śānta rasa* in the vast Buddhist literature produces an ineffable joy born out of our supreme knowledge. We experience this joy and understand what beauty actually is-the beauty that is lasting, elevating and sublime, the beauty that is the highest good, the beauty born out of internal harmony and not out of external symmetry and proportion.

References

1. ञातपरिञ्ञा, तीरण परिञ्ञा and पहानपरिञ्ञा see pp.38-39, of. पपंचसूदनी, Vol. I.
2. यं अनिच्चं तं दुक्खं यं दुक्खं तदनत्ता,
3. Quoted from *Buddha and the Gospel of Buddhism* by Ananda K. Coomaraswamy.p.324.
4. *ibid.*, p.26.
5. *ibid.*, p.52.
6. *ibid.*, p.56.
7. *ibid.*, p.83.
8. *ibid.*, p.85.
9. *ibid.*, pp.121-124.
10. *The Middle Length Sayings* Tr. by I.B. Horner pp.73-74.
11. 1. O thou of perfect from and beauty rare,
    Of fairest parts and lovely to behold,
    Exalted One ! thy colour like fine gold,
    Thou valiant spirit, with the dazzling teeth,
    Whose body shows the features that betray,
    The man of perfectly adjusted parts.
    Psalms of The Brethren, p.311.
12. Quoted from *Buddha and the Gospel of Buddhism* by Ananda K. Coomarswamy, pp.263-264.
13. Quoted from *The Number of Rasas by V. Raghavan, p.43.*
14. *ibid.*, p.26.
15. *Psalms of the Brethren*, p.186.

Buddhist Literature and Śānta Rasa

Rasa is the distinguishing feature of a work of art. If it does not delineate *rasa*, it cannot properly and legitimately deserve its name. All works of art, great or small, primarily concern themselves with the delineation of different kinds of *rasas* like *śṛṅgāra* (love) *hāsya* (laughter), *karuṇāa (compassion) and vīra* (heroic activities) etc. Man is endowed with sentiments like love and laughter etc. which are called *sthāyī bhāvas* (permanent dispositions) and the depiction and delineation of these *bhāvas* in a work of art produce *rasa*. Bharata in his *Nāṭya Śāstra* has enumerated nine such *sthāyī bhāvas* and nine *rasas* corresponding to them. Out of these nine *rasas, śānta,* according to him and many others, is very difficult to delineate in a work of art particularly in a drama. Great tragedies by Shakespeare which are judged as the chiselled masterpieces of world literature also do not go beyond describing pity and terror and at most, they delineate other *rasas* like *hāsya* (laughter)[1] but not *śānta*. In *King Lear* we find an attitude of resignation and a sort of satisfaction born out of 'ripeness'. This attitude of resignation has an element of inevitability.

Men must endure
Their going hence, even as their coming hither;
Ripeness is all.[2]

Judged from this point of view Buddhist literature takes off from where other imaginative literature lands. Whereas other literature deals with the eight *rasas* like *śṛṅgāra, hāsya, karuṇa* etc. Buddhist literature, particularly *Theragāthā* and *Therīgāthā* deal with *śānta rasa*. The *theras* and *therīs* have realised the true nature of things, have experienced ineffable joy born out of the peace following such realisation and have given expression to it tin heir verses. The result is the sublime poetry primarily delineating *śānta rasa*. Thus the tenor and tone of Buddhist literature strike quite a different note.

Most of the verses contained in the *Theragāthā* and *Therīgāthā* are sublime expressions of the mental state of desirelessness of the *theras* and *theris*. It is clear from them that these *theras* and *therīs* in spite of their various kinds of sufferings or perhaps because of them, have meditated and discovered the source of ineffable bliss. This they called *'amataṃ padaṃ* or *nibbāna* a state where they feel that they have become cool (*sītibhūto*)[3] and free from the three kinds of fire[4] which used to burn them before they realised this state. In these two books *śānta rasa* has been delineated.

We know that physical beauty is the basis of love (*śṛṅgāra*) between the lover and the beloved. But in the *Theragāthā* and *Therīgāthā*, we find a different kind of attitude towards physical beauty. It does not cause attraction here but it causes repulsion. Lord Buddha did not put a premium on physical beauty as he knew with his three kinds of *pariññā*[5] (understanding) that beauty is very short-lived. Physical beauty is characterised by *aniccatā* (impermanence) and *dukkha* (suffering). At one place he says, "Beauty is noting to me, neither the beauty of the body, nor that that comes of dress."[6] Physical beauty is only illusory and short-lived. There is nothing in it to be proud of. There are many references in the *Tipiṭaka* where Lord Buddha has revealed his attitude towards physical beauty. To Abhirūpanandā[7] who was infatuated with her perfect physical form, he proved its transitoriness by conjuring up a more beautiful woman who aged and faded in course of a very short period. The sight caused anguish in Abhirūpanandā and she soon became disillusioned. What Lord Buddha says to Sundarinandā with regard to this body reveals once for all his attitude to physical beauty :

Behold, Nandā the foul compound, diseased
Impure, compel thy heart to contemplate,
What is not fair to view. So steel thyself
And concentrate the well composed mind.[8]

In the case of many *therīs*, we find the same attitude. Aḍḍhakāsī ultimately gets tired of physical beauty :

But irksome now is all my loveliness;
I weary of it, disillusionized.[9]

Vimalā's[10] 'bloom of her beauty' intoxicates her for a short time and when truth dawns upon her she applies herself assiduously to attain the ineffable *nibbāna*. Khemā[11], proud of her physical beauty, learns the transitoriness when she sees a celestial nymph conjured up by Buddha passing from youth to old age. When she sees that the nymph has broken teeth, grey hair and a face full of wrinkles, she realises that the body is vile and a 'foul seat of disease and corruption'.

Ambapāli-this once famous Thais of India-contemplates her wasted charms in her poem. It not only epitomizes her beauty, grace and charm but it also expresses powerfully her painful realisation of their transitoriness:-

Glossy and black as the down of the bee my curls once clustered.
They with the waste of the years are like unto hempen or dark cloth.
Fragrant as casket of perfumes, as full of sweet blossoms the hair of me.
All with the waste of the years now rank as the odour of hare's fur.
Wrought as by sculptor's craft the brows of me shone, finely pencilled.
They with the waste of the years are seamed with wrinkles overhanging.
Beauteous the arms of me once shone like twin pillars cylindrical.
They with the waste of the years hang feeble as withering branches.
Like to the coils of a snake the full beauty of yore of the thighs of me.
They with the waste of years are even as stems of the bamboo.[12]

The description of physical beauty is so powerfully and glowingly done here that it can compare with the description of beauty given by any great poet of any literature of the world. But Ambapāli, at the same time, expresses her tragic feelings of her 'wasted charms' very poignantly. In her we find the mood of disenchantment and disillusion. She sees the deep trenches dug by her old age in her beauty's field and expresses her tragic experiences as deep as Macbeth's and King Lear's. But like them she does not stop there. She realises the impermanence of her beauty as also the transitoriness of worldly pleasures. This devastating realisation makes her change the course of life and apply herself assiduously in her *sādhanā* (meditation) to attain *nibbāna*-a state of desirelessness. Uptill now she had tried her best to achieve only two *puruṣārthas* viz. *artha* (wealth) and *kāma* (sensuous pleasure); this tragic realisation sparked off in her an energy which enabled her to work tirelessly for drying up all her passions with the fire of wisdom and attain what is called the greatest of all *puruṣārthas-nibbāna*. She developes what is called *nirveda* as a result of *tattvajñāna* (real knowledge) and all her feelings bring in their wake a mood of quietude-a mood of desirelessness. This gives rise to a different kind of aesthetic and spiritual joy called *śānta rasa*. What once was love for physical beauty has sublimated into love for the ineffable *nibbāna*. Verses ascribed to Ambapāli embody *śānta rasa* and give rise to supramundane pleasure inasmuch as they express not only the transitoriness of the beautiful things of the world but also as they express higher understanding of the real nature of things i.e. *tattvajñana*.

There have been a lot of discussions about the *sthāyī bhāva* of *śānta rasa*. It appears from these discussions that *Śama* is really its *sthāyī bhāva*. Namisadhu defines the *sthāyī* of *śānta* as: "*samyagjñānam sthāyībhāvah. Vibhāvastu śabdādi viṣayasvarūpam. Anubhāvo janmāditrāsādayah.*[13] Ānandavardhana[14] gives *tṛṣṇākṣayasukha jñana* and *Mammaṭa*[15] gives *nirveda* as its *sthāyī bhāva*.

Without going into detail it can be said that *tattvajñāna* and *vairāgya* are the *vibhāvas (sthāyi bhāvas)* of *śānta rasa*. Each of these helps the other and shades off into the other. Abhinavagupta says that 'in *śānta* one can see and enjoy the *anubhāvas* viz. the slow disappearance of *kāma* (sensuous pleasure) *krodha* (anger) and other evils and though the whole world becomes *vyabhicārin* for the *śānta*, such *bhāvas* like *nirveda* and *jugupsā* for worldly objects...and *śraddhā* will stand out prominently, as more intimate accessories, *abhyantara aṇgas.*[16] *Śānta rasa* is born out of a state which is characterised by the absence of pain, pleasure, jealousy and attachment. Bharata says :

Na yatra duḥkhaṃ na sukhaṃ na dveṣo nāpi mātsaryḥ,
Samaḥ sarvabhūteṣu sa śāntaḥ prathito rasaḥ.[17]

There are many verses in the *Therīgāthā* which express this kind of mental state. They describe their sufferings poignantly but their sufferings do not hinder them from rising higher spiritually. As a matter of fact, they give them the insight which dawns upon one when one developes *paññā* (wisdom). *Therī* Uttarā exults in the following verses :

Well have I disciplined myself in act,
In speech and eke in thought, rapt and intent.
Craving with root of craving is o' ercome.[18]
Cool am I now: I know nibbāna's peace.

This *'nibbāna's* peace' is nothing but *śānta rasa*. And this peace follows when all kinds of desires, *lobha, dveṣa, moha* and other evils are annihilated, when 'every throb of lust'[19] is rooted out and when ignorance is overcome. Sumedhā in her well known verses denounces sense desires and enjoys freedom from them.

'Like the sharp blades of swords are sense desires,
Like the poised heads of snakes prepared to dart',
'Like blazing torches, 'and like bare known bones.'
Transient, unstable are desires of sense,
Pregnant with ill and full of venom dire,
Searing as heated iron globe to touch,
Baneful the root of them, baleful the fruit,
As fruit that brings the climber to a fall,
Are sense desires; evil as 'lumps of flesh'
That greedy birds one from the other snatch;
As 'cheating dreams; as 'borrowed goods' reclaimed,
As spears and javelins are desires of sense,'
'A pestilence, a boil, and bane and bale,
A furnace of live coals, 'the root of bane,
Murderous and the source of harrowing dread.[20]

Sumedhā has understood the real nature of sensuous

pleasures and says that those who indulge in their lusts must suffer incalculably. She renounces all her desires and turns to that 'that groweth never old'. She wants to work out her own salvation and see the truth and liberty. Such examples from the *Therīgāthā* can be multiplied *ad libitum.*

The *therīs* of the *Therīgāthā* express their longing for *nibbāna* which is the ineffable bliss. They also long for extinguishing all desires. The result is the sublime verses embodying *śānta rasa.*

The verses in the *Theragāthā* also bear ample testimony to the fact that they also delineate *śānta rasa.* Without citing verses of many *theras,* I would like to give here a few verses as samples from the verses uttered by Bhūta which will make clear the tone and tenor of the poems contained in the *Theragāthā.*

When in the lowering sky thunders the storm-clouds' drum,
And all the pathways of the birds are thick with rain,
The brother sits within the hollow of the hills,
Rapt in an ecstasy of thought:-no higher bliss,
Is given to men than this.[21]

Thera Bhūta expresses here the ineffable joy that one gets in meditation in a lonely place far away from the madding crowd. The destruction of *lobha, dveṣa* and *moha* qualifies a *thera* to become a *sādhaka* (practitioner of meditation) and attain *nibbāna.* The sailing clouds in the sky, the verdurous woods, and the graceful peacock do not arouse their passions as they generally do in other imaginative literature, but help them sit in deep meditation and attain wisdom and *nibbāna.* If we make a study of the way the objects of Nature have been treated in the *Theragāthā,* it will be clear that they inspire the *theras* to practise meditation and attain *nibbāna.* Even the moon which plays a significant role in Romantic literature inasmuch as it arouses the passions of the lover and the beloved, plays a sublime role here. A therā who has attained prefect equanimity is "even as the moon on the fifteenth day sails in clear sky without a stain."[22] One who has destroyed all cankers and is free from all impurities, is like the full moon. Thus the treatment of Nature in the *Theragāthā* has been done in a sublime way and the objects of Nature treated in this way go a long way in delineating and expressing *śānta rasa.*[23] The *theras* and *therīs* describe in their verses the supreme bliss that they have got after attaining freedom from *rāga, dveṣa* and *moha* and different kinds of *āsavas,* rising above pain and pleasure and ultimately attaining a state of desirelessness. This mental state, hard to acquire, gives rise to an inner harmony which is called beautiful. Inner harmony follows destruction of all evils and defilements and attainment of real knowledge.

It will not be out of place to say that Buddha has added a spiritual and ethical dimension to the concept of the beautiful. Beauty gives pleasure, and inner harmony alone can give supreme pleasure. Therefore, real peace can follow inner harmony. What is physically beautiful cannot give real and lasting pleasure, but what is spiritually and morally beautiful can give unbounded and supreme bliss.

The subject matter of the *Udānas* of the Buddha, the verses of the *theras* and *therīs* and the *Dhammapada* is the deeper understanding of the real nature of things and the supreme bliss followifng attainment of *paññā* (wisdom). Lord Buddha has himself expressed the supreme bliss that he felt after putting an end to all his desires and attaining the highest wisdom and Buddhahood in these words:

Anekajāti samsāraṃ sandhāvissaṃ anibbisaṃ,
Gahakāraṃ gavesanto, duḥkhā jāti punappunaṃ,
Gahakāraka, diṭṭho'si, puna gehaṃ na kāhasi,
Sabbā te phāsukā bhaggā, gahakūṭaṃ visaṅkhataṃ,
Visaṅkhāra gataṃ cittaṃ, taṇhānaṃ khayamajihagā.[24]

Thus we find that the subject matter of Buddhist literature is *nirveda, vairāgya,* atainment of knowledge and realisation of *nibbāṇa.* In Asvaghosa's *Buddhacarita* and *Sāriputta Prakaraṇa* also the subject matter is the same. Therefore, it will not be wrong to conclude that a great bulk of Buddhist literature delineates *śānta rasa.*

References

1. *Śṛṅgāra hāsya karuṇa raudra vīra bhayānakāh,*
Bibhatsādbhuta sanjñau cetyaṣṭau nātye rasāh smṛtāḥ,

Bharata, *Nāṭya ṣāstra*, VI, 16.
Ratirhāsaśca śokaśca krodhotsāhau bhayaṃ tathā,
Jugupsā vismayaśceti sthāyibhāvāh prakīritaḥ,

ibid., VI. 18.
Mokṣadhyātmasamutthastattvajñanārtha hetusaṃyukyah,
Naihśreyasopadiṣṭaḥ śānta raso nāma sambhavanti,
ibid., VI., *kārikā* following 83.

2. Shakespeare, *King Lear*, Act, 5, scene II.
3. C.A.F. Rhys Davids, *Psalms of the Sisters*, p.19.
4. *Rāga* (the fire of lust), *dosa* (the fire of anger) & *moha* (the fire of bewilderment).
5. *Ñāta, tīraṇa and Pahāṇa pariññā.* See *Papañcasūdanī nāma Aṭṭhakathā* vol.I.pp.38-37. ed. by U. Dhammaratana & U. Jagrabhivaṃsa.
6. Quoted from *Buddha and the Gospel of Buddhism* by Ananda K. Coomaraswamy, p.324.
7. *Psalms of the Sisters*, p.23.
8. *ibid.*, p.56.
9. *ibid.*, p.26.
10. *ibid.*, p.52.
11. *Ibid.*, p.81.
12. *ibid.*, pp.121-124.
13. Quoted from *The Number of Rasas* by V. Raghavan, p.43. Also see Rudrata's *Kāvyālaṃkāra*, Ch.XV,15-16.
14. *ibid.*, p.43.
15. Mammaṭa, *Kāvyaprakāśa*, Ch.IV.35. *Nirvedasthāyibhāvaisti śanto'pi navamo rasah.*
16. *The Number of Rasas*, p.26.
17. *Nāṭya śạstra*, Chapter VI, *kārikā* following 83.
18. *Psalms of the Sisters*, p.19.
19. *ibid.*, p.30.
20. *ibid.*, pp.171-172.
21. *Psalms of the Breathern*, pp.246-247.
22. *Ibid.*, p.186.
23. See author's article entitled *Nature in the Theragāthā*
24. "Many a birth have I traversed in this round of lives and deaths.

Vainly seeking the builder of this house. Sorrowful is repeated birth.

O house-builder, you are seen; never again shall you build the house. All your rafters are broken; Your ridge-pole is shattered. My mind is gone to dissolution; I have attained the end of craving.

(*Dhammapada, Jarāvagga* translation by A.P.Buddhadatta Mahathera.)

Buddha's View of Harmony

Oxford English Dictionary defines harmony as "agreeable effect of apt arrangement of parts." The second meaning according to the same dictionary is "combination of simultaneous notes to form chords." "Sweet or melodious sound," is the third meaning.

If we look at Buddhism either as philosophy or religion we find all these meanings relevant in its context. Buddhism does not only stress the cultivation and development of inner harmony which is its primary concern but also emphasises the cultivation and development of social harmony which Buddha considered equally important for leading a good and peaceful social life. Our life can be sweet and melodious only when harmony in respect of social and spiritual life is achieved.

It is true that Buddha's supreme concern was the achievement of spiritual harmony but in his Discourses with various people he came across or who came to see him in his sojourn in the different parts of India for long fortyfive years he found occasions to talk of social harmony as well. His incidental remarks in this connection are worth taking into consideration. I think it would be better if I bring out Buddha's view of harmony in this short paper.

Let us first take social harmony. How to achieve social harmony is a great problem. What Buddha has said in the context of achieving social harmony makes the first meaning of harmony clear.

Harmony does not mean equality. Perhaps equality of mankind is a myth, a fiction, a something which cannot be realized. We know that the governments of some countries have tried their best to put into practice the theories propounded by great pioneers of social and economic equality like Marx and Engels but do we in actual practice find equality in those countries ? However much they have tried to bridge the gap between the rich and the poor, some sort of gap still remains unbridged. It is very heartening to note in passing that the efforts of such governments have indeed gone a long way in annihilating the gap between the rich and the poor and in ameliorating the miserable conditions of the latter. Poverty is caused in society partly by mismanagement but it is also caused by the results of one's past actions. Even if the theory of *kamma* is not applied to explain the difference between one man and another in respect of their poverty, at least the difference in respect of intellect and intelligence must be put down to the past actions of men. According to the actions performed in past lives one man is different from another. Why there is difference between one man and aneother is beautifully explained by Nāgasena to king Milinda. I will not quote here at length the relevant passage but I would refer the curious readers to this famous passage in the *Milindapañho*. Even if one were to explain the difference between one man and another on the basis of the different combinations of genes which are themselves complex, their complexity and different permutations and combinations can be ascribed to different past actions.

Lord Buddha essentially believes in a sort of inequality of men but he suggestes at the same time that despite these differences harmony in social life can be acheived for leading a peaceful and happy life. He has explained how social harmony can be achieved very clearly in one of the *suttas* of the *Dīgha Nikāya*. The *Kūṭadantasutta* which chiefly throws light on the concept of *yajña* incidentally has something to say on how social harmony can be achieved. King Mahavijita expressed his desire to perform a *yajña* to his priest who advised him to do so only when corruptions of all sorts are removed from his kingdom. To levy fresh tax when corruptions were rampant was a wrong activity. So long as corruptions were there, it was not proper to perform a real *yajña* for gaining merit. *Yajña*, he explained, does not mean slaughtering of innocent animals like cows, bulls, calves, heifers, goats, hens or pigs but it actually means removing poverty from kingdom and making it free from thieves, dacoits and highwaymen who make life in the kingdom unsafe. But the million dollar question according to the priest is why do they commit theft, dacoity and murder ? The answer is that they do not have much to live on. Some people are poor, so in order to eke out a living they produce discordant notes in society. They threaten and torture people and make them part with all that they have at pistol points as it happens very often these days. If they have sufficient to live on, they will not create troubles. Not only poverty but unemployment is also a serious problem. The minds of the young men who are unemployed are devil's workshop. If they have jobs to do and have sufficient food to eat, they will not think of engaging themselves in such immoral and risky activities. As a consequence, there will not be corruption. The priest of the king had put his finger on the causes of corruption and other kinds of evil in society and advised the king to give enough to the farmers and cattle rearers so that they may not feel any difficulty in raising a crop and rearing cattle respectively. The businessmen must be provided with enough capital to set up and run their business. And, last but not least, all citizens should have jobs for which the king should pay them. In this way all people of society will do their jobs and there will be no one who will be a thief, a dacoit or a criminal. I think this is the most effective way of achieving social harmony. This apt arrangement of the various constituents of society will produce an agreeable effect.

We also find here a theory that punishment is not a sure cure of social evils and malaise. Corruption and crime cannot be eradicated completely by punishing criminals. It is true that particular criminals will be punished and annihilated but there will be many in whom the seeds of corruption and crime will remain dormant and they will raise their ugly heads in due course. So degradation, banishment, fines, bonds and death sentence cannot put a stop to all such criminal and corrupt activities. The priest of Mahavijita thus puts his finger on the real causes of corruption and crime and advises him how the various constituents of society will act in unison and produce the sweet music of peace and prosperity.

Not only that, he also advises the king to seek the permission of four categories of people in society like the *Kṣatriyas,* vassals of his, or his ministers and officiates or Brāhmins of position or the householders of substance in his kingdom to perform *yajña* so that they may gladly part with their money for enabling him to meet the expenses of a *yajña.* The priest says that on no account they should be compelled to give money. Today force and compulsive methods are used to collect money but this is not a sure and safe method of establishing harmonious relationship between the king and his subjects or between government and people for that matter. What Buddha has said here is, indeed, the basic thought for achieving social harmony among the various constituents of society.

Buddha's primary concern, as I have said earlier, was the achievement of inner harmony. This may also be called spiritual harmony. One of the ways by which this sort of harmony can be produced is to practise the four *Brahma vihāras* viz, *mettā* (love), *karuṇā* (compassion), *muditā* (syampathetic joy) and *upekkhā* (equanimity). Love "has the characteristic of devotion to the aspect of (other's) welfare". It has the function of offering welfare. If one seriously thinks of doing good to others and offering them welfare he can go a long way in resolving any discordant note in society. He will think well of all without any exception and will not have hatred for any one. It is hatred for others that creates troubles. Struggles begin and violence of all kinds follow. The attitude of love for all without any exception is so sublime that one who adopts and cultivates it, will radiate love. In the *Vāseṭṭha sutta* Lord Buddha described the method of practising *mettā Brahmavihāra* in the following words. "He (practitioner of *vipassanā* meditation) continually relates to the beings in one direction (such as north, with a mind endowed with love, then likewise to the beings in the second, the third, and the fourth direction and in the same way to the beings upward, downward and across. He continually relates everywhere equally to the entire world beings with a mind endowed with love-a mind that is untroubled, vast, enlarged and measureless". The meditative cultivation of love is particularly effective for counteracting anger. Compassion as described in the *Visuddhimaggo* by Buddhaghoṣa "has the characteristic of devotion to removing other's suffering. It has the function of not enduring other's suffering. It is also practised in the same way as love and if it is cultivated while practising meditation, it becomes particularly effective for counteracting harmfulness.

The third *Brahma vihāra* is sympathetic joy or *muditā* which "has the characteristic of rejoicing". You rejoice at somebody's being fortunate, in other words, you have joy for his fortune as Brutus says, "As Caesar loved me, I weep for him, as he was fortunate I rejoice at it; as he was valiant, I honour him; but as he was ambitious, I slew him" If one cultivates *muditā* while practising meditation he can counteract displeasure.

Equanimity the fourth *Brahmavihāra* "has the characteristic of devotion to the aspect of even-mindedness with regard to sentient beings." In other words, it is feeling of neither pleasure nor pain that accompanies various states of consciousness."

When we relate to all beings with a mind endowed with love we wish "May all beings be happy". When we relate to all beings with a mind endowed with compassion we wish "May all be liberated from suffering of all kinds and misfortune." When our minds are endowed with sympathetic joy we wish like this : "You beings are rejoicing, it is good that you are rejoicing, it is very good", And when our minds are endowed with equanimity we observe others' suffering and happiness and think, "these appear because of that individual's own past activities". The meditative cultivation of equanimity is particularly effective for counteracting lust.

If we practise these *Brahmavihāras* we can achieve harmony which can go a long way in our spiritual development. We can get rid of anger (*kodho*), harmfulness (*doso*) and lust (*rāgo*) and cultivate love, compassion, sympathetic joy and equanimity. If all of us practise these *Brahmavihāras*, the world will be an ideal place-a veritable paradise to live in. I do not mean to say, however, that all will begin to do so overnight and all will do so in equal measure. But even if they are practised by some persons on a small scale, the wrold will be a better and happier place in that proportion.

We know that the Greeks had propounded the theory of fluids in our body. They spoke of four chief fluids viz., blood, phlegm, choler and melancholy. If they are in right proportion, one's life is balanced but if one of them is in greater proportion than others it becomes unbalanced and he becomes what is called 'out of humour'. i.e. the harmony of life is disturbed. Our Āyurveda śāstra also speaks of *kapha, pitta* and *vāyu.* We feel well when all these are in equal proportion and are held in check.

Buddha speaks of three *akusala hetus viz., lobho, doso* and *moho* which are the springs of immoral actions and he says that for a finer and better harmony to achieve, they are not only to be held in check but they are to be replaced by *alobho, adoso* and *amoho*. Buddha has elaborated the method of eliminating the *akusala hetus* and cultivating the *kusala* ones to replace them.

Thus harmony can be achieved-harmony of both kinds-spiritual and social. No note will play a discordant role and sweet music of peace and happiness will come into being by a kind of superior spiritual orchestration.

Aesthetics of Buddhist Art

When we read a poem or a work of art or see a statue we like to know what it is that makes it a poem or a work of art or a statue. This enquiry lands us into the domain of Aesthetics. Aesthetics is an independent discipline which makes a systematic study of art and beauty, their essential meanings, their values and relations. In short, Aesthetics is the philosophy of the beautiful. Artists of all types worth their names make beautiful things and thus create the taste of the people and educate it.

Aesthetics of Buddhist art means the principles which underlie this particular art. What were the causes that gave rise to this art and what were the influences which helped its growth? As the principles of this art, like those of others, have not always remained the same, so it is difficult to deal with them in so short a span. What I would do here is just to point out some of its salient features and try to explain why the Buddhist art developed the way it did.

In India art is inseparably connected with life. Art for the sake of art seldom inspired artists. They generally created works of art only when they felt sure that their works would ennoble human nature, make life better and help people realise the ends of life, viz. *Dharma*, *Artha*, *Kāma* and *Mokṣa*. The artists tried their best to depict and describe all that can harmonise truth beauty and good. Art draws its sustenance from life. Consequently, the purposes and ideal of life find their expression in art. The principles a man lives by govern the art he produces.

This essential feature of Indian art must be borne in mind while analysing the aesthetics of Buddhist art. Buddhist art is not severed from life but like other Indian arts, draws its sap from the Buddhist ideals of life. As we know, the *summum bonum* of life according to Buddhist religion is *Nirvāṇa* which is a quiet state of desirelessness. Buddhist art always keeps this high ideal in view and tries to depict the serenity and tranquillity which the Buddha felt under the Bodhi tree after extinguishing all desires (*taṇhā*). The highest goal according to Buddhist philosophy and religion is a state of desirelessness. Even the desire to achieve that state of desirelessness should not be there. Desires which keep on multiplying in life for various reasons and cause a man to be born again and again have to be annihilated so that a state of quietness and calmness is achieved.

Of the two kinds of literature secular and religious, the former describes human feelings such as love, laughter and anger etc. whereas the latter largely depicts the ninth *rasa* which is called *śānta* by Bharata - the writer of the *Nāṭya śāstra*. And, therefore, *nirveda* which means being non-attached to the beautiful objects of senses is also described here. In the *Visuddhimaggo*-a Pali text written by Buddhaghoṣa it has been described in detail how a *yogāvacara* (practitioner of Buddhist meditation) can develop *nirveda*. In the *Satipaṭṭhāna sutta* Buddha himself has described how *nirveda* can be achieved by reflecting precisely on this body itself which is encased in skin and is full of impurities. Thus reflecting he comes to realise the real nature of the seemingly beautiful objects of the world which are characterised by *anicca* (transitory), *dukkha* (suffering) and *anatta* (non-soul) and has no grasping for any object, howsoever beautiful it may appear and has no *taṇhā* which is at the root of our suffering. Buddhist literature including Buddhist philosophy and religion is primarily concerned with the spiritual journey of a man steeped in suffering to the glorious mansion of *Nirvāṇa* which is a state of complete freedom from all kinds of suffering, physical, mental and cosmic.

The obvious fact of our life is suffering. Buddha made a deep probe into it and put his finger on its cause, realised that we can get rid of our suffering provided we follow the eightfold noble path (*Ariyo aṭṭhangiko maggo*). This eightfold path has three important milestones of *śīla, samādhi* and *prajñā*. Buddha's teachings uniquely combine in themselves an insight into human psychology and the ehical rules which will help a man transcend his baser nature and realise the highest goal of human life. By observing the rules of discipline, i.e., *śīla* one can gain control over one's sense-organs and purify one's physical and vocal actions. This, in turn, enables him to concentrate his mind. Gradually he developes what is called the *vipassanā* meditation and comes to realise the true nature of things. The more deeply he realises this the more keenly he practises virtue and he is better able to purify himself. He does not allow any form of *taṇhā* to rise in himself. Thus he realises supreme bliss.

In the light of all that has been said it is now easy to understand what constitutes beauty according to the Buddhist way of life. A life well lived from the point of view of Buddhist ethics will constitute beauty. One who is completely purged of the impurities such as greed, hatred, anger and ignorance and has developed an insight into the real nature of things with his pure consciousness is the embodiment of truth, beauty and goodness. Therefore in many Buddhist statues the emphasis is not on depicting physical beauty but on the inner nobility and calmness arising from one's purity. A *yogāvacara* is required to practise the four *Brahmavihāras* i.e. *mettā* (friendship for all creatures) *karuṇā* (compassion for all suffering creatures), *muditā* (gladness at the success of others) and *upekkhaā (equanimity)*. These four are called the sublime states of consciousness. Cultivating these higher states of consciousness gives rise to supernal beauty.

It is this supernal beauty which artists aimed at while making statues of the Buddha. They have tried to depict the inner quietness which he had realised. They never tried to depict his physical beauty which is nothing in comparison to his inner spiritual beauty. There are many statues of Buddha where he is shown practising deep meditation with indrawn eyes. The half-closed eyes depict infinite compassion and sympathy that he had for the suffering humanity. There is nothing sensuous here, nothing that glorifies the flesh. Even in the Gandhāra art which does lay emphasis on the physical form such high ideals of Buddhist life are depicted.

In the beginning Lord Buddha was held in so high a reverence that artists never dared to make a statue of him or carve him in stone or bronze for they thought that they would not be able to do justice to the personality of the Buddha. In the early Buddhist art no figure of the Buddha is seen. But the Buddha is represented by symbols. Sometimes a horse and a *chhatra* (umbrella) would symbolise the presence of the Buddha. Apart from that, he would be symbolised by a lotus. Lotus has been the highest Indian symbol in art, religion and cosmology of life floating in the surface of creative waters. According to Vasudeo Sharan Agrawal, "It is the flower opening its petals to the rising Sun. Śurya is the symbol of Brahma, the Supernal Sun in heaven and the lotus is the flower of life blossoming on earth; it is the visible sign of consciousness (*prāṇa*) in matter (*bhūta*)"[1]

Becasue Lord Buddha attained enlightenment and became the living symbol of *prāṇa* so in early Buddhist art his presence is symbolised by the lotus. There were other symbols too. Bodhisattva's entrance into mother's womb was symbolised by a great white elephant entering into the womb of Maya Devi which she saw in a dream. The Great Renunciation (*Mahābhiniṣkramaṇa*) is symbolised by the horse Kanthaka standing on the bank of river Anoma. Sometimes his presence would be indicated only by the Bo tree. There was another way of depicting the presence of the Buddha which was done now by legends and now by actions of stories. In Bhārhūta the reliefs have the simplicity of actual statement, in Sanchi the exuberance of pageants and the form of ideals. These narrative reliefs, as has been observed by the great art critic Stella Kramrisch," carved in stone are one of Buddhism's contributions to Indian sculptures."[2] According to her, "it was in the South East Deccan, in Andhra, during the second century A.D. that sculpture became conscious in a degree comparable to the moment prior to realisation when the Buddha abandoned the world, the luxuries of the court, and the pleasures of the senses. The teeming compositions in Amravati with their innumerable figures, so slender and langourous, strong and passionate, tell the stories of the Buddha in this, his last, and in former incarnations, in a mood of withdrawal from life."[3] She further says, "This one surpassing state keeps the compositions as taut as a drawn bow string. There is no release in these reliefs; the arrow is not loosed from the profusion of life and intoxicating beauty that wreathes the gestures in a design of parabolic curves. The limbs of the figures are those of dancers who reach out into the void. They bend over their mortal youth. At no other moment has Indian sculpture been so acutely sensitive."[4] At Nagarjunakonda if one sees the statues one will discover that the "faces look inwards, reflecting the conquest and imminence of Release in the mirror of detachment, with concentrated, indrawn expressions and clarity of form."[5]

There are some other statues and images of Lord Buddha which depict *Bhūmisparśa mudrā*, *Abhaya mudrā* and *Varada mudrā* and sensitively depict great moments in the life of the Buddha. Thus Buddhist art is inspired by the high ideals of the Buddhist way of life and the teachings of the Buddha.

References

1. V.S. Agrawal, *Indian Art*, p.53.
2. Stella Kramrisch, *The Art of India*, p.32.
3. *ibid.*, p.32.
4. Stella Kramrisch - *The Art of India*, p.32.
5. *ibid.*, p.33.

Vipassanā - a Distinct Contribution of Buddhism to World Culture.

'Indian culture abroad' is a very intriguing subject on which volumes have been written and can still be written, because there are many ingredients of culture which travelled from India to different neighbouring countries and struck their roots there. These include all aspects of life, social, political, religious and spiritual and they range from the grossest to the subtlest. We all know that the message of Buddha was carried alive from this country and elements of Buddhism planted into the hearts of the people of a particular country to cater for their spiritual needs. The ennobling effects of his message can still be seen in the way of life of a country where Buddhism is a living religion.

In this paper I will talk about the *vipassanā* form of meditation and the great influence it has exercised on the minds of the Burmese people. Why I have taken up *vipassanā* to talk about will be at once clear from what I say below. This form of meditation which disappeared from the land of its origin has been in practice in Burma without any interruption over the centuries and it has been brought back to India in its pristine form in the recent past. This form of meditation which Buddha practised to put an end to sufferings of all kinds such as physical, mental and cosmic, is a distinct contribution made by the Buddha to world culture. It is also a great contribution by Indian missionaries to Burmese culture. Once this form of meditation was taken to Burma by Indian monk missionaries it was learnt by Burmese monks. It struck its root, had its luxuriant growth and became a part and parcel of the way of life not only of monks but also of the lay people at large.

It is really a matter of great happiness that what was once

taught by India to Burma is being learnt by her in this century. Vipassanācārya Sri Satyanarayan Goenka - a Burmese citizen of Indian origin, has brought back this form of meditation from Burma and has been trying to make it popular for the last several years. His yeoman's services can be compared with those of Ācārya Buddhaghoṣa who translated the whole of Pāli *Aṭṭhakthās* back into Pāli from Sīhalī and thus brought back our forgotten treasure.

We may feel proud to know that the *vipassanā* form of meditation is a distinct contribution to world culture, particularly, in the field of *yoga*, by one of the brilliant sons of India but it is also none the less a matter of pride to realise that this form of meditation was preserved in its original form by the Burmese people and they have returned the spiritual heirloom to us without damaging it in any way. *Vipassanā* is now, as ever has been, woven into the pattern of life of the Burmese people.

Let me explain here in brief what *vipassanā* is. Then only we shall be able to assess its quantum of influence in our life and the role it plays in purifying our life. The word *vipassanā* is composed of prefix *vi* and root *pas* which means to see. *Vipassanā* thus means seeing in a special manner. If one practises *vipassanā*, he develops special powers in him to see things as they are without reacting to them which we do in ignorance. By practising *Vipassanā* we develop *prajñā* (insight) with which we see the real nature of things, develop non-attachment and purify our mind which is polluted by our hydra-headed desires for the various objects of the world.

The importance of *vipassanā* can be seen if we know the nature of our mind. It is fickle and unsteady, according to Buddha.

Phandanaṃ capalaṃ cittaṃ durakkhaṃ dunnivarayaṃ /
Ujuṃ karoti medhāvi usukārova tejanam //

"As a fletcher makes straight his arrow, so does the wise man make straight the mind, which trembling and unsteady is difficult to guard and restrain". Our unsteady mind keeps on roaming from one object to another and thus amasses sensations which cause *taṇhā* (desires) and bind us to the wheel of birth and death, causing immeasurable suffering to us.

Buddha taught us a way out of suffering. If we can stop fending for our senses we can go a long way in reducing our desires which form the seeds of our rebirth. Mind has got to be controlled. But how can we do so ? By practising four *satipaṭṭhānas.* viz. *kāyānupassanā, vedanānupassanā, cittānupassanā* and *dhammānupassanā.* This is nothing but *vipassanā* which helps us in developing awareness of all the states of body, of different kinds of feeling, of our various forms of consciousness and also of the various principles of *dhamma.* Thus *vipassanā* does not only help us in keeping an alert and watchful eye on all the sense doors through which sensations keep on pouring in our mind and make us crave for them which in turn cause our suffering but also enables us to penetrate into the conceptions like *santati paññati* (conception of series), *ghana paññati* (conception of solidity), *puggala paññati* (conception of personality) and so on. Gradually we realize the ultimate truth and come to know that matter is nothing but a mass of vibrations by observing the physics and chemistry of our body. We realize that all *dhammas* are in a constant state of flux and they are characterized by *anicca* (impermanence), *dukkha* (suffering) and *anatta* (non-substance i.e.) no soul theory. That is why Buddha has said explicitly that the only way to purify oneself and put an end to all kinds of suffering, to achieve insight and to realize *nibbāna* is to practise four *satipaṭṭhānas* i.e. *vipassanā.*

''Ekāyano, ayaṃ, Bhikkhave, maggo sattānaṃ visuddhiyā, sokaparidevānaṃ samatikkamāya, dukkhadomanassānaṃ atthangamāya, ñanassa adhigamāya, nibbānassa sacchikiriyāya, yadidaṃ cattāro satipaṭṭhānā.

How do we practise it ? In the beginning a moral foundation is laid. The practitioner takes a vow to abstain from killing, stealing, sexual misconduct, lying and using intoxicants. In a ten-day workshop concentration is sharpened during the first three days through sustained observation of our breath going in and coming out which in the words of Ācārya S.N. Goenka provides 'a bridge between the known and the unknown'. First of all we take a small area below our nostril and observe pressure, pain, lightness, numbness, tingling sensation, heat, cold etc. We see them clearly as we acquire concentration of mind more and more and then gradually move along all the parts of our body. This has three advantages. First, we realize the true nature of *dhammas* and secondly we succeed in yoking our mind to our breath so that it may not wander uncontrolled. A wandering and roaming mind must of necessity bring in a large number of sensations which cause desires in us. The third that comes a little later when insight dawns on us is that we observe whatever happens in our mind and body without reacting to them. In ordinary life when we lose our temper our brows are arched, our fists are closed, our teeth are set, our eyes become red and we are full of tensions. A chain of reactions set in causing us incalculable harm. All of this can be stopped if we develop equanimity through *vipassanā*.

Although *vipassanā*-the technique of purifying mind and realizing *nibbāna*, has been discovered and taught by Buddha, it can be practised by followers of all religions because the subject of meditation according to it is human breath common to all humanity and the vow that one has to take for a moral foundation includes codes of conduct common to all religions.

It is for this reason that Buddha called his *dhamma* explicit and clearly explained. He says that it is a *dhamma* which produces results here and now.

"Svākkhāto Bhagavatā dhammo, sandiṭṭhiko, akāliko, ehipassiko, opaneyyiko, paccattaveditabbo viññuhī ti."

This unique technique of purifying oneself was completely forgotten in India. Its re-introduction to the land of its origin has a very interesting story. Sri S.N. Goenka - a business magnet of Burma suffered terribly from migraine and had to use morphine to kill the pain he suffered from but that also he could do only temporarily. He consulted practically all the best doctors of the world, spent a huge amount of money but he was not cured. Then he was advised by one of his friends to go to U-Ba-Khin-a *vipassanācārya* who also worked as Accountant General in Burma. U-Ba-Khin taught him to practise *vipassanā* which had a miraculous effect on him. The monstrous migrain was gone. He was then convinced of the efficacy of this form of meditation. Setting aside his material business of crores of rupees, he took to the spiritual business of imparting this technique to all people belonging to all races and religions and it is he who brought this technique from Burma to India in its pristine form.

Vipassanā (insight meditation) goes a long way in removing the heaps of impurities dumped in our mind in our several previous lives due to our own actions, frees us of our mental tensions and cures us of our psycho-somatic diseases. In the words of *vipassanācārya* Goenka, " meditation is an art of living. We must train our minds not to run away from problems but to go to their depths, to find their causes and then eradicate them. The mind has accumulated so much negativity-anger, hatred, aversion, fear, jealousy and passions. We have to free ourselves of these."

Meditation camps are held in jails also. Criminals have practised it and the results have been wonderful. They feel changed and wish to live a pure life.

This form of meditation can be practised anywhere and everytime in all situations of life and anybody can practise it. Its growing popularity is an indication of the fact that *vipassanā* is a distinct contribution of Buddhism to world culture.

As far as Burma is concerned, *vipassanā* has deeply affected the life of Burmese people, so much so that training in *vipassanā* even for a short while is regarded as essential for all people working in office or elsewhere. It has become a way of life.

INDEX